UNNATURAL HARVEST

HOW GENETIC ENGINEERING IS ALTERING OUR FOOD

Ingeborg Boyens

Doubleday Canada

Canadian Cataloguing in Publication Data

Boyens, Ingeborg, 1955–
    Unnatural harvest : how genetic engineering is altering our food

ISBN 0-385-25749-X (bound) ISBN 0-385-25789-9 (pbk.)

1. Food—Biotechnology. 2. Food—Biotechnology—Moral and ethical aspects. I. Title.

TP248.65.F66B69 2000   363.19'2   C98-932858-9

Cover images by Photodisc
Cover design by David Hunter/Fizzz Design Inc.
Text design by Kim Monteforte/Heidy Lawrance Associates
Printed and bound in Canada

Published in Canada by
Doubleday Canada, a division of
Random House of Canada Limited
105 Bond Street
Toronto, Ontario
M5B 1Y3

TRN 10 9 8 7 6 5 4 3 2 1

In memory of my mother,
who always had time and appreciation
for the wonders of the table

CONTENTS

Acknowledgements

It is a daunting challenge to write a book—doubly so when it is about science and you can not claim a list of doctoral degrees. I am indebted to all those people who accepted the notion that the story of genetic engineering in food is as much a story of ethics and public policy as it is of science.

I am grateful to those who paved the way for this book with their excellent volumes on agriculture, food, and biotechnology. Thanks also to those often unacknowledged people who maintain food-related news services on the internet. Also thanks to Nancy Westaway who helped with research when panic seemed to rule. Offering me valuable interpretations for all this information were Arthur Shafer, Ann Clark, Murray McLaughlin, and many others.

My appreciation goes to the people who shared their thoughts and stories with me in an effort to personalize a sometimes difficult subject. Dot Wilson, Dean Moxham, and Michelle Brill-Edwards are struggling valiantly for their personal and ethical independence in changing times.

Thanks go to the CBC for teaching me that it is not enough for an issue to be important, it also has to be relevant. My colleagues at *Country Canada* were tolerant of my naiveté and supportive of my efforts, regardless of their own opinions— particular thanks to John Drabble and Nigel Simms for their assistance.

The Manitoba Arts Council financially supported this project. At Doubleday Canada, John Pearce and Kathryn Exner were unflaggingly encouraging. Thanks go to Kathy Vanderlinden, who edited the manuscript.

This book would not have become a reality without the calm support at home of my husband and personal in-house editor, Gregg Shilliday. Thanks, Gregg, for putting up with my often unsolicited observations on food, usually at dinnertime.

Introduction

*Science is a first-rate piece
of furniture for a man's
upper chamber,
if he has common sense on
the ground floor.*
Oliver Wendell Holmes, 1872

For thousands of years, the world's food was grown on farms
that looked much like my grandfather's homestead. His operation was tiny—manageable by his standards, but inefficient
by the measure of today's industrial agriculture. The cows all
had names; the pigs rooted in the dirt; and the labor force was
made up of oft-complaining sons and daughters. Food—the
growing, harvesting, preparing, and eating of it—was a shared
obsession. Later, like many of his generation, my grandfather
sold the farm and moved to town. Although he still rose at
dawn, the telltale line on his forehead marking the boundary
between peaked hat and farm sun slowly faded.

In much the same way, the family farm has faded too. More
than seventy-five thousand small and medium-sized Canadian
farms disappeared from 1976 to 1996. In the United States, the
numbers are equally remarkable: in 1917, there were 6.5 million
farms; by 1993, there were only about 500,000 farmers still
working the land. In the 1970s, U.S. Secretary of Agriculture

Earl Butz forecast the future when he told farmers, "Get big or get out."

Today, like most of us, I live in the city, far from where food is produced. And also like most of us, I no longer have a personal connection to agriculture. The cycle of food production has become a wonder and a puzzle. With the modern magic of preservatives, refrigeration, and long-distance transport, peaches and tomatoes appear in the supermarket even when a defiant layer of snow blankets the country. It is only occasionally that I recall—through the hazy fondness of memory—the canning jars filled with pears, crab apples, and peaches lined up in neat rows in the basement coldroom to help us survive the long, hard winter.

On the brink of the new millennium, those of us lucky enough to live in the developed world are denied almost nothing in terms of food. We do not have to sit on a tractor under the unrelenting prairie sun to bring home a bushel of wheat for bread. We do not have to roll up our sleeves on a sweaty August day over a boiling water bath of mason jars. And yet a broad array of exotic foods never seen in our grandparents' day is arranged for our easy purchase in the produce aisles of the local supermarket.

In the lexicon of progress, food and farming have become agribusiness. There may have been costs as people abandoned the country for the city, but agriculture has achieved monumental productivity improvements since World War Two. In the early years of this century, living according to the rhythms of the seasons, in watchful apprehension of what nature might deliver, my grandfather was able to support about ten people from the bounty of his farm. One of today's modern North American farms sustains as many as one hundred people. In 1930, it took an hour of farm labor to produce a bushel of grain; in the 1990s, a bushel is generated in less than a minute.

At the same time, food has evolved from a lovingly tended and prepared staple of life into just another packaged commodity. After the losses and the limitations of the war years, a typical supermarket delighted customers by offering them a selection of about a thousand items, most of them fresh, cured, or canned. Today, new food processing technologies have resulted in assembly-line manufacturing on a massive scale. Granola bars, instant energy shakes, dehydrated pasta sauce mixes, and other examples of edible progress now arrive on store shelves as quickly as advertising campaigns can be drafted. In 1995, there were fifteen thousand products to be found in the aisles of a typical Canadian supermarket. American food emporiums boasted even more edible innovations—in 1989 alone, twelve thousand new foods were introduced to the U.S. market.

The fine print on the back of a typical box of today's food lists a string of mysterious artificial ingredients with long chemical names—tricalcium phosphate, dipotassium phosphate, diglycerides, silicon dioxide, and of course, the ubiquitous artificial flavors. More and more, the items available to eat are made up of substances that bear only a passing resemblance to traditional foods. We might think a frozen pizza is made of flour from milled wheat, tomato paste from crushed, vine-ripened tomatoes, mozzarella cheese from milk, and sausage from animals. In fact, the flour may be a chemically restructured mix of soy and wheat, the tomato paste may be "extended" with colored starch, the mozzarella may be a vegetable oil imitation, and the pepperoni may have been formed from textured soy protein.

These are the new essential ingredients of manufactured

food—a nutritional fuel designed for modern convenience. In our frantic urban world, most people place a low priority on food. Unlike stay-at-home moms of the past who served up meat and potatoes with predictable regularity, today's mothers routinely squeeze dinner in between work and the evening's soccer practice. It is more likely we stop at a drive-through for a burger in our car than plan a meal with ingredients that have to be peeled, diced, and boiled. A recent survey found that American consumers spend fifty-two percent of their food dollars dining out. In most North American kitchens, heating is practiced much more frequently than cooking. The essential kitchen appliance these days is the microwave oven, ever ready to zap that frozen pasta, pizza pocket, or burrito from the local corner store. Manufactured food makes the harried North American lifestyle possible.

Along with convenience, price is a fundamental consideration in our eating habits. Supermarket flyers, boosting the best price on everything from cantaloupes to pop, bulk up our Sunday papers. Pizza delivery services advertise two-for-one, three-for-one, sometimes even four pizzas for the price of one. North Americans spend less on food than any other industrialized society. In 1950, the average American family spent one-quarter of its income on food; by 1990, that had dropped to one-tenth. In Europe, food and drink costs twice what it does on this continent, yet consumers appear to accept those prices.

In these waning years of the twentieth century, our society's demands for convenience, a good bargain, exotic global foods, and healthful eating have set the table for foods produced by science, not by Mother Nature. Spurred by the lure of profit, corporations are now using biotechnology or genetic engineering—the insertion of genes from one species to another—to transform our food. Science, with a free-enterprise twist, is taking full advantage of our indifference and our appetites to create new life.

The comforting memories of my grandfather's Old McDonald-type farm are now being replaced by the cold reality of plants and animals born in the laboratory petri dish. Already, sixty percent of processed or manufactured foods—everything from cookies to ice cream to baby formula—contains genetically engineered soybeans. In the first decades of the new millennium, the majority of our food will be the product of genetic engineering. In the future supermarket produce section, the shelf life of genetically altered tomatoes will be measured in months rather than days. On the dairy shelves, milk will be generated by cows drugged with growth hormones designed to ensure huge milk yields. In the meat department, the chicken will come from birds genetically manipulated not to mind their otherwise intolerable caged existence.

The first wave of genetically engineered foods and crops began to quietly appear on the international market in 1996; hundreds of products are now in the pipeline for development and approval. By mid-1998, sixty-four modified crops had been approved in the United States and Canada, the heartland of biotechnology. In the European Union, where a new generation of "food activists" has launched a full frontal assault against biotechnology, only a handful of engineered crops had been approved.

The pace of biotechnological growth in just the few years since the first appearance of biotech crops is astounding. In 1996, soybeans genetically engineered to be resistant to the herbicide Roundup were grown on one million acres in the U.S. In 1997, the acreage swelled to nine million; in 1998, to twenty-five million. By the year 2000, manipulated crops are expected to cover nearly 150 million acres of land throughout the world—that is, eighty-one percent of the arable land in North America, ten percent of Asia, eight percent of Latin America, and one percent of the crop land in Europe. As the *New York Times* proclaimed in May 1998, "Biotechnology's knowledge machine is running at Silicon Valley speed."

The industry that plans to deliver this version of scientific progress to the marketplace is dominated by huge global business conglomerates in the new life sciences field. The industry operates on an international scale, but is mainly commanded by American companies that once focused on the production of synthetic chemicals but have graduated to foods with the support of the U.S. regulatory and economic environment.

The new biological ability of genetic engineering places modern society at the brink of a fundamental revolution—one that some liken to the Industrial Revolution of the 1700s.

Richard Godown, former head lobbyist with the Biotechnology Industry Organization, said in a 1994 TV interview, "The advent of recombinant DNA technology is comparable to the discovery of quantum physics." Sano Shimoda, president of BioScience Securities, a California biotech research firm, boasted at the 1998 U.S. National Forum on Agriculture that agricultural biotechnology will "rank on the Richter scale alongside major transforming technologies such as the steam engine, the transistor, and the computer." In early 1997, *Business Week* magazine put its own stamp of approval on the industry, declaring the next one hundred years "The Biotech Century," a time of a lab-based technological revolution that will propel "the grand, tumultuous pageant of human history."

The revolutionary changes forecast by *Business Week* are quietly being wrought in corporate laboratories far from the eyes of the people for whom they are intended. Unlike other revolutions, where the control of the state is seized from the faltering hands of the dominant class, this one is being forged by the business class for the sake of corporate and shareholder profits. At a 1997 lecture in the Maryse series entitled "Science at Work," David Ehrenfeld, who teaches biology at Rutgers University, said bluntly, "Excluding military spending on fabulously expensive, dysfunctional weapons systems, there is no more dramatic case of people having their needs appropriated for the sake of profit at any cost."

New test-tube foods are arriving on store shelves now thanks to the acquiescence of government regulators, particularly in North America, who see biotechnology as a valuable growth industry. Yet most consumers are unaware of this food revolution and have not even asked themselves: Is this what I want? Is this technology safe? Should there be limits on what science can do? Or even, Should biotech food be specially labeled? As British science writer Nigel Calder warned, "We are sleepwalking towards the revolution."

The imagination of science fiction writers has often conjured up a world of manufactured life. In 1932, long before science identified DNA as the building block of life, Aldous Huxley created a future in *Brave New World* that warned of dehumanization in the face of unbridled scientific progress. Food, in Huxley's utilitarian new world, was a dismal carotene sandwich, a slice of vitamin A pâté, and a glass of champagne surrogate.

And long before it evolved into a horror movie cliché, Mary Shelley told the story in *Frankenstein* of a gifted scientist working at a time of rapid scientific progress in the early 1800s. By exploring the fate of both creator and his creation, she asked the question that grows even more pressing as we are about to step into a new age: How far should science go in altering life?

The "foods" that are beginning to grace our dinner tables

have been dubbed "Frankenfoods" by the media. They are not, however, obvious monsters. These test-tube foods are generally indistinguishable from what we consider the products of nature. There are no labels or other signs to indicate that they are the edible creations of an unnatural harvest.

We are living in a time of immense scientific progress that makes a mockery of the imaginings of science fiction writers. We are routinely assaulted by news of cloned creatures, headless frog embryos, luminescent green mice, and "successful" experiments to grow a human ear on the back of a mouse. Hollywood seeks to entertain us with stories about dinosaurs brought to life from a snippet of DNA (*Jurassic Park*) and future genetically engineered societies where embryos are perfectly doctored in petri dishes (*Gattaca*). The fact that science is about to propel us into a world where the majority of our food will be engineered in laboratories has frightening implications for the environment, for human and animal health, for the global food system, and for the biodiversity of our planet.

The biotechnology industry argues that in two decades of experience with genetic engineering, no mutant viruses or bacteria have escaped to pollute the environment. No laboratory workers have fallen ill from their brush with unnatural lifeforms. And they insist that rigorous testing has ensured there are no risks to human health. To those who question these claims, scientists and regulators would say simply: "Look at our record. Trust us."

Despite these assurances, however, no one can predict the long-term impacts of genetic engineering. Science has been wrong before. How else did we get the ozone hole, thalidomide, and Chernobyl? An advertisement in the June 30, 1947, edition of *Time* magazine offers an unsettling comment on our faith in the future by celebrating a chemical that would later be universally condemned for its impact on the environment. "The great expectations held for DDT have been realized," it reads. "During 1946, exhaustive scientific tests have shown that, when properly used, DDT kills a host of destructive insect pests, and is a benefactor to all humanity."

Science is neither intrinsically good nor evil. At issue is how science is used. For example, biotechnology's application in the development of new pharmaceuticals may indeed offer the key to significant breakthroughs in the medical health field. But when it comes to genetically engineered food, the benefits, beyond those to shareholders, are ephemeral. Indeed, the risks seem much more real. Mae-Wan Ho, a reader in the department of biology at the U.K. Open University and a fellow of the U.S. National Genetics Foundation, told the Green Conference on Genetic Engineering in Brussels in March 1998, "Science is not bad, but there is bad science. Genetic engineering is bad science working with big business for quick profit against the public good."

Arthur Schafer, a bioethicist and the head of the Centre for Professional and Applied Ethics at the University of Manitoba, notes that proponents of every new technology are inclined to exaggerate the benefits and underestimate the risks. Decisions tend to favor the fast march forward to what is believed to be a better world. However, this new biotechnological revolution is particularly dangerous because advancements are happening so quickly. "We've had more than a century to adapt to the Industrial Revolution, to steam and coal," he says. "The changes now are coming at such a rapid pace that our flexibility, our ability to adapt, is being subverted."

Although my early years were shaped by the natural cycles of traditional farm life, I too have been guilty of sleepwalking toward the biotechnology revolution. As an adult, I fueled an urban-based career in journalism with a diet of processed foods, reheated by the inevitable microwave. It was not until I took on a job in 1992 as a television documentary producer for the Canadian Broadcasting Corporation's *Country Canada* that I stepped into the sphere of modern agribusiness. Naive in the ways of today's farming, I had to learn that pigs are kept in huge factory-like buildings, that no one uses a milking stool, and that those endless, weedless breadths of crops are produced only by a rain of pesticides.

And I discovered that science is routinely doing what Aldous Huxley did not even imagine: mixing and matching species to create new life. It is easy to be caught up in the excitement of a new technology, to be carried away by the enthusiasm of the scientific community. It is, after all, remarkable to see a genetically engineered potato plant resolutely repel the assault of a laboratory-induced infestation of Colorado potato beetles. There is something amazing about a month-old tomato that looks just as red and plump as it did the day it was picked.

But through my research into agricultural issues, I have had a unique opportunity to open the door a crack on the rarely seen world of multinational biotechnology. This book does not presume to analyze the techniques of science; there are other volumes that do that. Instead, it attempts to assess the implications of a new technology that is quietly, almost secretly, revolutionizing the production of the most basic staple of existence: food.

Biotechnology extends humanity's power over the forces of nature as has no other technology in history. Its proponents promise benefits, but downplay the risks to human health, the environment, animal welfare, and biodiversity. With genetic engineering, we assume control over the hereditary blueprints of life itself. Should we expect that such unprecedented power to alter life is without hazard? Should scientists in corporate laboratories race ahead without an ethical framework? What are the actual benefits? This book aspires to provoke a debate on these and many other important questions—questions that need to be addressed before we step any farther into the unknown.

1

THE GENE JOCKEYS

PIG NO. 6707, AS HE WAS CHRISTENED WITH SCIENTIFIC detachment, was born one sweltering July day, ominously enough, in 1984. He was scrawny at birth, weighing less than one kilogram. Too lethargic to shoulder his way past his five brothers and sisters to his mother's teats, his every move was nonetheless monitored by a team of lab-coated molecular biologists and geneticists. After all, No. 6707 was no ordinary swine destined for the abattoir and the meat counter. He was the triumphant culmination of a nine-year scientific effort by the U.S. Department of Agriculture to cross the line between hog and human.

No. 6707 and his siblings were born on Animal Husbandry Road by a process that had little to do with the birds and the bees. They were conceived when scientists at the Beltsville research center outside Washington, D.C., flushed eggs from a sow that had been treated with fertility drugs and mixed them with boar sperm in a petri dish. At the time, this was a relatively routine procedure in the reproductive sciences. It was the next step that broke new ground. Dr. Vernon Pursel and his team took a gene that normally regulates human growth and micro-scopically injected it into the pronucleus of a single-cell hog embryo. Then they crossed their fingers, hoping the human growth hormone gene would somehow find its way into the chemical building block or DNA of the pig, producing a hog that was more like a human being—leaner and bigger.

Those were the early days of a revolutionary new science called genetic engineering. There was no guarantee the human genes injected into the pig cells would affix themselves onto the swine DNA, essentially becoming part of the pig's genetic blueprint. Indeed, one earlier litter created at the lab showed no evidence of the human growth hormone trait. Genetic engineering was apparently a hit-and-miss business.

With this litter, the research team was once again in for an anxious wait. Tissue samples from the piglets had to be sent to a lab in Philadelphia so DNA analysis could verify whether the human gene had been incorporated in any of the baby pigs' genetic makeup or genome. When the test results finally arrived two weeks later, they prompted the scientists to break open the champagne. Two of the six newborns exhibited signs of the foreign gene. One expressed the human trait only sporadically, the other had the human gene fully incorporated in his genome. That was No. 6707. He represented an enormous step forward for science. The genetic framework of mice and rabbits had been manipulated in the lab, but this was the first time scientists had managed to artificially engineer a farm animal—an animal with a complicated genetic structure and the potential for profit. "We felt like we were on top of the world," Pursel remembered.

But the self-congratulations were short-lived. Ominously, No. 6707 and others who were later "successfully" engineered had thick, leathery skin and unusually long bristles. They were indeed leaner than their conventionally born cousins in the pig world—downright skinny, in fact—but they never grew larger. Many of them became blind, sterile, and so arthritic they could barely stand. They died or had to be euthanized after a short and painful life. It seems their scientific creators could not control the release of the growth hormone gene in appropriate proportions at various points in the animal's development. It was as if the growth hormone faucet was on constantly. One scientist told the *Washington Times*: "We are at the Wright Brothers' stage compared to the 747. We are going to crash and burn for a number of years."

As the news of these crash-and-burn experiments trickled from the scientific press to the popular media, they ignited a public outcry. The accounts seemed to confirm fears that in some modern-day take on Mary Shelley, scientists were quietly mixing up monster foods in the lab. People were alarmed about the morality of using human genes to develop livestock. If the procedure had worked, would eating pork become an act of cannibalism? What about the ethics of what seemed to be porcine torture? "We had people tear us apart, rip us up one side and down the other saying we'd done these terrible things to these animals," a perplexed Pursel told the press. "Well, that wasn't our intention." (Pursel had taken the most frail of the piglets home to tend them overnight in his bedroom closet.)

It took twenty-five litters before the Beltsville researchers gave up on the project, finally acknowledging that the public would not accept cross-species experiments. In 1988, they suspended their attempts to use human genes in the manipulation of hogs. Today, that phase of research is studiously brushed under the carpet. The center's own glossy brochures obliquely refer to the fact that the lab "produced the first transgenic farm animals" without mentioning any of the embarrassing details.

It is unfair to castigate Pursel and his team. After all, they were simply building on the foundation that science had laid for them. They were only doing what a modern education had taught them to do. Their understanding of the notion of progress had propelled them to discover something new, and then proceed without much apparent concern for the consequences.

The Beltsville researchers were following up on groundbreaking work launched ten years earlier. In 1973, two cell biologists from California, Herbert Boyer and Stanley Cohen, had become the first to cross nature's boundary between the species. They did it by reshaping the essential building blocks of life.

The form and function of all living things are controlled by genes, tiny segments of the chemical deoxyribonucleic acid or DNA. A DNA molecule is a long chain—the familiar double helix or twisted ladder—with many thousands of bases along the chain. A gene is a stretch of DNA, one thousand to two thousand bases in length.

DNA is like a long string of pearls. Each pearl, representing a gene, occupies its own special place in the necklace critical to its correct function. Each gene has its own set of on–off switches to produce a protein at the right place, time, and quantity that in turn ensures appropriate structure and function. Each cell in a living thing, whether a brain, blood, or leaf cell, contains a double-helix set of thousands of genes.

The chemical language of DNA, made up of the same four fundamental molecular units, is the same in all life, but the genes in an organism are arranged in different patterns to make up its unique blueprint. It is the sequence of its genes that determines whether the cell belongs to a rose or an elephant. However, it was the similarity of these genetic building blocks in all living things that intrigued Boyer and Cohen. Using enzymes, they were able to snip slices of DNA or genes from two unrelated bacteria and stitch them together to create a completely new form of life. The process was called recombinant DNA or genetic engineering. The product was called transgenic life.

That work launched a whole new field of science. The next milestone came in 1982 when scientists unfurled a genetically engineered version of the "town and country mice." The cover of *Nature* magazine heralded the achievement with a photo of a supermouse, its DNA boosted with a human gene, posed next to a puny, conventional mouse. *Business Week* breathlessly prophesied the miracle science would create "a dairy cow as big as a elephant," able to produce six thousand gallons of milk per year. There would be beef cattle as long as stretch limosines, square chickens that were all breast meat and no feathers, turkeys as large as sheep.

However fanciful those predictions, recombinant DNA research quickly advanced from mice to rabbits and then to the ill-fated pigs—a progression from bacteria to complicated mammals in just a decade. And today, after more than two decades of experience in genetic modification, it is possible to snip, insert, stitch, edit, program, and produce just about any new combination of living things. Nowadays, scientists routinely redesign the biological blueprints of life, transferring genes from one species to another. They are not all creating hog-humans, but they have acquired a power that nature had never before allowed.

Researchers are now using genes from chicken embryos and insect immune systems to make potatoes more disease resistant. They hope to use the gene that regulates the way Arctic flounders protect themselves in freezing water to help delicate berry plants withstand frost. And Chinese scientists have already succeeded in transplanting a gene from a Mongolian fish into a beet, to allow it to be planted earlier and harvested later.

Yet however bizarre or unsavory such manipulations may seem to laypeople, scientists maintain there is nothing frightening or unnatural about jumbling up genes from different species. Biotechnology, they say, is simply a modern tool in the old science of plant and animal improvement. It is a way to use nature's instruments to serve human needs—the basic application of science. And genetic engineering or gene splicing is just one technique in the biotechnology toolbox.

Scientists argue that biotechnology is as old as agriculture itself. Long before anyone knew what genes were, they say, people were using biotechnology to improve plants and animals and to process and preserve food. From the earliest days of agriculture, ten thousand years ago, farmers noticed minor variations in the different plants and animals they tended. Over time, they learned that these variations were passed from parents to offspring. Farmers would choose seeds from the best plants hoping to produce better crops, or would breed their best animals in an effort to develop healthier, more productive livestock. According to this view, people also harnessed biological processes to make foods—for example, cultured yeast and bacteria have been used for centuries in baking, brewing, and cheese making.

It was not until the nineteenth century that people put a scientific framework around this anecdotal understanding of breeding. The Austrian monk, biologist, and botanist Gregor Mendel experimented with peas and concluded that traits are inherited by what we now call genes. Mendel's theories, extraordinary for a man of God and for a man of his time, paved the road for modern selective breeding.

Science-based selective breeding has produced many of the familiar varieties and hybrids we see in our gardens, farms, and supermarkets. However, it can be a laboriously slow procedure—in animal breeding, for example, creatures have to grow to sexual maturity before they can be bred again. Even in the plant kingdom, where nature has not imposed such rigorous time challenges, selective breeding is cumbersome. When two whole plants are crossed, all the genes from both plants get jumbled up. Because of this, breeders spend years "backcrossing" the mixed-up plant with the well-known plant they started with, again and again, to slowly breed out the many genes they do not want. At this rate, even traditional plant breeding can take a very long time, often ten to twelve years.

Genetic engineering is obviously much faster and, scientists say, more precise. In recombinant DNA work, only the one gene that confers the desired trait is moved into an organism that may have as many as 100,000 genes. Genetic engineering has in effect liberated crop and animal breeders from letting the birds and the bees roll the dice for them. It has transformed heredity—the passing of inheritable characteristics from parent to offspring—from a natural, random event into a process that can be artificially controlled and exploited.

Scientists also note ruefully that conventional breeding has limits—previously inviolate limits imposed by nature. Sexual crosses can only occur in the same or closely related species. This constrains the genetic sources that breeders can draw on to enhance desirable characteristics. For example, a donkey and a horse can produce a mule, but a horse and a dog will produce nothing at all.

Now, genetic engineering lets scientists ignore the genetic constraints in nature. The benefits of this new, improved world of human creation, they say, are obvious. And anyone who suggests there is something unnatural about genetic engineering is simply allowing emotions, not scientific facts, to rule them.

But it is plainly wrong to suggest that biotechnology is not a major departure from the way life has evolved naturally until now. When most people use the term "biotechnology," they are not thinking about some fifteenth-century peasant mixing a keg of beer. They are referring (as I do) to the newfound ability of humans to cross the line between the species, even between the animal and plant kingdoms. In the lifetime of the planet, the boundary between the species has always been sacrosanct. Where in nature do we find DNA from a fish, a spider, a virus, or a bacterium introducing itself into the DNA of a vegetable? It was almost as if nature had drawn a line in the sand that humans could not—and perhaps should not—cross.

It is true that we have been domesticating, breeding, and hybridizing plants and animals for centuries. But in the history of such tinkering, we have always been constrained by the natural limits imposed between the species. Today's molecular biologists seem to assume there is nothing particularly sacred about the concept of a species. As they see it, the important unit of life is no longer the organism, but the gene. They view life from the vantage point of the chemical composition at the genetic level. Life seems to be merely the aggregate representation of the chemicals that give rise to it.

There are two ways to assess the benefits and risks of biotechnology—from a scientific point of view and from an ethical perspective. The biotechnology industry often shies away from ethics, pretending that ethical discussions are somehow inappropriate in a modern world. Instead, it clings to the safer scientific terrain, claiming it as its own, and pointing to the irrefutable evidence of its scientific "facts."

However, biotechnology is not nearly as exact a science as the industry would have us believe. The genetic road map or genome of countless plants and animals has not yet been defined. Only in the cases of extremely rudimentary organisms, such as bacteria, have the sequence of genes in the DNA been completely deciphered, although even here its functioning is not completely understood. The human growth hormone gene was spliced into everything from mice to hogs because it was one of the earliest genes to be identified and mapped. By the late 1990s, after a decade's work, scientists on the massive, $3-billion, international Human Genome Project had managed to catalog only half of the 100,000 genes in the human body.

Recent research also tells us no genes work in isolation from others. Genes are arranged along the DNA necklace in groups, or families. The function of a given gene in a group is dependent on all the other genes in the same family. Genes and the proteins they give rise to have evolved together to form an intricate network of finely balanced functions, the complexity of which we are only now beginning to understand.

Biotechnology, critics say, is like throwing a book through the window of a library and imagining it will land in its appropriate slot on the shelves. That is, science may be able to get a foreign gene into the genome of another organism, but it has still not figured out how to direct that gene to a specific location. In many cases of this so-called precise science, genetic engineers have simply been lucky. For example, a company that developed a tomato with an unnaturally long shelf life was actually trying to find the mechanism that would allow it to create a blue petunia. The creation by German researchers of a four-pound potato, big enough to feed a family of six, was an accidental by-product of their program to investigate the breakdown of sugar in potatoes.

Often researchers have not been so lucky, inventing fish that sprouted bulbous lumps, lettuce that did not develop heads, carrots so hard they would break a tooth. Luck, both good and bad, plays a big role in this so-called rational science.

In fact, the knowns of biotechnology are minute; the unknowns are vast. Each part of the most basic gene manipulation has difficulties and implied risks—for example, the use of vectors. It is not enough for scientists to identify an attractive gene; they have to find a way to get the gene into the cells of a host organism. To do this, they routinely use highly active genetic parasites as vectors, like molecular Trojan horses. These genes are derived from viruses. Unlike most viruses, which can survive and multiply in only a limited range of species, these are lab-engineered to be active in a wide range of host DNA environments. They are essentially designed to combat the natural defences a cell would throw up to potentially infecting foreign DNA.

The most common vectors used in genetic engineering are transgenic combinations of natural genetic parasites from different sources. The most widely used carrier in today's plant biotechnology is derived from a tumor-inducing plasmid derived from the soil bacterium *Agrobacterium tumefaciens*. In animals, vectors are constructed from retroviruses, which can cause cancers and other diseases. A vector commonly used in fish, for example, has a framework from the Moloney marine leukemic virus, which causes leukemia in mice, but can infect all mammalian cells. It has components from the Rous Sarcoma virus, which causes sarcomas in chickens, and from the vesicular stomatitis virus, which causes oral lesions in cattle, horses, pigs, and humans.

Mae-Wan Ho of the U.K. Open University says the low success rate of recombinant DNA work shows the use of vectors is often fatal. She challenges what many genetic scientists think of as routine science. In the July/August 1997 edition of *The Ecologist*, she writes, "Genetic engineering bypasses conventional breeding by using artificially constructed parasitic genetic elements, including viruses, as vectors to carry and smuggle genes into cells. Once inside the cells, these vectors slot themselves into the host genome. The insertion of foreign genes into the host genome has long been known to have many harmful and fatal effects including cancer of the organism."

Despite the uncertainties and difficulties of biotechnology research, the pace of progress is accelerating at a dizzying speed. Today, the ability to identify and use genetic information is doubling every one to two years. And as biotech research zooms forward, most people do not even know it is going on, let alone follow its path.

However, it has become a tenet of current thinking that science must be allowed to work unfettered for the sake of human advancement. One of the defining characteristics of the modern age is our unqualified faith in the ability of science and technology to improve our lives. In a 1989 survey, eighty-eight percent of Americans thought the world would be better off because of science and technology. However, those people did not necessarily understand science—the same poll showed twenty-one percent of respondents thought the sun revolved around the earth.

In a secular age, science has become the religion of North American culture. Although few of us realize it, we pay tribute at the altar of science every day with our reliance on computers we do not understand, VCRs we cannot program, and appliances we cannot repair. But though we may not understand science, our children are supposed to grow up to become computer programmers and the cure for cancer should be available in a neat pink pill. And so biotechnology speeds on, buoyed by the faith of a public that believes science knows what it is doing.

When "Dolly," the first mammal to be cloned from adult cells, was created at Scotland's Roslin Institute, a reporter asked one of the scientists, Ian Wilmut, about the ethics of cloning. His reply: "I am only a scientist." Although many biotechnology researchers like to pretend there is no ethical dimension to their work, or if there is, it does not concern them, the new science clearly involves a range of ethical and moral issues. Theologians say it severely violates the natural order of life and contravenes the basic principles of most religions. Although religions hold widely different views on how life developed, they share a belief that the earth is not an accidental phenomenon but an intelligently organized system. The species boundaries are an essential part of that system's structures.

In the spring of 1998, representatives of several faiths—Hindu, Buddhist, Christian, and Jewish—joined forces in a suit aimed at compelling the U.S. Food and Drug Administration to label genetically engineered foods. They argued that the FDA's decision not to label violated fundamental religious freedoms defined by the constitution. In their submission, they said: "A considerable portion of the population is religiously motivated to avoid all genetically engineered foods as they view the production of these foods to be incompatible with proper stewardship of the integrity of God's creation." Indeed, with no labeling of gene-spliced foods, vegetarians and followers of religious dietary restrictions do not know if they are eating genetic material from animals or even from humans.

Many scientists have warned of far graver dangers. Erwin Chargaff, the biochemist often referred to as the father of molecular biology, wrote in his 1978 autobiography *Heracliteon Fire*: "I have a feeling that science has transgressed a barrier that should have remained inviolate." In case there is any confusion about his meaning, he goes on to describe genetic engineering as a "molecular Auschwitz" that poses a greater threat to the world than the advent of nuclear technology. "I consider the attempt to interfere with the homeostasis of nature as an unthinkable crime."

George Wald, the 1967 Nobel laureate in medicine, also advised science to go slow in its exploitation of the new technology. In 1976 he wrote in *The Sciences* journal: "It is all too big and is happening too fast. So this, the central problem, remains almost unconsidered. It presents probably the largest ethical problem that science has ever had to face. Our morality up to now has been to go ahead without restriction to learn all that we can about nature. Restructuring nature was not part of the bargain. For going ahead in this direction may be not only unwise, but dangerous. Potentially, it could breed new animal and plant diseases, new sources of cancer, novel epidemics."

But the words of caution, whether from religion or science, have not had much impact on slowing the current pace of biotechnological progress. That progress is being managed now by a new corporate world order. The ability of science to move DNA from one species to another is being rushed from the hands of lab-coated researchers to those of product-oriented profiteers.

2

FROM PETRI DISH TO PRODUCE AISLE

NEW LIFE IS BEING FASHIONED IN LABORATORIES, EXPERI-
mental farms, and greenhouses across North America, often
right under the noses of an unsuspecting public. A passing
motorist would barely remark on the picture-perfect image outside of Calgary, Alberta, as several cows and their calves lope
over the crest of a hill and into a copse of trees, a Stetson-
hatted cowboy on horseback in cantering pursuit. It is just
one more western cliché come to life—no cause for alarm.
There are no mad scientists here, no monsters strapped onto
a laboratory bench, not even a sign along the road advertising
"researchers at work."

Yet the bucolic motif obscures what could be the plotline
for a Michael Crichton thriller. The genetic makeup of one of
these cows and twenty of her offspring includes a human inter-
feron gene that gives the cattle an immunity to shipping fever,
a disease that strikes one-third of calves when they are trans-
ported to the feed lot. The mother cow was born through a

process similar to that of the Beltsville hogs. Luckily, she developed none of the deformities that afflicted her distant cousins in the pig world. When she grew to maturity, her eggs were fertilized in the lab, manipulated in the petri dish, and then inserted into a number of surrogate mothers. Some of the calves that were subsequently born had the human gene passed on to them by their genetic mother. By 1996, six generations of cattle had been born with the genetically engineered immunity to shipping fever, showing no outward sign of their manipulated DNA. These mutant cattle manifest only the calm bovine expressions of contented cows.

The horseback rider, a self-described cowboy at heart, is molecular geneticist Bob Church. Church is the former head of the medical research program at the University of Calgary and founder of the pioneering transgenic program that gave life to these cattle. He is seen by many in Canada's scientific community as the godfather of biotechnology, but he speaks in the matter-of-fact tones of a prairie rancher. Scuffing the ground with a booted toe, he suggests that gene splicing is not much more complicated than using "nature's scissors, Scotch tape, and Xerox machine" to produce new life. His casual manner gives no hint of the three years of effort it took to produce a viable embryo with a foreign gene that would grow to be the mother of a new life-form.

Transgenic life also thrives on a chunk of expensive real estate in West Vancouver. The West Vancouver Fisheries and Oceans lab is a modern, low-slung building with a breathtaking view off Marine Drive. Behind the chain-link fence and the security of yet another lock, Bob Devlin and his team store the living products of their efforts at gene splicing. Instead of borrowing a gene from the human genome, they have tinkered with the growth hormone gene naturally found in trout and salmon and then re-inserted it into fish embryos, so it is expressed not in the pituitary gland but through the liver of the fish. This way, the normal blocks on the growth hormone are lifted. The procedure prompts the fish to grow faster and as much as thirty-seven times larger than they normally would. In large galvanized vats, the silver flanks of the outsized fish crowd their siblings—the ones that did not express the giant trait. A genetic engineering success story. But if you look closely among the shimmering streak of fish, you will see lumps and bumps that Mother Nature never scripted. These are the evidence of a troubling side effect of this experiment in genetic engineering: about twenty percent of the oversized fish have sprouted inexplicable bulbous growths, signs of cartilage run amok.

These monster fish and the human-boosted cattle are not likely to appear in your supermarket tomorrow. The British Columbia Salmon Farmers Association has already declared it wants nothing to do with the mutant fish, even though fish farmers would benefit from growing bigger fish with the same portion of feed. The association has said consumers are not ready for this kind of technology. The amiable Bob Devlin, a man with a broad and easy smile, is philosophical about the indictment of his marine progeny. He says it will be 2010 before all the kinks are worked out of the system—and by then, consumers will surely accept the technology.

Bob Church also has no intention of taking on what might be an unreceptive marketplace. He says his transgenic cattle were never intended for the slaughterhouse and the meat counter. His was an experiment in pure science.

Both Church and Devlin enjoy a luxury shared by few other researchers in biotechnology. Supported by academic and government dollars, they are in search of progress, not profit. Their innovations will be limited to the experimental stage, the metaphorical petri dish. However, most of their colleagues in the field labor in corporate labs and have the assignment of transforming research from the test tube into products destined for supermarket shelves.

The brave new world of genetic engineering is controlled not by academics in ivory towers, but by businesses with their eyes on products and profits. This corporate approach to science is led by huge multinational, vertically integrated pharmaceutical, chemical, and seed companies, notably Monsanto, DuPont, Novartis, AgrEvo, and Dow AgroSciences. The players in this corporate drama have large public affairs budgets and government relations departments designed to persuade consumers and governments they need what the biotech industry has to offer. Biologist Mae-Wan Ho describes this industry as an "unholy alliance between bad science and big business."

However, these purveyors of genetic engineering are not proposing to force hog-humans, monster fish, or transgenic cattle on consumers. Polls show that most consumers around the world find the transgenic manipulation of animals repugnant. So those kinds of experiments are being left in the lab— at least for now. Instead, corporate biotechnology has prepared a menu of far more palatable items—crops and plants spliced with what can be presented as innocuous genes from basic bacteria.

The products of biotechnology have been slipping silently into the marketplace throughout the waning years of the twentieth century, largely without any kind of labels. By late 1998, bioengineered crops had been tested in forty-five countries, in about twenty-five thousand field trials, on sixty different crops. More than thirty-one million acres of commercial crops had been planted in 1997—up from six million in 1996. Most appeared in North America, the heartland of research and development in genetic engineering in food. The U.S. was the world's most enthusiastic cheerleader for the technology. In early 1998, fifty-seven companies and agencies had produced crops and foodstuffs waiting for approval from the U.S. government. Canada followed suit and gave the green light to thirty-nine gene-spliced crops and foods, including thirteen canola varieties, fourteen corn, and three tomatoes. Almost all of these foods were herbicide-resistant crops, like soybeans and canola, engineered to be used hand-in-glove with a company's trademark pesticide, or crops, such as potatoes and corn, with a built-in pesticide to help repel insects. Although three genetically engineered tomatoes had been approved in Canada, none were actually available for sale.

Most test-tube foods are absorbed invisibly into edible products that appear on grocery shelves. For example, although most people have never seen soybeans—either natural or manipulated—they are ubiquitous. As a valuable source of protein, they are pressed and ground into sixty percent of the processed food prepared for consumption. They are one of the world's richest, cheapest, and most readily accessible proteins. Soybeans appear in the oil we sprinkle on salad; in margarine, mayonnaise, baby food, and ice cream. Equally, no labels appear on bottles of canola oil even though gene-spliced canola is mixed with conventional canola. So, conceivably, every container of canola oil in the grocery store contains some oil derived from engineered seeds.

The biotechnology industry has been enthusiastic about a global marketplace it estimated would be worth $6 billion by the year 2005. However, outside North America, test-tube foods have been a harder sell. By late 1998, Japan had approved twenty such products, but there was growing consumer unease about the government's decision not to label them. Masae Wada, deputy chairperson of the Japanese consumer group The Housewives Association, recently told the press, "It's strange that there are no laws on the distribution of genetically modified products, while laws exist on agricultural chemicals and foodstuff additives. There are too many unknown factors, including the effect on human health." The Japanese Consumers Co-Operative Union also reflected what appeared to be growing public concern when it announced it would begin testing for the presence of genetically engineered foods in early 1998, starting with identification of modified soybeans.

The European Union went further. By late 1998, its complicated regulatory procedure had approved only nine genetically engineered foods for import, and no manipulated crops at all were cultivated in European countries. Despite vigorous corporate opposition, the European Union imposed labeling rules, and protests against manipulated crops and foods were daily news fare. Even what might be regarded as a routine field trial of engineered seeds in Great Britain was open to sabotage from scythe-wielding housewives and farmers under the auspices of a civil disobedience movement.

Despite these setbacks in Europe, the biotechnology industry resolutely stuck to its strategy: the development of innovations that would return a worthwhile profit. The first order of business was the creation of "designer foods," intended for upscale consumers in the developed world who could afford the premium price. Researchers have, for instance, been busy trying to develop a single-serving head of lettuce, tiny salad-ready vegetables, fat-free french fries, and tiny tomato plants suitable for the apartment-dwelling urban gardener.

In Canada, the Chateau des Charmes winery in Niagara-on-the-Lake, Ontario, was working with university researchers to develop cold-hardy grapes, crossed with genes from a cousin of wild broccoli, capable of extending the limited Canadian wine-growing season. Researchers in Hawaii were attempting to genetically engineer a decaffeinated coffee bean. Coffee is the world's most traded commodity after petroleum and precious metals; the market for decaf coffee is estimated at $25 billion a year.

The first genetically engineered whole food to appear on store shelves, in 1994, was a designer tomato named the Flavr Savr, which promised—for a hefty price—to deliver summertime taste in the winter. Fresh tomatoes year-round are not something most people in the world expect—except, that is, for North Americans. Americans and Canadians spend $4 billion a year on tomatoes—each consumer eats an average of eighteen pounds a year, more than any other produce except lettuce and potatoes. Although tomatoes are enormously popular, shoppers complain about the tasteless versions they find on supermarket shelves throughout the winter. In one poll of consumer satisfaction, grocery store tomatoes rated thirty-first of thirty-one fruits and vegetables.

Biology is to blame for the winter tomato's poor marks. The ripening of a tomato is the natural beginning of the rotting process. You cannot have one without the other. The brilliant red of a ripe tomato is a certain sign that it is about to rot, nature's way of ensuring continuation of the species. The tomato you buy in January in Toronto was likely grown in Mexico. It was picked from the vine when it was still green, firm enough to withstand the long trip north but too firm to redden and to start developing flavor. Along the route to the supermarket, it was gassed with ethylene, a chemical found naturally in the fruit. The ethylene gives the tomato its red color, but regretfully nothing in the way of flavor.

A small California biotech company named Calgene recognized an obvious opportunity for profit in the tomato market. So it spent eight years and $20 million trying to figure out how to defy nature. Finally, in the early 1990s, Calgene researchers identified the gene in the tomato that prompts rotting, learned how to copy it, and inserted a duplicate of the gene backward into the tomato's genetic road map or genome. This so-called "antisense" technology canceled the original gene's normal function and delayed the natural process of decline. The procedure extended the tomato's life by seven to ten days. The result was supposed to be a tomato perhaps not quite as good as the homegrown version, but tasty enough to merit a premium price in stores.

A cynic might speculate that the lengthened life span simply gives Calgene the ability to grow tomatoes even farther away from the intended marketplace. The extra days of life would then be absorbed by the complicated fresh fruit and vegetable distribution system that sometimes sees trailer-loads of tomatoes sidelined until the right buyer—at the right price—shows up. However, Calgene insisted that its tomatoes would be allowed to show the first blush of red before they were picked.

Before the Calgene tomato could get to the produce aisles, it ignited a vigorous debate in the United States about biotechnology and the public interest. The scientific community, led by Calgene's then CEO Roger Salquist, insisted that the tomato was no more dangerous to human health than any other variety produced through conventional breeding.

Jeremy Rifkin, a prominent American social and economic critic, became the biggest burr in the side of the biotechnology industry and Calgene's attempts to create a bionic tomato.

Rifkin set up the Pure Food Campaign in the early 1980s as part of his well-established Foundation on Economic Trends, which in turn organized a national network of chefs opposed to scientific tampering with food. Although no modified foods were then commercially available, thousands of restaurant entrances began displaying next to the Visa and MasterCard symbols a decal showing the DNA helix slashed by a red bar. A generation of "food activists" was poised to orchestrate "tomato smashings" as a visible, and telegenic, sign of protest. Rikfin himself, with his polished, confrontational media style, made regular appearances on television to target the tomato: "We are talking here about a technology more powerful than any in history in that it can remake the genetic blueprint of life itself. . . . It may be benign or it may turn out to be toxic or mutagenic. Our position is better safe than sorry."

Salquist, ever on the offensive, dismissed Rifkin as "a slime-bag" and his efforts to malign the engineered tomato as "ridiculous." The U.S. Food and Drug Administration apparently agreed with Salquist—after four years of reviews, hearings, and media musings, the tomato finally got the green light from the FDA on May 15, 1994. "We've won the game," said Salquist. "These people spent ten years trying to come up with arguments and not one of them has held water."

On the day the FDA granted its approval, the Pure Food Campaign directed its attentions to Davis, California, home of Calgene and the heart of the state's tomato country. However, the food activists appear not to have understood what comfortable roommates science and agriculture were in Davis. The town is essentially built around the University of California campus, which produces a new crop of agricultural research graduates each year. So when a Pure Food Campaign activist flew in from Chicago to organize a protest in front of the local State

IGA, fewer than ten people showed up to drop a few ripe tomatoes into a coffin-shaped cardboard box with the word "death" scrawled on its side. The lackluster protest provoked little interest; inside the store, about one thousand pounds of the Flavr Savr tomatoes sold in their first three days on the shelf. And biotechnology was launched onto the American marketplace.

But despite the Flavr Savr's feisty entry onto the market, a precarious future for the tomato had been foreshadowed by its long development. The lengthy debate about risks and ethics, along with distribution problems, sapped Calgene's financial energy. Although it had planned to move into Canada by 1995, Calgene was forced to retrench. By late 1998, the Flavr Savr had not appeared north of the Canada–U.S. border. Nor had it made significant inroads into the global marketplace.

Calgene had applied for approval of its tomato in the United Kingdom in 1994, but favor there was held up for more than a year as scientists and regulators debated the implications not of the ripening-retardant gene, but of an additional gene spliced into the tomato as a "marker." Scientists routinely add a second foreign gene to an attempted fusion to let them know when the experiment has actually worked. Unfortunately for scientists, new DNA is taken up infrequently by cells. In a plant experiment, only a few of perhaps thousands of plantlets growing in a petri dish will incorporate the desired gene, and, without a marker, it is impossible to tell which ones. In Flavr Savr, the marker gene was taken from common *E. coli* bacteria, and resists the powerful antibiotic kanomycin, which is administered orally to patients before surgery. All the plantlets were exposed to the antibiotic; those that survived were known to have incorporated into their DNA the marker gene and, along with it, the gene that retards the ripening process. The concern was that the antibiotic-resistant trait in Flavr Savr might be transferred to the digestive tracts of people who ate the tomatoes. Calgene produced documentation showing this would not happen, and approval was finally granted, although not all fear evaporated.

In spring of 1996, in search of an infusion of capital and an established distribution system, Calgene went into partnership with the U.S. pharmaceutical giant Monsanto. By 1997, the partnership had evolved still further—Calgene was no longer a small upstart company; instead, it was one hundred percent owned by Monsanto.

Sometime in 1996, the tomato silently disappeared from American supermarkets and from the media spotlight, although both Health Canada and British regulators had by that time approved it for import. Critics say the tomato failed because it had a soft skin and peculiar taste; Calgene meanwhile insisted it had pulled the tomato off the market because it found it could not keep up with the demand.

While Calgene was struggling with its business affairs, several other companies honed in on the lucrative fresh tomato market. The FDA gave its approval to three other genetically engineered, long-lasting tomatoes. The DNA Plant Technology Corp. (DNAP), also of California, developed a tomato it claimed would survive on the shelf for forty days. This wonder tomato was produced by manipulating the gene that triggers the natural production of the hormone ethylene. The company called this discovery "trans-switch" because it switches off the natural reddening process. It is a system that apparently also works on bananas, squash, and other fruits and vegetables. Like Calgene, DNAP teamed up with a huge multinational produce distribution company in 1996. And like Flavr Savr, DNAP's Endless Summer tomato silently disappeared from the marketplace sometime later.

Although the early efforts eventually failed, designer tomatoes are sure to be on store shelves in the early years of the new millennium. Some have been incorporated into processed food in the United States since 1995. And for several years, the Zeneca Group's long-lasting tomatoes were crushed into paste for sale in Sainsbury and Safeway stores across the United Kingdom. The company created its bionic fruit through a modification that slowed down the action of an enzyme that causes it to rot. In a curious contradictory message, British consumers seem to have accepted this clearly labeled product despite widespread concern about genetic engineering in food—perhaps because it is priced ten percent lower than others on the shelf. By the end of 1997, the company reported it had sold 1.6 million cans of the manipulated tomato puree.

Other fruits and vegetables with an artificial shelf life—squash, melons, and bananas, for example—are on the way too. In the future supermarket, fresh produce may not have to be kept on ice or sprinkled with a fine rain of cooling water. Of course, this application of biotechnology may satisfy an upscale demand for designer foods, but it does little to resolve the bigger questions that will confront agriculture in the twenty-first century, such as how to feed hungry nations that cannot afford designer prices.

In addition to wealthy consumers, corporate biotechnology has targeted the beleaguered farming community as a prospective market for its products. Since agriculture began, farmers have fought against the vagaries of nature: hail in August that flattened crops bursting with vitality; hoards of grasshoppers descending on a crop, the sound of their munching clearly audible across the fields. Biotechnology appeals to the longing for control over these plagues, promising a world in which farmers could withstand anything nature threw at them—an attractive prospect for a shrinking community that has had to deal with ever-rising costs and limited returns. Biotechnology presents itself as the magic bullet for a host of agricultural problems. According to the public relations party line, the new science could create plants that would reduce the need for fossil fuel-based chemicals. It could fashion drought- or salt-tolerant crops—a valuable attribute if the threatened greenhouse effect does raise temperatures and sea levels.

However, whether or not these noble aims are possible, they are not how the industry has launched the new science. What corporate biotechnology has chosen to do instead is to create a palette of herbicide-resistant crops. These are crops designed to be used with matching herbicides, made—no surprise here—by the same companies that created the crops. In other words, the seeds of the biotechnology revolution are being sown to ensure the sale of specific chemicals.

The first genetically engineered crops were designed to be resistant to a broad-spectrum herbicide like glyphosate or glufosinate ammonium, capable of killing not only weeds, but all plant life. This was the most popular early application of the new technology. The Organization for Economic Cooperation and Development (OECD) reported that seventy-five percent of field trials of genetically engineered crops around the world in 1995 were testing herbicide tolerance. In 1996, the results of those trials blossomed into commercial crops—two canolas were planted in Canada; a herbicide-resistant soybean, cotton, and corn were all grown in the United States. By the end of the millennium, herbicide resistance will be engineered into almost every crop grown in North America.

Herbicide resistance appeals to farmers because it allows them to cut back on their chemical spraying. A crop like canola, for example, normally requires tender loving and expensive care. As many as fifteen different weeds attempt to smother the seeds that produce the highly desirable cooking oil. Farmers often have to treat canola with several passes of herbicides aimed at foxtail, wild mustard, or other unwanted vegetation. It costs at least $40 an acre for the herbicides to treat conventional canola, plus the labor and effort of spraying.

In contrast, herbicide-resistant canola allows a farmer to hook up his chemical sprayer only once. After the plants show their first blush of green in the spring, the field is doused once with a broad-spectrum herbicide such as Liberty, Basta, or Roundup at a cost of about $20 an acre. Within three days, the wild oats, mustard, and everything else touched by the spray will wither in the country sunlight—that is, except for the gene-spliced canola. It will stand bright and green in a sea of shriveled, graying weeds.

Consequently, companies are able to claim that the genetically engineered, herbicide-resistant crops are good for the environment because they lessen the amount of chemicals required to grow them. At the same time, of course, they ensure that farmers buy their made-to-order herbicides. From the corporate perspective, a winning strategy, at once environmentally friendly and profitable!

By 1998, twenty-seven corporations had initiated herbicide-resistant plant research, including the world's eight largest manufacturers of pesticides—Bayer, Ciba-Geigy, ICI, Rhone-Poulenc, Dow Elanco, Monsanto, Hoechst, and DuPont. AgrEvo, a joint venture of Hoechst and Schering, created a canola and a corn that would be immune to its glufosinate ammonium herbicide Liberty. The Liberty Link strategy would also be applied to other crops. Monsanto launched a whole lineup of crops designed to be used with its popular glyphosate herbicide

Roundup. By late 1998, there was Roundup Ready canola, corn, soybeans, and cotton, with more products to come. Harvey Glick, Monsanto's director of research in Canada, said in an interview in 1996, "Certainly we realise some value from this opportunity, but our corporate philosophy has always been if technology is good for the farmer, it will also be good for Monsanto and everybody else in the agricultural community. And we know technology is good for Canadian farmers." In 1998, thirty percent of North American soybeans were herbicide resistant, as well as ten percent of the corn crop, twenty-seven percent of cotton, and forty-five percent of canola.

Fewer herbicides would indeed be needed with herbicide-resistant crops as long as nothing goes wrong. But the fear is that the herbicide-resistant traits will spread in the wild, creating unkillable superweeds. Every major commercial crop has a weed in its family line; wild mustard, for example, is a cousin to canola. And, of course, there is no way of stopping the wind or bugs from carrying pollen beyond the edges of the field. The corporate spokespeople, however, argue that if a weed were to become tolerant to Roundup or Liberty, any other herbicide in the existing chemical arsenal could be pulled in to do the job. So much for the much-touted reduction in chemical use!

An editorial in the *New York Times* on December 8, 1997, suggested that herbicide-resistant technology "offers the wrong solution to the needs of farmers who grasp at any economic advantage. This may make sense in terms of corporate profits, but it makes no sense at all in terms of the resources that really matter—the health of the land and the people who live upon it."

One of biotech's herbicides raised alarms in 1997, when the Environmental Protection Agency temporarily banned the

use of bromoxynil, which had been implicated in causing cancer and birth defects, by strictly interpreting an act that requires
"a reasonable certainty of no harm" from the aggregate exposure to a chemical. Much to everyone's chagrin, it was made
known that Calgene had had a bromoxynil-resistant cotton on
the market since 1994—one of the first products of the herbicide-
tolerant trend. This connection with a suspicious chemical was
surely not biotechnology's finest hour. The magazine *New
Scientist* suggested in a January 1998 editorial that it might be
better if biotech research "were to concentrate on creating
better products rather than designing crops that require toxic
chemicals." Jane Rissler, spokesperson for the Union for
Concerned Scientists, said bluntly, "The sole use of this cotton
is to expand the use of a very dangerous pesticide." However,
later in 1998, the FDA changed its mind about the ban, and
bromoxynil-resistant cotton bloomed in the southern U.S.

Next to herbicide-resistant plants, bug-killing crops are the
hottest category of bioproducts designed for large-scale agriculture. By 1998, corn, potatoes, and cotton with a built-in
resistance to insects had been approved by Canadian and
American regulators.

Researchers took a gene from a lowly soil bacterium,
Bacillus thuringiensis (Bt), and inserted it into the crop of
choice. Bt is a natural organic pesticide that was discovered
more than thirty years ago and developed into a product widely
used by the organic industry.

Monsanto was essentially first off the block in 1996 with
potatoes engineered to be toxic to the Colorado potato beetle,
the most damaging insect pest in potato fields. The beetle
has been devastating to potato crops across North America,
often stripping plants of ninety percent of their leaves when
it strikes. Monsanto's researchers spent eight years developing

its New Leaf potato, a Russet Burbank spud that generated Bt in its leaves and was as deadly to the beetle as a chemical spray.

NatureMark, the Monsanto subsidiary formed to market the defensive New Leaf potatoes, tested its crop in field trials in Atlantic Canada in 1995. Then it irritated consumers and the federal government by releasing the potatoes grown in these trials to supermarkets without notice or identification. The potatoes could not be differentiated from other Russet Burbank potatoes on the shelves.

In spring of 1996, Monsanto moved to rectify its public relations blunder. Armed with a comprehensive marketing strategy, New Leaf potatoes were sold to twenty-five Sobey stores in the Maritimes in the weeks leading up to Easter. Playing up the fact that no chemicals had been sprayed on the potatoes, the pest-lethal spuds were billed as "great tasting, fresh and grown in a different way." Monsanto's advertisements appealed to consumers' environmental awareness. "By selecting foods made from NatureMark plants, you are supporting our vision of a cleaner environment and a healthier world," the marketing plan enthused. Consumers responded as hoped, snapping up fourteen thousand ten-pound bags in just five days. And in the 1996 growing season, farmers across Canada planted several thousand acres of New Leaf potatoes for both seed spuds and the general market.

Next, in 1996, Monsanto introduced insect-resistant cotton and several varieties of Bt-spliced corn to American farmers. At the same time, Ciba Seeds, soon to merge with Sandoz to become Novartis, a multinational company based in Switzerland, entered the Canadian market with a corn variety that would repel European corn borers. Borers reduce corn yields by five to ten percent each year by laying eggs in the whorl of the plant, then feeding on the leaves and boring into the stalk of the plant. By the next growing season, Monsanto and Dekalb Genetics had also jumped into the Canadian market for bug-proof corn. In 1998, ten percent of corn in North America had a built-in Bt gene, thirty-five percent of cotton was insect-resistent, and the University of Guelph estimated that twenty percent of potatoes grown in Canada were outfitted with a bug-proof gene.

Corporate biotechnology likes to say it is creating new crops that will reduce the need for agricultural chemicals. Indeed, the Bt organism, a staple of organic farming, is considered to be benign to humans and to many other insects and birds. However, Bt is being engineered into so many kinds of crops that scientists expect it will be only a few years before pests build resistance and ruin the organic pesticide for everyone. It is routine for insects to attempt to evolve to survive. "It's just insane," said Mike McGrath, editor-in-chief of *Organic Gardening* magazine, in 1996. "They have taken one of the best tools we have and now are going to ruin it." And, of course, once Bt is no longer effective, farmers will have to use synthetic chemicals in its place.

In Canada, agronomist Pat Lynch set off a biotech skirmish when he told *Ontario Farmer* newspaper that corn companies were spending too much time and effort developing new bioengineered traits instead of focusing on what was really needed—better yields. As a consultant for the multinational food processing giant Cargill, Lynch was speaking pure biotech heresy. Lynch quipped that the Bt gene should be renamed the "B.S. gene" because of all of the rhetoric it has generated. He told the farm newspaper that traits are being introduced purely for marketing reasons, not because they will benefit farmers. Herbicide-resistant corn was not something for which farmers were asking. Instead, Lynch said, "The marketers told the breeders 'that's what we want'."

Indeed, "what the marketers want" is a hallmark of the biotech universe. So far, what they have wanted, and have been able to get, has been bug- and herbicide-resistant crops, a few designer foods, gene-spliced soybeans in packaged cake mixes, unnaturally long-lasting tomatoes in cans of sauce. But the avalanche is set to begin. About three thousand genetically engineered foods are said to be lined up for approval in the next few years. By 2005, industry observers predict that nearly all of North America's arable land will be planted with crops laced with foreign genes, and most of the fruits and vegetables in our grocery stores will be products of genetic engineering. At some point in the next century, almost every food we now consider natural will in fact be a human creation.

In this silent and seemingly inexorable food revolution, the congenial plaid-shirted farmer we knew from the past will play only a small role. Instead, it will be orchestrated by a few huge multinational corporations with their eyes focused firmly on the bottom line. How the transformation came about, and its implications for the future, is one of the most interesting— and disquieting—aspects of the biotech story.

3

IS BIGGER
BETTER?

TWENTY YEARS AGO, AMERICAN RESEARCHERS BEGAN TO
break away from the confines of the university world and set
up shop with young entrepreneurs. Together, they planned to
merge the classical sciences with the practical product-oriented
aims of technology.

It was the 1970s and there was still a breath of innocent
optimism in the air, which infused the hopes and aspirations
of these unlikely partners. They dreamed of creating better
plants and animals to help feed the growing population that
threatened to bring the world to the brink of starvation. And
they imagined their small upstart companies would take on
the warhorses of industry and hit the big time, much as Apple
had done in the computer realm. Wall Street looked on with
approval and gave the movement official recognition with a
name: biotechnology.

The marriage of science and manufacturing was con-
summated in 1976 in the medical biotechnology field when
Genentech became the first company to commercialize recombinant DNA technology. Genentech's stock underwent the most

rapid price increase ever seen in stock market history, climbing from $35 to $89 per share in its first twenty minutes of trading. It was a fabled start to a new industry. The media were just as exuberant as the stock market, heralding biotechnology as a financial and technological gold rush.

In those halcyon days, agricultural markets were viewed as potentially as rich as medical ones. Gene splicers talked of creating new foods, improving the taste and nutrition of staples, and fighting world hunger. In response, agriculture start-ups were bankrolled with enthusiasm by America's well-established venture capital community. Thanks to supportive tax and investment laws, the entrepreneurial spirit that gave birth to the nation embraced the new scientific frontier. In the first decade of the industry's growth, several billion dollars were funneled into fledgling biotech firms.

The rest of the world eyed the United States with wonder and envy. One after another, countries devised industrial strategies that targeted biotechnology for their research and development dollars.

In those days, small was beautiful. *Business Week* magazine wrote, "When it comes to biotech innovation, big companies like Monsanto are counting on the little ones to lead the way." Calgene, the innovative, California-based company that would later break new ground with its Flavr Savr tomato, was the one of the "little ones" leading the way. As the legend goes, Calgene got its start when Norman Goldfarb read about biotechnology in *Newsweek* magazine. Having worked in the developing computer business in Silicon Valley, Goldfarb was convinced that anything was possible. With some family money at his disposal, he persuaded a friend, Raymond Valentine, a genetics professor at the university campus in Davis, to offer a hand developing scientific innovations in the plant world.

Together, they set up shop in a garage in a Davis suburb—that is, until the city took issue with all the UPS trucks delivering chemicals and forced them to relocate.

Despite the prevailing optimism, investors in Calgene and other new firms soon found it took longer than they expected to translate lab-based research into profitable products. It was difficult to genetically manipulate plants and animals and still create a food that was safe to eat. There was little question of public support for a valuable new drug, but consumers were much more wary of gene-spliced food. And in addition to lengthy product development, there were also regulatory delays as a host of government agencies wrestled with how to ensure that genetically engineered foods were safe. Investors began to drift away.

Calgene managed to graduate from its garage beginnings and develop the science to create a long-lasting tomato. The company's researchers were convinced they had tapped into the financial mother lode when they discovered how to flip around the gene that controls ripening in a tomato. In retrospect, that was the easy part. The company spent years getting the necessary approvals from the U.S. Department of Agriculture, the FDA, and the EPA before it could offer consumers a taste of its tomato innovation. Roger Salquist, the quick-talking, bluntly outspoken entrepreneur who became president of the company in 1984, says he spent much of his time scavenging the country for the funds required to keep the firm afloat. "Wall Street is a fickle bunch of sheep," he said in a curt indictment of the investment community and its advisers. The upshot was that Calgene suffered multimillion-dollar losses.

The fantasy of the upstart entrepreneurs began to collapse in 1985, when Genentech, the first of the nervy newcomers to commercialize biotechnology and the one that had been expected to make the big breakthrough, was taken over by the Swiss pharmaceutical giant Hoffman LaRoche. That appropriation set the course for a very different future. Large multinational chemical and pharmaceutical companies began to dabble in the new science, establishing their own in-house agricultural biotechnology programs. In the mid-1980s, they began to use their deep pockets to establish dominance in the business by acquiring biotech companies of all sizes. The new leaders in agricultural biotechnology were very familiar names: Monsanto and DuPont in the United States, Hoechst and Ciba-Geigy in Europe, Mitsubishi and Ajinomoto in Japan.

The trend to "bigger is better" was in keeping with the global environment. Small entrepreneurial companies had existed only in the United States, where tax incentives encouraged venture capital investments. Elsewhere in the world, where investment habits were more conservative, there were few start-up companies. There were none at all in Japan, a country where biotechnology had progressed significantly. In Japan, for example, the new science had long been controlled by large multiservice companies that in turn were supported by a well-established network of government funding and research.

American biotechnology had strayed substantially from its roots, now embracing the big-business model presented by the rest of the world. The new brand of biotechnology had little to do with altruistic ideas about creating better plants and animals or solving world hunger. The revolutionary science was now more and more controlled by the product-oriented corporate world, rich in finances and influence.

The trend to buyouts continued unabated through the 1990s. By the middle of the decade, the name of the game became mergers, acquisitions, collaborations, and technology swaps. Company rosters were shuffled so often in this version of "merger mania" that what resulted was a confusing corporate maze, and a concentration of business interests in fewer and fewer hands. The British newspaper the *Guardian* wrote in September 1997 that the power and strategic control the companies were amassing would "make the oil industry look like a corner store." The *Guardian Weekly* followed up in December: "With astonishing rapidity, a tiny handful of companies is coming to govern the global development, production, process and marketing of our most fundamental commodity —food."

It would have taken a detailed playbill to keep the mergers and buyouts straight. As an example of the kind of activity that confounded the investment community, AgrEvo bought Plant Genetic Systems of Ghent, Belgium. Calgene, the makers of the Flavr Savr tomato, purchased a licensing option from DNAP, the makers of another long-lasting tomato. Novartis, the giant created through the merger of Sandoz and Ciba Seeds, acquired the New Jersey-based Merck & Co.'s crop protection business. Back in 1989, Dow Chemical had joined forces with Eli Lilly to create Dow Elanco. Dow Elanco in turn bought the small upstart biotechnology company Mycogen. Then Dow Chemical moved to pay Eli Lilly for the remaining shares of Dow Elanco and reincarnated itself at the beginning of 1998 as Dow AgroSciences.

After frantic purchasing of their own, three huge giants were left standing to dominate the field: Novartis; DuPont, which bought a twenty percent share in the world's largest seed company, Pioneer Hi-Bred; and Monsanto, which teamed up with Cargill, the international food-processing company.

By the late 1990s, the few small companies that had managed to survive in the early years finally lost their footing and sold out out to acquisitive multinationals. The poster company for the "small is beautiful" crowd—Calgene—surrendered to Monsanto. The move was an ironic postscript to the *Business Week* story of years earlier that had predicted companies like Monsanto would have to count on the "little ones" to lead the way. Roger Salquist, the man who had been heralded as Calgene's entrepreneurial hero, said the company could not continue to bankroll the technology. "Monsanto can always print money with Roundup," Salquist commented, referring to what had become the world's most popular herbicide.

There was a sense of disappointment in the investment community as it observed the new landscape. In its 1997 annual review of the industry, Ernst & Young management consultants said, "For the ag-bio sector, the handwriting may be on the wall. The sector's leading companies have all ceded ownership or control to larger agricultural companies." The company concluded that multinationals' domination of the market "possibly signalled the end of entrepreneurial ag-bio in the United States."

But many viewed the corporate concentrations from the perspective not of shareholders and their profits but of a community losing its control of food to a few powerful agribusiness interests. In tracking consolidations in the seed industry, the Rural Advancement Foundation International (RAFI) described the first half of 1998 as a dramatic punctuation of corporate concentration that had begun two decades before. It reported that the top ten companies had $7 billion or thirty percent of the commercial seed trade. "The global seed trade is now dominated by life industry giants whose vast economic power and control over plant germ plasm has effectively marginalised the role of public sector plant breeding and research," RAFI wrote in its July/August 1998 communiqué.

Monsanto, the St. Louis-based chemical and pharmaceutical giant, exemplifies what the U.S. biotechnology industry has become. It is the company all the critics like to hate, and they routinely refer to it as the "Pac Man" of the industry, the "shark" in the pond, the "Monster company."

It started small itself in 1901. Its first product was saccharin, supplied exclusively to the youthful Coca-Cola company. After World War One, Monsanto moved into chemicals. In the 1920s, it became an important producer of aspirin, and in the subsequent decades it developed a swathe of new products, including detergents, plastics, fibers, machine controls, and silicon wafers. The 1970s would later become a source of embarrassment for Monsanto, as it supplied Agent Orange to the U.S. government for its scorched earth policy in Vietnam. In the last two decades, Monsanto's name has been synonymous with its blockbuster products, the artificial sweetener NutraSweet and its agricultural herbicide Roundup.

The company that introduced NutraSweet and Agent Orange to the world was dismissed in the 1980s as boring and geriatric. *Barron's* magazine was direct: "Say 'biotech' and chances are you'll think anything but 'Monsanto,' a lumbering 94-year-old chemical maker in St. Louis." However, the company was determined to change those perceptions and set out to recast itself as the leader in America's biotechnology business. In its bid to debunk old thinking, Monsanto displayed the quote from *Barron's* on the cover of its 1995 annual report. Robert Shapiro, who came on as chairman and CEO in 1993, explained, "The reason we put the quote on the cover is that it captures the sense of astonishment and disbelief many people still feel when they begin to understand what Monsanto is becoming."

In the early 1990s, the company was not the biggest player in the biotechnology game—on a global scale, Bayer-Hoechst,

DuPont, Novartis, Dow Elanco, and Rhone-Poulenc were larger. But Monsanto's nervy, pioneering attitudes attracted attention beyond its size. It was the first company to introduce a menu of biotechnology products to the world—bovine growth hormone, the New Leaf potato, Bollguard cotton, and Roundup Ready soybeans and canola. Another fifty new drugs, foods, and crops were said to be in the research pipeline.

Genetic engineering was helping Monsanto earn handsome profits. In 1996, net income reached a record $885 million. The firm's share price rose from $14 at the beginning of 1995 to $39 by the beginning of 1997. On an indexed basis, Monsanto's total shareholder earnings increased more than 350 percent from 1992 to 1998. In 1996, the company's generous returns to shareholders—sixty-two percent of the year's total return —won it a spot on the nation's Fortune 500. Wall Street analysts were as enthusiastic as they had been in the early days of biotechnology. Monsanto, they raved, might become the Microsoft of genetic engineering.

In the mid-1990s, Monsanto launched a ferocious buying spree. It started in 1994 with American Cyanamid, the maker of a group of agricultural herbicides. Then came Agracetus, Asgrow, Calgene, DeKalb Genetics, and Delta & Pine Land. Monsanto secured its distribution network by spending an estimated $1.2 billion to buy Holden Foundation Seeds, a major U.S. corn seed producer, and two of its seed distributors. Then it moved to expand its global influence by buying the international operations of Cargill in Central and Latin America, Europe, Asia, and Africa for $1.4 billion. Then came Plant Breeding International Cambridge from the U.K.-based Unilever for about $525 million. Monsanto clearly had a prodigious appetite. Sano Shimoda, of the research firm BioScience Securities, said at an agricultural conference in 1997 that Monsanto "was set to become one of three or four companies such as DuPont and Novartis to dominate the field."

In the middle of its feeding frenzy, convinced that biotechnology was the path of the future, Monsanto took a dramatic step in its effort to become the leader in the global biotech business. In 1996, it declared its intention to "start over." After ninety-five years, it decided to unceremoniously hive off its massive $3-billion-a-year chemicals business, the original heart of the firm, into a new company called Solutia. What remained —the agricultural products, food ingredients, and pharmaceutical divisions worth around $6 billion a year in sales—would become a new "life sciences" company called Monsanto, which would use biotechnology to develop new foods, drugs, and foods enriched with pharmaceuticals.

"Life sciences" was the new moniker to describe the corporate ability to control all steps of the life and food cycle from DNA to dinner plate. It was the marriage of food ingredients, medicine, and agricultural products. There were already other life sciences players on the court—notably Novartis. With 100,000 employees and operations in seventy-five countries, Novartis was undoubtedly the world's largest life sciences company. Monsanto was the poor country cousin with just twenty-eight thousand employees before the split.

Monsanto hoped that by breaking down the old barriers between its agriculture, food, and pharmaceutical divisions, it would enter the global arena. "Monsanto has been moving towards a future in life sciences for the last decade," the 1996 annual report declared. The new company "will be an even tougher, lower-cost, more aggressive competitor than it is today." Shapiro said the reorganization, along with the shopping expedition, had positioned Monsanto for the future. "Once the pending transactions are completed and a new corporate infrastructure is in place, we will have the capabilities we will need as a life sciences company to quickly move our agricultural biotechnology products into the marketplace; to launch our major products in our pharmaceutical pipeline and to connect the areas of food and health."

However, the split and the multibillion-dollar shopping spree would test the company's financial mettle. To offset its own possible vulnerability to takeovers, Shapiro orchestrated a $33 billion merger with American Home Products, a massive drug company that produces weight loss aids and contraceptives as part of its pharmaceutical menu. The merger, announced in June 1998, was to be one of the largest deals in American corporate history. Monsanto would immediately became the world's number one agrochemical company, number two seed company, number four pharmaceutical company, and among the top five veterinary drugs companies. However, in October 1998, Monsanto and American Home Products announced that they had both agreed to call off the deal for unspecified reasons. Monsanto was left looking financially strained. In November 1998, Shapiro announced the company would attempt to raise $4 billion to fund its recent seed company acquisitions through a series of financing transactions, and a combination of divestitures and cost reductions. Up to one thousand jobs would be eliminated and another fifteen hundred would be affected by the sale of "non-core assets." Yet Shapiro remained publicly optimistic, predicting Monsanto would be back and growing soon. "The period from 1999 to 2001 will be one of execution in the marketplace and delivery for our shareholders," he said.

Monsanto may have been recreating itself as a life sciences company, but like many in the burgeoning biotechnology field, its roots were thoroughly chemical. The companies beginning to rule biotechnology had all dominated what the agriculture industry euphemistically called crop protection. It was no accident that in 1997, according to three independent industry estimates, world pesticide sales grew for the third year in a row. The *Pesticide Action Newsletter* estimated that the top ten global agrochemical companies enjoyed sales totaling $4.2 billion in 1997, up twenty-one percent over the previous year.

Monsanto was building its strength on profits from its hugely successful herbicide Roundup. First introduced in 1974, Roundup was enjoying a new lease on life two decades later —an astounding persistence in an environment where farm chemicals are regularly supplanted by new products.

The herbicide had gone through three growth spurts and was about to start a fourth. Roundup began its life as a premium-priced herbicide for high-value crops. In the mid-1980s, Monsanto dropped its price, allowing it to infiltrate lower-value markets. The third phase of growth was based on the increasing use of the herbicide in conservation tillage. That is, instead of turning over the earth to expose and dry out weed roots, allowing precious soil to be blown away, farmers began to kill weeds with a chemical like Roundup and plant their crops right into stubble-covered fields. Roundup's fourth growth burst would be based on biotechnology and crops engineered to be resistant to the chemical. The proposed menu of Roundup Ready crops was extensive: soybeans, corn, canola, and cotton, to begin with.

Although Roundup is due to lose its patent protection in the U.S. in 2000, the herbicide's position in the marketplace seems secure. Nineteen ninety-five was a banner year for the all-purpose weed killer and the company sold another twenty percent more the next year—three times as much as it did in

1990. Monsanto's 1996 annual report conceded that this kind of growth could not continue for ever but affirmed that "the profitability of Roundup herbicide could be sustained at least through the 1990s."

The company's confidence in the chemical was underscored by its investment of more than $200 million in 1995 and 1996 to increase its worldwide manufacturing capacity. That kind of commitment would continue in subsequent years with plans for another $180 million in manufacturing capabilities. Selling its herbicide was clearly the route to profit for Monsanto, the "life sciences" company. In information collected by the *World Crop Protection News*, Monsanto was the globe's biggest chemical seller, with sales in 1997 of $3.16 billion.

Although biotechnology has left its small, entrepreneurial roots far behind, the industry has borrowed one of the best lines from that heady era. It argues that only biotechnology can create new productive foods and crops to feed a global population that will double to ten billion by 2050. To feed that population, farmers would have to produce as much food in a single year as has been grown in the whole history of farming. The production challenges are numbing. Yet corporate biotechnology, cloaked in the mantle of humanity's benefactor, repeats its mantra that only genetic engineering can do the job.

This logic has won biotechnology supporters, many in high places. Former U.S. president Jimmy Carter wrote a piece in the *Washington Times* in July 1997, lauding the new science as a way of forestalling global famine. "Responsible biotechnology is not the enemy; starvation is. Without adequate food supplies, we cannot expect world health, or peace." Reflecting his government's staunch support of biotechnology, U.S. Secretary of Agriculture Dan Glickman told the World Food

Summit in Rome in November 1996: "Today the world's population is increasing by the equivalent of a New York City every month, a Mexico every year and a China every decade. Without biotechnology, we will be forced to exploit highly erodable farm and forest land. This may meet our short-term needs, but in the end, our legacy to future generations will be a barren earth. . . . Biotechnology can give us a quantum leap forward in food security by improving disease and pest resistance, increasing tolerance to environmental stress, raising crop yields and preserving plant and animal diversity."

In theory, Carter, Glickman, and the other proponents of biotechnology are right. The prospects for feeding a growing and hungry world with conventional agriculture are not good. Currently, three billion people face poverty and hunger in the world's least developed nations. That number is sure to rise as the world's population climbs. Biotechnology might be capable of easing this crisis if it concentrated, for example, on creating a healthier or more productive rice plant that the developing world could afford to buy. However, so far the industry seems much more interested in creating profitable products such as designer foods for the industrialized world.

In the 1960s, significant new developments in breeding, chemicals, and equipment launched dramatic productivity improvements. This so-called Green Revolution accelerated yields in the industrialized world, but developing countries did not benefit from the same productivity improvements. Farmers there could not afford the expensive equipment and agricultural chemicals demanded by the new approach to farming. In much the same way, commercial biotechnology is unlikely to take hold in the developing world, where it is most needed. Poor farmers in Africa and Asia will not be able to afford the chemicals or the premium seeds the industry prescribes.

The inequitable distribution of food among the wealthy and the poor is a complex problem that science alone will not be able to solve. The challenges for developing countries are daunting: among their many needs are economic and political reform, education, land reform, debt relief, agricultural infrastructure, strict deforestation policies, realistic government food subsidies, and family planning. During the famine of the early 1990s, for example, Ethiopia was still exporting food. Millions were left hungry because factional warfare prevented food from being distributed where it was needed.

Delegates at an international meeting of leading agricultural scientists held in India in July 1997 concluded that science would not be enough to meet the food shortages expected in the next millennium. The scientists, including many who spearheaded agriculture's Green Revolution, said the world should not count on a repeat performance. On the threshold of the new millennium, agricultural productivity is indeed leveling off. Food production is growing at its slowest rate in four decades, and is on the decline in ninety countries, including forty-four in Africa. Biotechnology would only be useful in feeding the extra two billion mouths expected in developing countries if access to it were free and democratic, much like agricultural research used to be.

International agencies are very aware that biotechnology is becoming a rich man's game. The International Service for the Acquisition of Agri-biotech Applications (ISAAA) was established with the hope of extending biotechnology to the developing world. In its review of field testing and commercialization of transgenic plants from 1986 to 1995, it found that ninety-one percent of the 3500 field trials of biotech crops in that period occurred in industrialized countries. Only two percent of trials took place in the developing countries of Asia—almost all of them in China—and very few took place in Africa. The report noted that most of the research was on modified corn, canola, and tomatoes—hardly staples in countries stricken with hunger. And the most popular trait tested in field trials around the world was herbicide tolerance, a technology that is out of reach for impoverished farmers in the same countries.

Yet the refrain continues from corporate biotechnology. Monsanto, for example, used global population growth as a key rationale for its radical restructuring. CEO Shapiro says his new life sciences company is what the world needs if people hope to feed themselves without resorting to despoiling the environment in an effort to scratch out more arable land. Shapiro's penchant for talking about "sustainability" in the face of a population increase and the feared environmental degradation that would go with it, prompted the *Economist* to dub him the "the green gene giant" in April 1997. The magazine was unabashedly enthusiastic about the new tone at Monsanto. "Rather than having to discuss toxic spills, Monsanto now talks about feeding the world."

Indeed, Monsanto does devote a small portion of its research and development dollars to biotechnology work in the developing world. The company's self-described philanthropy includes sponsoring a handful of research projects in these countries. The aim, says Monsanto, is to produce social good, not just commercial goods.

One example was Monsanto's collaboration with the U.S. Agency for International Development in the early 1990s to bring Florence Wambugu and several other scientists from Kenya to St. Louis to work with Monsanto researchers on a project to redesign the African sweet potato. The sweet potato is a major food crop for poor people throughout Africa, but it is routinely decimated each year by a virus. The feathery

mottle virus can reduce crop yields by as much as eighty percent. The scientists studied gene-splicing techniques with
Monsanto scientists, hoping to adapt the techniques to give
the potato resistance to the virus. "Giving this knowledge and
technology has greater implications than just handing over a
bag of food," Wambugu told the *St. Louis Post-Dispatch* in
1992. "If you have knowledge, you can change Africa." Many
of Africa's food shortages are a direct result of a failure to invest
in research to improve local crops. Over the years, science in
Africa has focused on improving cash crops for export, not on
developing food for starving Africans. The Monsanto project
was exceptional. Typically, in the past, African scientists were
brought to the U.S. to work on crops like corn and soybeans,
which are not particularly useful to their home countries.

Other collaborative programs between developing countries
and the private sector in the developed world include about
a dozen projects put together by ISAAA. For example, with
funding from the Rockefeller Foundation, Monsanto donated
protein genes to Mexico to allow Mexican researchers to
develop virus-resistant potatoes. Pioneer Hi-Bred contributed
to the development and transfer of several diagnostics for
maize diseases to Brazil. And Sandoz transferred a marker gene
in cassava to Africa and Latin America.

The international development community concedes that
corporate biotechnology could help feed a world in which, even
now, 200 million children are chronically hungry. But in order
to make a real difference, it would have to do much more than
fund a few philanthropic projects. Joel Cohen, of the U.S.
Agency for International Development, said in an interview that
for biotechnology to succeed in the developing world, "the
tremendous potential of private industry must be tapped." No
such undertaking looks imminent.

Bioethicist Arthur Schafer has little faith that biotechnology will ride to the rescue of a hungry world. In fact, he says, "It may be that it will annihilate Third World food production. It may eliminate the need for cocoa because through genetic engineering we may be able to grow it in Canada; we won't have to import from poor southern countries. We will eliminate the need for their agriculture altogether.

"It's so easy to say it's going to benefit these poor people. That's not why it is being introduced. It's being introduced to make money."

Making money is clearly the focus of the biotechnology business. The corporate strategy even strives to ensure that farmers in the developing world pay dearly for the proceeds of the new science.

In traditional agriculture, farmers routinely hold back some seeds each year for the next year's crop or buy a truckload of seed from the neighbor down the road. It is estimated that three-quarters of farmers in North America hold back seed. In the world of farming, that is viewed as plain common sense or neighborliness. However, from a corporate point of view, it is pirating, much like what is practiced routinely in the software industry.

Seed companies have long struggled with how to break the natural cycle of seeds, which perpetually produces new seeds for planting. They have done so, in part, by creating hybrids that either will not reproduce in the subsequent year or will reproduce inferior crops. Biotechnology has bettered those early attempts. In 1998, Delta & Pine Land and the USDA announced they had won a patent on what they called the "Terminator," a gene that would prevent the germination of seeds the second year. Soon after, Monsanto bought Delta & Pine Land

and its Terminator gene. By the end of 1998, it was moving to convince the USDA to give Delta & Pine the exclusive license for the seed-sterilizing technology.

After the Terminator came the "Verminator," a new chemically activated seed killer. The Verminator does its deed by switching on rodent fat genes that have been bioengineered into seeds. Its developer, the U.K. company Zeneca, planned to apply for patents in fifty-eight countries. "The Verminator is a broader, more pervasive variation on the Monster's Terminator," said Pat Mooney, executive director of Rural Advancement Foundation International (RAFI). Other biotech companies were apparently working on other strategies to limit the long-standing practices of farmers around the world.

In the interim, biotechnology companies resorted to charging royalties from seed companies to get their return. Monsanto opted for an even more aggressive strategy—going straight to farmers for payment. Under Monsanto's plan, farmers have to sign a "Technology Use Agreement" if they want to use Roundup Ready or the company's Bt crops. Under the agreement, producers must first attend an enrollment meeting, then agree not to keep the seed or to sell or give away seeds for planting purposes. They must also allow Monsanto agents to inspect their property for up to three years after planting the crop. There would be no trust-on-a-handshake on Monsanto's part.

It was a brash strategy aimed at a farming community that had always prided itself on its autonomy. Monsanto's move was designed to retain gains for proprietary research and to enhance profits. It also effectively weakened the independence and inter-dependence of farmers. In many ways, this was vertical integration right down to the farmers' fields.

Ever ready with its public relations machine, Monsanto countered any anxiety in the agricultural community with testimonials from farmers. Steve Richards of Lashburn, Saskat-chewan, was quoted in an advertising supplement entitled "Fields of the Future" as saying: "If companies are unable to get a return on their investment, it's unlikely new technologies will continue to come to market. The Technology Use Agreement can be a win-win situation if producers are shown the potential return."

However, their first year with Monsanto's biotech crops gave farmers a direct lesson in how far the company was prepared to go to guarantee its return. To enforce the TUAs, Monsanto hired Pinkerton security and solicited tips from seed cleaners, farm supply dealers, seed company sales representatives, and other farmers about producers they suspected of saving seeds. In Canada, there were reports of one grower who bought a TUA but was found to have a quarter section more of Roundup Ready seed in the ground than he had paid for. He settled by paying a penalty. Another producer who had grown and harvested Roundup Ready canola without a TUA was required not only to pay a fine, but to turn over the proceeds from the crop.

However, a little simple math shows that Monsanto will hardly be struggling to get a return on its research investment. The company was charging farmers a user's fee of about $5 per bag of soybeans. That works out to about $10 an acre. In 1998, American farmers were expected to grow thirty million acres of Roundup Ready soybeans. That adds up to about $300 million. Add to that the cost of the matching herbicide —another $540 million. Even after calculating the costs of maintaining a distribution and marketing force, the proceeds from one year's worth of Roundup Ready soybeans certainly pay for the development of the technology—plus return a tidy sum to shareholders.

The United Nations Food and Agriculture Organization estimates there are 1.4 billion poor people around the world who depend on farm-saved seed for their food security. That fundamental convention of farming is now being challenged by the technology use agreement strategy, the Terminator and the Verminator. Monsanto and Pioneer are also both said to be working to develop a hybrid wheat. Until now, small grains cereals such as wheat and rice—the two staple crops that much of the world depends on—have defied efforts to hybridize them and to take them from farmer control.

Twenty years ago, before biotechnology was invented, no one spoke about owning a life. Today, companies refuse to take a scientific step without protecting their "intellectual property" with a patent. Patents guarantee that competitors cannot borrow a firm's ideas without paying for them.

Invariably, these patents protect single genes, the genes that will infuse plants or animals with new characteristics. From the patent perspective, genes are not just the building blocks of living things, they are the keys to new products. In the world of biotechnology, genes are not viewed as living things, but simply as chemical carriers of information.

Patents have a history in the U.S. that goes back more than two hundred years. Thomas Jefferson, the owner of a large plantation and an inventor and scientist himself, drafted America's first Patent Act in 1793. He argued that patents were necessary so "that ingenuity should receive a liberal encouragement." There is no reason to believe he ever intended the law to cover life-forms. Indeed, for almost two hundred years, the idea that humans could hold patents on microbes, plants, animals, or their genes was roundly dismissed. Congress, in fact, refused to cover new plant varieties under the patent legislation, opting instead to enact specific and more limited protection schemes for plants. Traditionally, patentable inventions were defined as being capable of some industrial application. Ideas, discoveries, artistic works, business schemes, and living things could not be patented.

In 1971, General Electric decided to challenge those conventions by filing a patent application for a bacterium that could digest oil hydrocarbons. Although the Patent Office rejected the application, in 1980 the Supreme Court ruled five to four that the oil-eating microbe was indeed a "human-made invention" and therefore patentable. It took another seven years for the U.S. Patent Office to interpret the Supreme Court decision in the case and essentially establish patentability for any living thing under the sun. What had been the unthinkable was suddenly accepted—a microbe, a plant, or an animal could be owned. In 1988, the world's first patent of a genetically engineered animal was granted to Harvard College for its development of the Oncomouse—a mouse that been genetically modified to develop a certain kind of cancer. By late 1998, the U.S. Patent and Trademark Office had claims to eighteen hundred genes, eighty-five mice, three rats, three rabbits, a sheep, a nematode, a bird, a fish, a pig, a guinea pig, an abalone, and a cow.

Patenting of life, with the exception of human beings, is now an accepted practice in many industrialized countries. Even the European Union, which had held out giving approval for more than a decade, buckled under industry pressure in 1997 and agreed to grant life patents. Canada has so far refused to bend to the corporate lobby. But the fact that it is a small market made its stand on patents hardly significant.

For a company to be granted a patent on a biotechnological innovation in the U.S., it has to prove that the invention is new, useful, and an advance on existing science. It often takes about four years for a patent to be approved. The application usually remains top secret; that, in turn, can hold up trials until the patent is granted. If a patent is proffered, the company is given the exclusive right to use, sell, or manufacture its invention for the term of the patent, usually seventeen to twenty years.

Most companies see patents as currency; for example, companies might exchange rights to one another's patented material through cross-licensing, or patent holders can earn income by licensing access to others. More than a hundred patents are issued for genetically engineered inventions each year in the U.S. In 1995, for example, they included a corn line from Pioneer Hi-Bred; a tobacco from Arizona Technology Development that expresses M-sexta, a protein that can block the digestion of insect pests; and a Bt process from Mycogen to combat flea beetles and alfalfa weevils.

In this scientific gold rush, companies vigorously stake their patent claims and defend their piece of intellectual turf with deadly earnestness. Patents are, after all, the lifeblood of the biotech business. Competing firms do not sit idly by when a patent is approved—their patent lawyers immediately assess whether the new patent overlaps with existing patents. For example, every aspect of Bt genes has been contested, from the promoters to markers. The legal infighting has pitted Novartis against Monsanto, Mycogen against Monsanto, DeKalb against Northrup King. To show what the stakes are, a San Diego jury ruled in March 1998 against Monsanto and in favor of Mycogen, awarding the company $174.9 million in damages on the basis that Monsanto had delayed providing access to an accelerated gene technology in accordance with a 1989 agreement.

In 1996, litigations were up sixty-nine percent over the previous two years. There were sixteen new legal cases involving the industry's biggest players—Pioneer Hi-Bred, Monsanto, Novartis, Northrup King, and AgrEvo. Almost all involved patents for transgenic seeds. Although each litigation costs an average of $3 million, it represents a potential market of about $100 million. There have been so many lawsuits in recent years over claimed patent infringements that even industry insiders have a hard time keeping track of who is suing whom. One thing is sure. Extended litigation saps the strength of weaker companies, furthering the consolidation of the industry.

Patents essentially give a company or an agency the opportunity to lock out competitors. In practice, that means that university researchers or regional and local seed companies that might have been engaged in valuable public research are also prohibited from using the patents. Patent rights thereby determine the number of researchers in the market. The big concern is that patents may actually curb research, by granting control of a commodity to a single company.

Government and university scientists have been blindsided by the many patents that now protect the kinds of advances they used to trade freely among themselves. A story in the *Kitchener-Waterloo Record* on April 13, 1998, reported the frustrations of John Dueck, director of Agriculture Canada's Eastern Cereal and Oilseed Research Centre in Ottawa. Dueck was engaged in crucial negotiations over the cost in royalties and license fees of getting some new advances to local farmers. "Frankly," he admitted, "some of us were a bit naive in the past."

Patents may effectively close the door on much public research and development, particularly in developing countries, where most of the world's anticipated population growth will occur. And patentable genes are often found in the rich ecosystems of the developing world. In pursuit of valuable genes for the health-care field, cell samples have even been taken from indigenous peoples, and the genes then patented. So rather than assisting the developing world, corporate biotechnology has been accused of "biopiracy" in its scramble for valuable patents. Before the patenting of life-forms, agricultural researchers in developing countries had access to nonproprietary technologies from the public sector. Now, advances in biotechnology are proprietary information, locked in by patents and controlled by multinational corporations intent on making profits.

In addition to their patent offices, the large multinational corporations that control biotechnology maintain well-staffed public relations departments. These units provide the spin on genetic engineering that will win over governments, consumers, and farmers. The first and most essential rule is to avoid the words "genetic engineering." This is, after all, a world in which nothing is as it seems. Sewage sludge is "biosolids." So genetic engineering becomes "novel traits." On the consumer front, the biotechnology sell emphasizes better taste (Flavr Savr tomato) or more environmentally friendly systems (bug-proof plants). Monsanto's New Leaf potato campaign obliquely claims: "Plant breeders were able to breed resistance to the Colorado potato beetle into this variety. No need for chemicals." And, of course, the industry continues its "education" program to teach people that biotechnology is no different from the quaint crossing of breeds that has long defined agricultural science.

On the farm front, AgrEvo introduced its Liberty Link canola to farmers with not one reference to gene splicing. "What does that matter to farmers?" remarked Steve Meister, the head of the company's public relations in North America. It is typically assumed that producers will accept whatever their local seed dealers tell them. Farmers are inundated with glossy brochures, advertisements, and television commercials featuring the approved language and the aggressive look of biotechnology—pumas, jaguars, and sumo wrestlers are all used to depict the force that scientific smarts will use to vanquish nature.

Extensive public relations budgets equip companies well for the essential persuasion of governments. Observers say that Monsanto spent millions of dollars up to 1996 in its unsuccessful effort to persuade Canada to approve bovine growth hormone (BGH) for use in milking cows. Some avenues of influence rely more on personal relationships than on big budgets. For example, Mickey Kantor, former U.S. trade representative and until January 1996, secretary of commerce, was appointed a member of Monsanto's board of directors. In 1997, Marcia Hale moved from assistant to the president of the United States for intergovernmental affairs to senior official with Monsanto to coordinate public affairs and corporate strategy in the U.K. and Ireland. After about six months, she returned to Monsanto's Washington office to handle international and "other matters," which the *Washington Post* described as a "sweet job." Josh King, a director of production for White House events who traveled extensively with President Clinton, left the staff in late 1997 to join Monsanto as director of global coordination in the firm's Washington office.

In summer of 1998, Monsanto launched a $1 million advertising campaign designed to convince recalcitrant Europeans that there was nothing frightening about biotechnology in food. Its advertisements in British newspapers inflamed groups opposed to the new science by listing their phone numbers. Claiming its intention was to be open and transparent, a

Monsanto spokesman said, "We believe food is so fundamentally important, everyone should know all they want about it." Monsanto turned up the temperature further by building its European advertising campaign around its "we will feed the world" motto. It appealed to Europeans not to be selfish. "Let the harvest begin," the ads read.

Many developing nations took umbrage at this very commercial strategy. Delegates of African countries participating in the fifth extraordinary session of the Commission on Genetic Resources in June 1998 asked for support in fighting Monsanto. "We . . . strongly object that the image of the poor and hungry for our countries is being used by giant multi-national corporations to push a technology that is neither safe, environmentally friendly, nor economically beneficial to us," their statement read. "We agree and accept that mutual help is needed to further improve agricultural productivity in our countries. We also believe that Western science contributes to this. But it should be done on the basis of understanding and respect for what is already there. It should be building on local knowledge rather than replacing and destroying it. And most importantly, it should address the needs of our people rather than serving only to swell the pockets and control of giant industrial corporations."

In late June 1998, at a financial conference in New York, Monsanto announced another plan whose humanitarian motives might have been expected to garner it international favor. The company would contribute $150,000 to an institute called the Grameen-Monsanto Center for Environment-Friendly Technologies, which would administer a plan to provide access to technology to very low income people. Monsanto's partner in this venture, the Grameen Bank, had earned global acclaim in the past for helping the entrepreneurial efforts of women caught in the grip of famine and economic turmoil.

This time, observers were less impressed by the Grameen Bank's decision to get in bed with an aggressive transnational corporation. Vandana Shiva, the recognized Indian environmentalist, wrote to Grameen's founder, Professor Mohammed Yanus: "When you announced your joint venture with Monsanto ... you reversed the movement and took a step to betray the interests of women you have served so far. The micro-credit scheme linked to the Grameen-Monsanto Center will create markets for Monsanto products, not the products based on the creativity of Bangledeshi peasants." Three weeks later, Yanus canceled the deal, explaining, "We were not informed of Monsanto's massive involvement in agriculture which the environmentalists at home and abroad have agreed is detrimental to the interest of the poor farmer."

Multinational corporations now comprise fifty-one of the world's one hundred largest economies—many have more clout than some countries. Some of the richest of these run the biotech industry, which continues to insist that its purpose is feeding the world and creating valuable new foods. The patent wars, ruthless business takeovers, and cynical efforts to buy support in consumer and government ranks are just part of the normal running of a modern multinational industry.

In the world of profit, bigger is definitely better. Biotechnology is no longer a small, upstart business with romantic ideas about providing goods and services to the public, and making some money in the process. The original founders of Calgene harbor no hard feelings about the transformation in the business, no sentimentality about the days gone by. Norman Goldfarb is back in the computer business, Raymond Valentine has retired, and Roger Salquist now describes himself as a "merchant banker" helping small entrepreneurial companies develop niche markets on the peripheral edges of the biotechnology industry. Perhaps it is old-fashioned to be concerned that global giants out for profit above all have taken control of a basic essential of life—food—and that governments and consumers, either through acquiescence or ignorance, are allowing it to happen.

4

BOOSTED BOVINES: A CASE STUDY

A JAGGED SMUDGE OF LIPSTICK PINK HANGS ON THE DAWN horizon. Frigid air clings like an arctic blanket over the American Midwest. Judy Klusman emerges from the barn, her booted feet crunching in the brittle snow. Grasped in her mitts are two pails loaded with milk bottles fitted with oversized nipples. She heads toward the calf huts—the surreal white plastic enclosures that shimmer in the first hint of daylight. Soon the only sound to be heard on this Wisconsin dairy farm will be the eager slurping of the calves as they tug on the artificial teats that act as their surrogate mothers.

This dawn ritual is Judy Klusman's favorite chore. The calves bellow softly and stomp the frozen ground in anticipation as she approaches. She is, after all, their nourishment, their lifeline. With her cheeks reddened by the chill and the rooster crowing in the distance, she is part of the age-old image of the dairy farm. All that is missing is the calico cat lapping at the milk pail. But the true picture of the modern, technologically based dairy business is inside the barn. There, the first shift of cows plods into the humid warmth of the tile-lined milking parlor from the open-air feeding stalls. The hired hand attaches the automatic milkers to the cows' swollen udders. The pure, white fluid is sucked into the sterilized, galvanized pipes of the milk pumping system.

Klusman is the fifth generation in a family line of dairy farmers to work this operation in Wisconsin. She transformed what was a classic family farm into a modern agribusiness. Her father milked sixty-eight cows morning and night in the traditional dairying pattern. Under her direction, about 130 cows shuffle into the milking parlor three times a day—the two full-time employees spend most of the day in the milking pit. Thanks to a protein-enriched diet and an intensive milking schedule, each cow produces an average of twelve thousand liters of milk a year. That's twice the state average and enough to have the Klusman operation listed among the top ten producers, on a per-cow basis, in the country.

Although she is charmed by the insistent tug of the suckling calves, Klusman is a hard-nosed businesswoman. She will ship the male calves off to market in mere days so their mothers' milk will no longer be needed for them. There is no room for unproductive sentiment here. Klusman's farm philosophy is about the bottom line; her language is peppered with references to "progressive farmers," "productivity goals," and "management tools."

This is February 3, 1994. Tomorrow, one more "management tool" becomes available for Klusman and other American dairy farmers looking for high milk production. February 4 is the day the U.S. Food and Drug Administration has set for the international chemical giant, Monsanto, to begin marketing recombinant bovine somatotropin (BST) or, as it is commonly called, bovine growth hormone (BGH). BST is a genetically engineered drug that when injected into a cow can elevate her milk production by as much as twenty-five percent. As the first gene-spliced food product to appear on the United States market, BST will set the course for the future of biotechnology around the world.

BST is a protein hormone that occurs naturally in dairy cattle. Scientists have known for fifty years that supplemental BST could boost milk production in lactating cows. However, it could only be extracted from the pituitary glands of slaughtered cattle. Until genetic engineering came along, there was no practical way to mass-produce BST. Gene splicers found a way to improve on nature by taking the gene that generates BST in cattle, inserting it into the *E. coli* bacterium, and then multiplying it in a fermentation tank.

Four companies—Monsanto, Eli Lilly, American Cyanamid, and Upjohn—were working on similar efforts to boost bovines, but only Monsanto was awarded the right to market its version. Genetically engineered BST must be injected into cows on a regular basis much as insulin is administered to people who have certain types of diabetes. Nine weeks after they give birth, cows are started on a regime of Posilac, as BST is trademarked, which is repeated every two weeks for about ten months, the normal lactation period for a cow.

Monsanto's engineered BST is virtually the same as the natural version—virtually, but not exactly. The company's synthetic model is constructed with an extra amino acid—an alteration that Monsanto scientists dismiss as inconsequential. Milk from American dairy farms is collected in giant tanker trucks, pooled, and delivered to processors for pasteurization. There is no effort to separate out the milk from farms that use recombinant BST. After all, the FDA ruled that milk from

BST-boosted cows cannot be differentiated from milk from untreated cows. For that reason, no special labeling is required for this brand of biotechnological progress. As of February 4, 1994, BST would simply slide into the milk supply as American cheese, butter, yogurt, ice cream, and infant formula.

In the early 1990s, BST generated what easily can be described as the greatest controversy in U.S. dairy industry history. The battle lines between opposing forces were clearly drawn—even language defined what perspectives people had. Supporters of the drug usually used the term BST. Those opposed opted for the more descriptive term, BGH or bovine growth hormone. (I have chosen to use BST most often because the term is scientifically more precise.)

Monsanto tried to convince consumers that BST was an innocent enough use of the new gene-splicing technology. However, Americans responded unpredictably. They were shocked by the idea of someone tinkering with what was always considered a pure, wholesome, natural food. For most Americans, nothing is more symbolic of health, nutrition, and clean-cut values than milk—it is the drink Mom pours you with her apple pie.

The FDA tested the political winds and decided it had better take its time considering the potential implications for human and animal health before it approved the drug. Monsanto pulled out all the political stops to help persuade the federal agency that synthetic BST would have little impact on the dairy business or on consumers' health.

University researchers, many of whose work rested on financial support from Monsanto, played their part. They produced fifteen hundred studies that affirmed the purity of Monsanto's new drug. More than twenty thousand cows were tested with the drug throughout the 1980s. This research was the basis for Monsanto's contention that there was no scientific reason to deny the approval of BST—there were no documented human health implications and veterinarians found that animals' health concerns could be adequately managed.

The experience of one research team did, however, ring some alarm bells. Three British scientists who analyzed data on BST for Monsanto charged that the company tried to block publication of their findings. Erik Millstone, Eric Brunner, and Ian White said that the firm stopped the printing of their 1991 paper that linked the hormone supplement to somatic cell (pus and bacteria) counts as a result of increased incidences of udder infections in boosted cows. In a tell-all article published in *Nature* magazine, they said they found much higher white cell counts in milk from treated cows than had been reported by Monsanto. "Until those data are in the public domain, some important questions about the effects of BST on animal health will remain unresolved," they wrote. Although this one study hardly negated all the other findings, it did show the extent to which Monsanto was prepared to ensure that the scientific literature was favorable.

Monsanto's application to the FDA was backed by an impressive lineup from political, industrial, and scientific establishments. The American Medical Association, the Association of American Dieticians, the International Dairy Foods Association, the National Milk Producers Federation, the Grocery Manufacturers of America, among others, all offered ringing endorsements for BST throughout the early 1990s. There was additional support from organizations like the National Institutes of Health and the United Nations World Health Organization.

Monsanto did what it could to forge potentially advantageous political alliances. According to confidential documents obtained by opponents of BST and handed over to the *New*

York Times, Monsanto used the friendship of Tony Coehlo, chief strategist for the Democratic National Committee, with then Agriculture Secretary Mike Espy to try to win favor for BST. Monsanto apparently prepared notes for Coehlo on how he was to broach the subject of the hormone supplement over dinner with Espy. "Let Secretary Espy know that companies like Monsanto will likely pull out of agriculture biotech if the Administration does not stand up to persons like Senator Feingold," the memo said. (Senator Russ Feingold, a Democrat from Wisconsin, had been responsible for organizing Congressional opposition to BST.) The briefing notes were leaked to the press before the dinner meeting happened, so it can only be speculated what impact Coehlo's lobbying on Monsanto's behalf may have had.

Several members of Congress accused three FDA officials of conflict of interest and ethical misconduct in their handling of the BST file. A subsequent thirty-page report from the U.S. General Accounting Office (GAO) detailed how a former Monsanto lawyer, Michael Taylor, a former Monsanto scientist, Margaret Miller, and Suzanne Sechen, a student of Monsanto's top scientist, all played key roles in the FDA's ultimate decision to approve BST. Taylor, for example, had been a leading Washington, D.C., lawyer representing Monsanto until 1991. After that, as deputy FDA commissioner, Taylor wrote the policy exempting BST and other biotech food products from labeling. Despite the extensive details in its report, the GAO concluded there had been only minor rule-breaking by the FDA employees. Vermont Congressman Bernie Sanders, who was one of the members to bring the complaint forward, remarked that while the GAO may have cleared the employees, it also proved that "the FDA allowed corporate influence to run rampant in its approval" of the drug.

No matter how diligently Monsanto worked to win support

for its invention, many Americans remained unconvinced. As BST would not make milk more nutritious or tasty, consumers wondered who other than Monsanto and large dairy producers would benefit from the new test-tube food.

BST became an easy target for the Pure Food Campaign. Rifkin and his group based their opposition to BST on ethical grounds, arguing that the hormone supplement would harm cows, affect human health, spell the end for smaller dairy farms, and needlessly tinker with nature's bounty. The campaign organized a network of chefs, school districts, and health-care institutions that vowed not to use genetically engineered products. It launched a series of court challenges with the hope of stemming the incoming tide of biotechnology in food. And, finally, there were demonstrations, events, and interviews to persuade the American people it was just plain wrong to fiddle with Mother Nature. "The battle will now be fought for the consumer," one Pure Food Campaigner told the press. "It will be fought in every grocery store, in every ice cream shop, in every pizza parlor."

The corner store battle seemed drawn between those who believed there was sufficient evidence of BST's safety and those who felt the ethical implications of the hormone called for caution. It took nine years for the FDA to consider the debate. In late 1993, the federal agency finally determined there was no scientific reason not to approve the bovine booster. Its findings showed that because BST is a protein-based hormone, it is broken down during digestion, rendering it inactive and incapable of having any effect in humans. In addition, the FDA concluded that well-managed BST-treated cows experienced no greater health problems than untreated cows who also produced high levels of milk. On granting BST a clean bill of health, FDA Commissioner David Kessler said: "This has been one of the most extensively studied animal drug products to be reviewed by this agency. The public can be confident that milk and meat from BST-treated cows is safe to consume."

Nowhere was the debate over BST more intense than in Wisconsin. There are thirty thousand dairy farmers in the state, almost as many as in all of Canada. For decades, Wisconsin produced more milk than any other state. The license plates here read "America's Dairyland." Wisconsin tourism struts the classic black-and-white Holstein motif proudly on aprons, hats, and mugs. In one shop window, the dairy paraphernalia—a neon cow light, Holstein cow pins, neckties in the cow pattern—are displayed with meticulous care. Huge fiberglass cows and giant mice eating immense cheeses greet travelers on the interstate. Dairy silos seem to rise with every turn in the road.

In early 1994, Judy Klusman had emerged as one of Wisconsin's most ardent BST supporters. Not only was she one of the state's most productive farmers, she was also a Republican representative in the state assembly. For her, the bovine growth hormone dispute had become as vicious as the abortion debate. Klusman had received crude messages on her answering machine; her son had been harassed at school. But she remained resolutely supportive of the genetically engineered hormone supplement. She had not yet ordered Monsanto's BST, but as a self-described progressive dairy farmer, she was matter-of-fact about her plans to use what she saw as a new technology. "I'm going to use any management tool that will help increase the productivity of my cows," she said. "This particular product is not capital intensive. I don't have to build on to my barn or add more cows to get more milk."

On release day, February 4, Klusman is decked out in an electric-blue suit and functional business pumps, a study in contrast from her working dairy farmer garb. She is taking her campaign to the state assembly, where she is trying to convince the Democratic majority that labeling of milk—either BST-treated or BST-free—should not be allowed. Wisconsin has no say over whether the drug is legal or not—that is a matter already settled by the FDA. However, state representatives cannot help but be dragged into a debate that is so central to Wisconsin's very definition of itself.

Brandishing the microphone like a nightclub singer, Klusman reminds her audience of state representatives that countless scientific studies have shown that BST has no impact on human or animal health. "If we don't think science is real, then let's get rid of it. Get it out of the school system." Her voice rises perilously in its passion, but the Democratic majority members remain impassive. "Science is not infallible," she determinedly continues. "But if we don't trust science, we are never going to progress. I mean, we are just going to stop and stand still. And I don't think people are ready for that either."

While Klusman warms up to her topic inside the shelter of the capitol, the stone figure named Wisconsin on the building's dome gazes down dispassionately on a demonstration beginning on the outside stairs. It is a bitterly cold day and about thirty protesters huddle on the granite steps, headbands, toques, and scarves bundled around their ears. They have braved the frigid temperatures to draw notice to what they call "Sour Thursday." Their placards read "Keep milk pure" and "Don't do drugs." One woman's face is obscured by a plastic Halloween mask shaped like a cow's face. In a show of defiance, one by one the protesters pour milk into a garbage pail adorned with a noose.

One of the demonstrators, toqued and scarved in natty red wool, is John Kinsman, a man introduced to the huddled group

as the "godfather." He is a real live dairy farmer in a collection
of students and young activists. When he speaks, the group
listens attentively. "Farmers do not want to shoot up their cows.
We have enough problems without that. We do not want to
produce a product that we ourselves will not drink or use."

Kinsman's farm philosophy is a world away from that of Judy
Klusman. On the Kinsman farm in the heart of the Wisconsin
Dells, the cows shuffle from the pasture when they are beck-
oned with an age-old call. They line up dutifully in their stalls
in the barn, their rear ends facing the central walkway. There
is no milking parlor here—Kinsman moves down the line,
hooking the milkers up to each cow as she stands in her place.
He milks thirty-six cows, about the state average. They each
produce about six thousand liters a year, once again average
for the state. The staff at the Kinsman operation are family
members, who don coveralls and rubber boots to assist in the
twice-daily milking. This is the kind of a place where a cat
still controls the barn mice and the calves still suckle on their
mothers.

Kinsman confesses his prime motivation as a dairy farmer
is not achieving increased productivity. He sees the farm first
and foremost as a home and the cows as a means of continuing the family farm. He has worked this operation for more
than thirty years, planting twenty thousand trees in an effort
to conserve the soil and beautify the landscape.

About fourteen hundred small dairy farms much like this
stopped operation in Wisconsin during the previous year, 1993.
Two of them were Kinsman's neighbors. He says their barns
and homes stand abandoned in a grim tribute to a business
in which costs and competition continue to escalate. Kinsman
predicts BST will only exacerbate the loss of smaller dairy
operations; indeed, a study by the White House Office of

Management and Budget agrees that one-third of American farmers will hang up the milkers for good once BST is approved.

Kinsman argues that there is no compelling reason to bring in BST. Only Monsanto, the biotechnology establishment, and large, technologically intensive dairy farms have anything to gain. American farmers already produce more milk than can be consumed. Contrary to free market ideology, the U.S. maintains an elaborate regulated milk market that compensates farmers for producing surplus milk that has to be junked. The U.S. government spent more than $10 billion to buy surplus dairy products throughout the 1980s. The Office of Management and Budget says BST will add $300 million to the cost of federal dairy support programs from 1994 to the year 2000.

Kinsman is also concerned about the impact BST may have on human and animal health. Although there have been many assurances about the safety of recombinant BST, he is worried about possible long-term effects—for example, the potential impact the synthetic hormone may have on human cancers. And, he notes that Monsanto's Posilac label itself lists a host of difficulties that cows may have if they are put on the drug plan. Ironically, farmers who sign up on the Monsanto program also get a $150 credit with their veterinarians. The company indicates that cows may suffer more udder infections, which will force farmers to use more antibiotics to control them. Kinsman says the situation is not only painful for the cows but, more significantly, may also result in more antibiotics slipping into the milk. The drug label also refers ominously to reproductive problems, digestive disorders, foot and leg ailments, and persistent body sores and lacerations. The BST strategy turns cows into milk machines, Kinsman says. "It's like running a car with the choke open all the time. The cow cannot stand it. Her body, the rest of her body can't keep up with that," says Kinsman. "You burn out your cows."

Kinsman is not even sure if the economic argument makes sense. Cows on Posilac, like all high-producing animals, need more nourishment. So after the additional feed costs, it is difficult to conclude the cows will make the farmer more money.

For now, there is not enough information to determine whether Kinsman's or Klusman's assessments are right. It will take several years of experience with BST to know whether its benefits outweigh its risks.

Before the release of BST in 1994, Monsanto executives had mused about making a billion dollars a year from the bovine milk booster. The industrialized world was supposed to be at the company's feet. First in Monsanto's plans came the U.S., then Canada, and then the European Union. But by late 1998, Canada's approval remained elusive, and the European Union declared it would not even consider approval of BST before the year 2000. Outside the U.S., the synthetic hormone seemed to have made incursions only in developing countries such as Malaysia, Namibia, and Mexico. The closest it got to the lucrative market in the European Union was Bulgaria, Turkey, and Russia. Financial and industry observers were beginning to suggest that the luster on America's first biotech food product was beginning to tarnish.

Monsanto, however, defiantly continued to release statistics that argued the recombinant growth hormone was a hit with farmers. Before the launch, Monsanto predicted seventy-five percent of America's 130,000 dairy producers would use the bovine booster. "A resounding success," the press releases trumpeted at the six-month mark, even though take-up had only hit the eleven percent point. In spring of 1996, Monsanto claimed seventeen thousand dairy producers, or about fifteen percent of the U.S. total, had purchased Posilac. By mid-1997, Monsanto was no longer releasing customer numbers. However, it did say there was a forty percent increase in sales in the first five months of 1997 compared with the first five months of 1996. About four hundred producers continued to join the drug plan each month, said Monsanto, delivering "steady growth" in sales.

But the cheery tone of the press releases was offset by some troubling business news at Monsanto. In late 1995, the company launched a ten percent discount sales package for farmers who signed up for a six-month contract. The critics interpreted the sales pitch as a sign of desperation. Monsanto also parted ways with the senior executives who had been assigned the task of introducing BST to the marketplace. Robert Deakin, the head of U.S. marketing and sales for Posilac, quietly resigned. After Robert Shapiro came on as the company's new president, Walter Hopgood, the head of the biotech division, left after twenty-two years with Monsanto to pursue "other opportunities." In Canada, the person in charge of the BST file, David Nattress, took an unexpected early retirement from the company. There was a terse "no comment" issued from both the individuals and the firm with regard to the departures.

However, industry observers were quick to offer their version of what was happening at the company. Monsanto became the target of endless rumors: "They are withdrawing the product." "They've given up." "They are writing off the millions they spent on research and development." The Pure Food Campaign said bluntly that BST had been exposed as a failure, thanks to a protest campaign that received more than sixty thousand phone calls and letters of concern, distributed more than two million "Consumer Warning" leaflets, and staged two hundred milk dumpings and protests like the one on the steps of the Wisconsin capitol.

According to John Kinsman, by 1995 it had become so politically incorrect to use BST, farmers who boosted their cows had the Posilac deliveries made to their vets or to their feed suppliers so the familiar Federal Express trucks would not be seen at the farm gate. Stock analysts got into the game, estimating Monsanto was losing $10 million a year. "I wouldn't be surprised if they were out of that business by year end," James Wilbur of Smith Barney Inc. said in *Business Week* magazine in 1996. Christopher Willis, a chemical industry analyst at Schroder Werthaim & Co., a New York investment banking firm, told the press: "As far as I can see, it's not going anywhere."

Even some within the biotechnology industry were privately suggesting BST had been a mistake—the decision to tinker with nature's nearly perfect food was a poor way to launch the era of biotechnology in food production. "From the point of view of the many advances of the biotechnology industry, this was an unfortunate product to lead with, in the sense that the public doesn't feel it has control over whether it uses it," Wayne Callaway of the Dairy Coalition, a lobby group representing U.S. milk producers and processors, told the *Washington Post.*

Confirmation of stunted sales seemed to come in late 1995. The respected industry magazine *Dairy Today* did a national study of dairy farmers and concluded that BST sales might have peaked. The survey of four hundred producers in twenty-one states showed that twenty percent had used the bovine booster. Of those that had not, eighty-seven percent said they never would. It seemed that few new customers were likely to materialize. The study also showed that forty percent of those farmers who had tried the drug on their animals had stopped it, citing economic, management, and health problems. In Wisconsin, the uptake was remarkably low; more than ninety percent of producers said they would not use the hormone supplement. Even in California, the land of large, highly technological dairy farms, BST usage was down at the end of 1995.

Monsanto had no choice but to concede BST sales were not as high as it had hoped. Jerry Steiner, Monsanto's director of U.S. marketing, said in late 1995 that "although operating results have improved, they haven't improved as much as we wanted them to." One of Monsanto's problems was the high currency-exchange rates it had to pay to have synthetic BST produced at its plant in Austria. Austria's currency had appreciated eighteen percent against the U.S. dollar in the early 1990s. Monsanto's solution was to announce plans to build a new production plant in Augusta, Georgia. The decision was a double-edged sword that would neatly reprimand Europeans for denying BST and reward Americans for approving it.

The newly formed Dairy Coalition was busy promoting the science of BST on Monsanto's behalf. But the company also felt it had to redirect its public relations campaign. In a low-tech but highly focused move, Monsanto decided to enlist farmers in its efforts to spread the gospel of BST. There were reports that some producers and family members were paid an hourly wage to speak at meetings, attend trade shows, or call on other potential Posilac customers.

However, even when the assurances were delivered by farmers in peaked caps and plaid shirts, consumers remained unconvinced about the safety of BST. In survey after survey, Americans reiterated that they did not like the idea of genetic engineering in a product that had once been the epitome of natural goodness. In summer of 1995, a survey by the University of Wisconsin showed that eighty-one percent of consumers rated BST as either a "poor" or "fair" idea. Despite all the guarantees of its purity, sixty-five percent of respondents said they were concerned about the potential health effects of consuming BST-produced milk. The results were surprising given that the product had been on the market for more than a year. Typically, concern about a new technology dissipates over time. In this case, consumers simply did not seem to trust science, business, or even the institutions set up to protect them.

However deep consumers' disapproval might have been, it did not translate into a drop in milk consumption. Fewer than one percent of consumers stopped buying milk or milk products in response to the BST scare. But about ten percent of fluid milk drinkers were choosing products labeled BST-free wherever they were available. The issue of labeling remained the key point of contention. A huge majority of consumers—more than ninety percent—wanted milk from BST-boosted cows to be labeled to distinguish it from nature's own. The dairy industry continued to argue that labels were unnecessary because the milk from boosted cows was no different from natural milk. However, its underlying concern surely was that labels would be bad for business.

Monsanto made its position on labeling abundantly clear in 1994 when it sued two small dairies that dared to label their milk BST-free. The dairies said they gave up on the labels rather than incur an expensive legal battle with a well-financed multinational. Monsanto followed up with letters to other dairies insisting they too cease and desist.

Although the FDA ruled that BST-boosted products did not have to be labeled, most states ultimately passed laws allowing processors to identify their milk or cheese as BST-free. What resulted was a confusing patchwork of state legislation.

Wisconsin, for example, approved a voluntary BST-free labeling law, despite Judy Klusman's vigorous speeches in the state assembly. By 1996, every dairy in Wisconsin, including the large cooperatives, had developed a BST-free line of products. Vermont went the farthest of all the states, requiring blue dots on all milk products from cows treated with BST. Vermont's proactive law was repealed in 1997 after a panel of judges ruled that it violated milk producers' freedom of speech.

Illinois refused to follow the example set by other states. It prohibited BST-free labels, even dispatching regulators to raid grocery stores in search of milk products with illegal labels. Three dairy companies, including the popular Ben & Jerry's Homemade ice cream company, launched a lawsuit against the state in the spring of 1996. A court judgment a year and a half later gave Ben & Jerry's and the other complainants the right to include a compromise label on their products outlining their opposition to BST. Ironically, the ice cream company was forced to admit that the cooperative from which it purchased its milk supplies would soon start allowing its members to use BST on their cows. Nothing in the world of boosted bovines seemed to be straightforward.

Despite a mountain of scientific studies supporting the safety of BST products, the public remained unconvinced. Anxiety escalated in January 1996, when Samuel Epstein, a professor of environmental medicine at the University of Illinois School of Public Health and chairman of the Cancer Prevention Coalition, published a study in a leading public health journal, the *International Journal of Health Services*, linking BST with breast and colon cancers.

Since 1986, independent scientists had expressed concerns about the potential impact of increased levels of insulin-like growth factor (IGF-1) in milk from treated cows. IGF-1 is a powerful, naturally occurring growth hormone in the blood of humans and other animals. The IGF-1 in cows and humans is chemically identical. It was found that products from cows injected with recombinant BST contain elevated levels of IGF-1, which it is believed can pass into the bloodstream of milk consumers. Ingested IGF-1 would ordinarily be broken down in the stomach, but the presence of casein in milk prevents such a breakdown.

Little is known about the hormone, but it is thought that increased levels of IGF-1 in humans can lead to elevated tumor rates as well as acromegaly, or gigantism, which is characterized by excessive growth of the head, face, hands, and feet.

Before BST was approved for use, the National Institutes of Health in the U.S. had appointed a panel of scientists, veterinarians, and a dairy farmer to review existing studies and consult with scientists, consumers, and drug company officials. The panel concluded that IGF-1 levels were not a problem since the amount in boosted milk was less than that typically found in human breast milk or even saliva.

However, different studies showed a huge variability in measured IGF-1 levels, and Epstein remained concerned. He determined that following absorption into the blood, high IGF-1 levels exert cancer-promoting effects on cells lining the colon and on breast cells. Epstein concluded: "The entire nation is currently being subjected to a large-scale adulteration of an age-old dietary staple by a poorly characterized and unlabeled biotechnology product. Disturbingly this experiment benefits only a very small segment of the agri-chemical industry while providing no matching benefit to consumers. Even more disturbingly, it poses major potential public health risks for the entire U.S. population."

The FDA moved again to reassure the public. It maintained that BST did not elevate IGF-1 levels in cows and, even if it did, the hormone would be broken down in consumers' gastrointestinal tracts by digestion; undigested IGF-1 would be excreted. "The suggestion that IGF-1 in milk can induce or promote breast cancer in humans is scientifically unfounded and misguided," the federal agency declared.

However, by 1998 further scientific studies supported a connection between high IGF-1 levels in the blood and breast, colon, and also prostate cancers. A study published in *Science* in January 1998 found a fourfold increase in the risk of prostate cancer among men with the highest levels of IGF-1 in their blood. And then another study of U.S. women published May 9, 1998, in *The Lancet* detailed a seven-times increase in the risk of breast cancer among premenopausal women with high levels of IGF-1.

Monsanto continued to fight challenges on the health front. When two investigative reporters working for the Fox television station in Tampa, Florida, prepared a documentary quoting Epstein and others, Monsanto sent in its artillery. A lawyer hired by the company dispatched a letter to the station stating that the discussion of any link between the use of synthetic BST and cancer "is the most blatant form of scaremongering." In a second letter, he wrote that Monsanto critics in all probability were "scientifically incompetent." Fox did not air the documentary series. The reporters filed a lawsuit and set up a Web site to publicize the story, claiming their bosses had suppressed the documentary pieces in response to pressure from Monsanto.

The milk industry and the FDA chose to ignore the scientific challenges to BST. In fact, by the late 1990s, the milk industry's powerful lobby was orchestrating a campaign to

increase milk consumption. Top U.S. health officials participated. For example, an advertisement showed U.S. Secretary
of Health and Human Services Donna Shalala with a glass of
milk in her hand and a "milk mustache" on her upper lip.
Shalala oversaw the FDA.

However controversial the effects on human health, there
was little disagreement that Posilac did have consequences for
animal health. After BST had been on the market for two years,
the FDA said it had received 1459 reports of adverse effects
on cows. The agency's two-year report offered a distressing
list of problems including mastitis or inflamation of the udder,
reproductive disorders, abnormal milk, and foot and leg ail-
ments. Yet somehow the FDA concluded that these results
were acceptable, if not routine. "Based on these reports of
adverse reactions to Posilac, FDA finds no cause for concern."

Jay Livingston, a farmer near Lisbon, New York, found
ample cause for concern after he introduced BST to his herd
of two hundred cows. "For the first couple of months on BST,
our cows seemed to be doing OK," said Livingston. "Their
milk production increased from forty to sixty-five pounds per
day. Then they went to pieces. We had a half dozen die and
the rest started experiencing major health problems." Livingston
stopped using the gene-spliced booster but continued to witness reproductive problems in cows long after they had been
off the drug. Multiple births, normally seen about one in one
hundred, became commonplace. In the dairy business, twin
births are not double the good news. They sap a cow's strength
and in just about all of the twin births, the calves are sterile.
At Livingston's farm, many of the cows and calves died.

The Wisconsin Farmers Union added to the depressing
account. It reported receiving complaints about BST from farmers in seven states on a telephone hotline. Producers who

called recounted stories of cows dying right after injection and of widespread health problems that forced them to drastically cull their herds. John Schumway, a farmer in Lowville, New York, said he had to send one-quarter of his two hundred cows to slaughter after starting BST. Melvin Vanheel, who milked seventy cows outside Little Falls, Minnesota, told the hotline he witnessed one spontaneous abortion following mastitis, lumps and open sores at the injection site, and heat stress. His vet told him to drop the drug.

These grim reports had little impact on the FDA, but it was a different story in Europe. Veterinarians in Germany, for example, resolved not to administer BST to cows on the grounds that it would violate their professional code of ethics, which forbids intentional harm to animals.

In addition to raising serious questions about cruelty to animals, the use of BST has raised a further concern regarding human health. At issue is the indirect effect the hormone supplement has in passing on antibiotics and antibiotic resisitance to humans. Since BST increases infections in cows, it also increases the use of antibiotics. Cows being treated with antibiotics are supposed to be pulled out of the milking line long enough for traces of the drugs to be flushed out of their system and their milk. Random tests are done to determine if milk has drug residues, and farmers can be fined if they allow polluted milk into the system.

In theory, there should be no antibiotic drug residues in the milk on supermarket shelves. In practice, however, it is not that simple. A Monsanto-sponsored study in Vermont published in December 1992 showed that BST-injected cows received four times the antibiotics for mastitis as untreated cows, with treatment lasting six times longer than average. In addition, seven times more milk was discarded from boosted cows than from drug-free animals. This extra pressure is being put on an already strained system. The FDA has conceded the difficulty of policing drug residues in milk. Of the eighty-two drugs that are known to leave traces in milk, only thirty are actually approved by the FDA. Many antibiotics used by farmers to treat their cows are technically illegal. The agency, meanwhile, has the capability to test for only about a dozen drugs, and it analyzes only five hundred samples a year. It is fair to conclude, therefore, that some antibiotic residues are appearing in the milk Americans serve their children.

By 1996, the U.S. dairy industry had suffered further erosion. In the two years following the approval of BST, another four thousand dairy farmers in Wisconsin had quit the business. This was good news for BST marketers. FDA records showed that it was younger farmers who were more likely to try the new barn biotechnology. Monsanto was watching those statistics with a calculating eye. U.S. marketing director Jerry Steiner predicted that thirty to forty percent of dairy farmers would leave the industry in the next five years. "A lot of older dairymen will retire. A new generation of dairymen will have different views."

John Kinsman is one of the older dairymen, but in late 1996, he had no plans to retire. Kinsman's work against BST helped catapult him to the head of a national organization that speaks on behalf of family farmers, the Family Farm Defenders. In the waning years of the century, he is as likely to be attending meetings in Europe or Washington as he is to be peering beneath the slapping tails of his cows. And mad cow disease, not BST, is on his mind.

Judy Klusman is one of the "new generation of dairymen with a different view." In late 1996, she became deputy house leader in the state assembly. Still using BST at the farm, she reported that her herdsman felt the cows were performing well on the supplemental hormone, suffering no problems that careful management could not fix. And although some farms still boasted signs declaring "we don't use BGH," the controversy had slipped from the political arena and from the front pages of the newspaper. For Klusman, that would mean she could use BST without censure. "It's pretty much calmed down, although some people still use the product as a whipping boy," Klusman said.

The U.S. experience stood as a case study for Canada. When the genetically engineered bovine booster appeared on the American market in 1994, the debate over the scientific safety of the product and its ethical implications repeated itself north of the border. A who's who of the business world lined up behind Monsanto, and the deck seemed stacked in favor of corporate biotechnology. Trade pressures under the North American Free Trade Agreement called for "harmonization" between Canadian and American regulations. Major agricultural colleges and universities in Canada, like McGill and Guelph, were receiving funding by the biotechnology industry to do research on BST. And there were suggestions that Monsanto was using its financial clout in an attempt to persuade regulators to speed up the approval process. In November 1994, the Canadian Broadcasting Corporation program *the fifth estate* reported that Monsanto had tried to make questionable payments to Health Canada officials, offering to pay as much as $2 million for approval to market BST in Canada without being required to submit data from any further trials or studies. It was all a misunderstanding, Monsanto protested. Canadian regulators had not understood that the offer of money was for research, not for grease.

Perhaps more so than their American counterparts, Canadian farmers tended to align themselves with consumers. After all, the average dairy herd in Canada is smaller, with about forty-five cows. And dairy production north of the U.S. border is regulated by a quota system. Farmers are prescribed how much milk they can harvest, so being competitive and producing more milk does not necessarily translate into higher earnings.

Several federal members of parliament with their eyes trained on the U.S. experience persuaded the House of Commons committee on agriculture to hold public hearings on whether BST should be allowed into Canada. In addition, the Council of Canadians, a nationalist lobby group born of the 1980s free trade debate, took on the BST challenge with vigor. In 1994, federal politicians' offices were flooded with letters from consumers alarmed at any suggestion that milk be tampered with. Calls for a moratorium on approval came from all corners, including the National Dairy Council of Canada, the National Farmers Union, the Ontario Nurses Association, and the Toronto Food Council.

Monsanto responded to the political pressure and voluntarily agreed to withhold BST from the market until July 1995. The government appointed a task force made up of industry, consumer, and department representatives to review in greater detail the costs and benefits of synthetic BST for the Canadian dairy industry, animal genetics, and consumers. When it reported, the task force made no recommendations, simply concluding there would be only limited gains and some significant losses in the dairy industry with the licensing of BST.

It had been assumed government regulators would approve BST as soon as the voluntary moratorium was lifted in July 1995, but the political and consumer lobby persevered. By early 1998, efforts to license BST were still on hold as the government agency formed two expert committees to reexamine the drug, one to look at the implications for human health, the other to examine the impact on cows.

In 1998, six scientists at Health Canada's Bureau of Veterinary Drugs accused their managers of pressuring them to approve drugs of "questionable safety" in order to please the industry. They filed a labor grievance claiming they had been subject to coercion, conspiracy, threats, intimidation, and defamation for failing to expedite approval of BST. Five of the scientists wrote an internal report concluding that Health Canada had not asked the U.S. manufacturer for enough data on whether milk from treated cows is safe to drink. Health Canada suppressed that document, forcing the Senate agriculture committee to resort to the access-to-information process to get a copy. When the document was finally leaked from other sources, it showed that the U.S. study that led to the approval of the hormone in that country had found that thirty percent of rats given BST reacted with increased levels of antibodies and some suffered thyroid lesions and cysts. Both the FDA and Monsanto had maintained that no negative effects on rats had been found.

Incensed at what they were seeing, senators sitting on the committee called for another ban. Former agriculture minister Eugene Whelan told the press, "No one can positively prove that this hormone will not do any harm ten or fifteen years from now." The colorful senator, who had served during Pierre Trudeau's Liberal government, added that if he were still minister and found farmers using BST, he would ban them from the dairy business. Whelan found support from senators of differing political stripes. Conservative Mira Spivak was active on the file. And Ottawa physician and Conservative senator Wilbert Keon was quoted in *The Western Producer* as saying,

"The motion before us could be seen as sending a reminder to Health Canada regulators to follow the principle of the Hippocratic Oath: 'do no harm.' The motion reminds our regulators to be very diligent. It asks that we do not harm our milk supply as such."

The pressure from politicians, bureaucrats, consumers and others continued to build. In January 1999, a report from the Canadian Veterinary Medicine Association gave the federal government the justification to turn down Monsanto's application. Health Canada said it rejected the bovine supplement not because of what the product might mean for human health, but because of the implications it had for the health of cows. The report cited udder infections, lameness, and fertility problems. Monsanto immediately announced its intention to appeal the decision. Robert Collier, who flew to Ottawa from Monsanto headquarters in St. Louis, told the press that the drug review process in Canada was not reliable.

With the U.S. administration acting as cheerleader, Monsanto continues to press for approval of BST elsewhere in the world. In late 1997, at the World Trade Organization, the U.S. successfully challenged the EU's right to impose a ban on BST-containing imports. Corporate biotechnology also strove to have the Codex Alimentarius Commission, the international body that sets standards on food safety as well as food products and drugs, approve a draft standard that would have allowed the use of BST around the world. However, a global consumers' lobby intervened and succeeded in mid-1997 in persuading delegates to reject that draft. At the same meeting, Canada voted against further study of BST. (That vote was lost.)

The regulatory system that so far has protected small Canadian dairy farms—and in part has kept BST at bay—will also be challenged at the World Trade Organization, probably in the early years of the millennium. Without this protection, dairy farmers will likely have to look to Posilac as a way to boost milk production and competitiveness. Until then, it is naive to think that BST-boosted milk is not in the Canadian dairy pool—either in U.S.-produced cocoa mix, granola bars, and single-serving puddings or in Canadian milk produced with BST smuggled across the largely unregulated border.

In five years of experience with BST in the U.S., Monsanto has relentlessly promoted its biological invention. Like much of what biotechnology has to offer, BST seems designed for the advantage of big business; in this case, the drug's creators. Over the years, farmers have learned how to get more milk from their cows through better feeding and breeding and without the risks that BST seems to pose. A genetically engineered bovine booster hardly seems necessary in countries that already produce more milk than they need. One lesson may be extrapolated from the BST experience—biotechnology may be a risky and ethically suspect solution to a problem that never really existed.

5

AN APPLE
A DAY

IT WAS ONE OF THOSE END-OF-AUGUST DAYS THAT CLOSES the door on summer indolence. The snap of approaching fall had blanketed the morning with a crisp dew. Although the sun shone in the midday sky, the day had a cool, back-to-school clarity. The day spoke of change.

In her office at the Unisys Corporation headquarters in the suburbs of Philadelphia, Dot Wilson laced up her sneakers, unaware of what lay ahead for her. As the U.S. field support manager for the information management systems company, Wilson spent much of her time traveling across the United States. This was one of those rare but welcome days in the office when she could join her colleagues on their daily lunchtime constitutional along the jogging path that meandered between the Unisys buildings.

A brisk three-mile course was routine for Wilson. At forty-four, she was in good shape, toned by an active life and time at the health club. But on this August day in 1988, halfway through the course, she was struck by a "strange sensation" of extreme weariness in her legs. She dismissed it as many would disregard a sudden ache or pain. But a week later, the sensation was still there; in fact, she was feeling "strange all over."

She went to see her doctor, who prescribed the normal battery of tests. When the results failed to point to an immediate diagnosis, Wilson and her mysterious symptoms were passed from one specialist to another. Her list of complaints soon grew longer: spasms, deep muscle pain, pins-and-needles prickling. Diagnosis, however, remained elusive. No one thought of the health food supplement, L-tryptophan, that her general practitioner had suggested she try just three months earlier for the insomnia she suffered on her road trips. L-tryptophan was considered innocuous—after all, it had been identified as the ingredient in warm milk that brings on sleepiness.

Over the fall, the change forecast by that late summer day took an ominous turn. In December, Wilson was compelled to take short-term disability leave to spend time in hospital for more comprehensive tests. Despite those tests, doctors could not come up with a sure diagnosis or a treatment plan. There would be no quick return to work for Dot Wilson. Now it was the spasms, the pain, and the worry that kept her awake at night. Once again, her physician recommended L-tryptophan, saying it "was no more dangerous than Rice Crispies."

The manifestations of illness seemed to intensify. By this point, she suffered an itchy rash, night sweats, and tight, leathery skin, along with the now tediously predictable spasms and muscle pains. About one year to the day of her last lunch-time powerwalk, things turned even worse for Dot Wilson. Her legs gave out altogether one day in her bedroom; her arms turned leaden soon after. Suddenly, inexplicably, this once active career woman was rendered quadriplegic, unable to turn in her bed or manage the most basic of bodily functions.

Not surprisingly, television became an essential in the limited life of the newly immobilized Wilson. In November 1989, she caught an evening news report about a puzzling new disease with symptoms just like hers. Eosinophilia myalgia syndrome (EMS) was striking Americans across the country. Some had died. The connection, it seemed, was that all of the victims had taken L-tryptophan. Within a week, all of Wilson's specialists had called her to say they had solved her puzzle.

At that time, L-tryptophan was considered a staple in health food stores in the United States. It had first become popular in the 1970s when it was heralded as a safe, nonaddictive treatment for insomnia, premenstrual syndrome, and depression. Six Japanese manufacturers produced the food supplement for the U.S. market. After several months of investigation, the EMS outbreak was traced back to just one of the six producers— the Tokyo-based petrochemical giant Showa Denko K.K. The company already controlled more than half of the American market, but in 1988 and 1989, it sought to boost the efficiency of its L-tryptophan production. Showa Denko altered its normal manufacturing procedures by introducing a new, genetically engineered bacterium called Strain V.

Showa Denko was not the first company to use genetic engineering in its production system. As many as one hundred other pharmaceutical and food companies had already harnessed the reproductive capabilities of genetically manipulated organisms to produce large quantities of a desired substance. Like other food supplement manufacturers, Showa Denko had routinely used a fermentation process, in which large quantities of bacteria are grown in vats and the required substance is extracted and purified. In this case, Showa Denko used Strain V in the fermentation system to convert nutrients into

L-tryptophan. The technique was like using a gene-spliced bacterium as a living factory.

According to U.S. law, the company was allowed to sell the L-tryptophan produced in gene-spliced bacteria without any safety testing because it and other firms had been selling the supplement produced in non-genetically engineered bacteria for years without ill effects. The method of production was considered immaterial. What was important was that the new product was "substantially equivalent" to the L-tryptophan that had been sold for years.

The company must have considered this a routine change. However, this seemingly minor tinkering apparently produced a toxic brew. Tests showed that Showa Denko's L-tryptophan was 99.6 percent pure, well within approved standards. But the tiny proportion of the compound that was considered "impure" contained between thirty and forty different contaminants. One of them, EBT, attracted particular attention from scientists because it was shown to cause some of the symptoms of EMS in rats.

That was 1989, the early years of the biotechnology revolution. No one was eager to blacken the reputation of the new industry. Showa Denko insisted genetic engineering was not responsible for producing the unexpected and toxic contaminants. Rather, it blamed another change in its production system. The company said it had coincidentally reduced the amount of activated carbon used for purification at the same time as it introduced Strain V.

The company's claims, however, could not be corroborated. When U.S. Food and Drug Administration inspectors went to Japan to check out the production plant, they discovered Showa Denko had erased all traces of the L-tryptophan production line. Despite repeated requests, the company refused to release samples of the genetically engineered bacteria. The FDA officials reported: "The team encountered refusals to provide information, access to records and areas routinely inspected." By destroying all stocks of the modified bacteria, Showa Denko eliminated data and destroyed possible evidence that could have been useful in solving the puzzle and perhaps finding an answer for those suffering the toxic effects of L-tryptophan.

Its frustrations aside, the FDA was no more eager to raise the specter of a deadly experiment in genetic engineering than was Showa Denko. The FDA had learned as early as November 1989 that the company had genetically engineered its bacteria. However, the agency neglected to reveal that fact until August 1990, when it was forced to respond to an article in *Newsday*. Another piece in *Science* magazine quoted scientists at the FDA as saying they were concerned about the "impact on industry" of a disclosure of the potential link between EMS and genetic engineering.

Luck was on the biotech industry's side. The FDA scheduled hearings into the L-tryptophan deaths, but the sessions dissolved into a debate on whether food supplements should be available for sale in health food stores. The well-financed and aggressive health food industry in the U.S. dominated the hearings, arguing that the existing regulatory system that allowed the sale of supplements should remain untouched. In 1990, the FDA opted for compromise, banning L-tryptophan, but continuing to allow the sale of other food supplements in unregulated retail operations.

Canada managed to sidestep the devastating epidemic that struck just south of the border. Under Canadian law, ingestible substances are either "foods" or "drugs"—there is no provision for "dietary supplements." Vitamins and herbs are unregulated, but as such are not allowed to claim therapeutic properties. (The law governing dietary supplements is currently under review.) Because of its claims of healing benefits, L-tryptophan would have been considered a drug in Canada and would have had to meet much more stringent regulations than it did in the United States. For example, the manufacturer would have been compelled to file details on its production processes and any changes it made to them. Perhaps not surprisingly, Showa Denko and the other manufacturers never bothered to apply for drug status in Canada and so L-tryptophan was not available for sale north of the U.S. boundary line.

The official toll in the first year of the EMS outbreak in the United States numbered 37 dead, 1535 permanently disabled, and more than 5000 temporarily afflicted. It was never definitively determined if the toxic assault had been caused by slipshod production—a consequence of Showa Denko cutting back on the level of its filtration—or on genetic engineering gone wrong. More than two hundred scientific studies tried to determine what happened. Based on fundamental chemical and biochemical principles, scientists deduced that the EBT contaminant was probably generated when the concentration of L-tryptophan within the bacteria reached such high levels that the molecules or their precursors began to react with each other. Richard Hinds, a Washington lawyer who represented Showa Denko, seemed to throw cold water on the notion that inadequate filtration was to blame for the toxic brew. He told *Science* magazine that the amount of powdered carbon used for filtration had varied before, dipping as low as it had for the virulent L-tryptophan, without ill effect.

Dot Wilson has a diagnosis now, but she will likely never know what it was about the seemingly innocuous little pill she got from the health food store that so changed her life. In the late 1990s, she still used a wheelchair, suffered constant pain controlled only by an arsenal of drugs, and endured an ever-increasing range of new problems, including heart, thyroid, and blood sugar disorders and a bout of breast cancer. She settled a lawsuit against Showa Denko in 1991, which has enabled her to live in relative financial comfort. Wilson is pleased that she has recovered some of her abilities—these days, she can prepare a cup of tea. However, one bitter irony remains: despite its advertised therapeutic benefits, L-tryptophan had never managed to coax her to sleep in an unfamiliar bed after a long day's work, but the rigors of life with L-tryptophan-induced EMS always leave her exhausted and bone-tired at night.

Wilson has given up her dreams of a cure. No research is being done into the mysterious disease that struck from such an unsuspected source. EMS hit with devastating ferocity, but in the realm of illness, its toll is considered small. The Dot Wilsons of the world do not have the political clout to demand answers. From its protected perch on the other side of the world, Showa Denko essentially has washed its hands of the matter, with only a handful of lawsuits left to be resolved. The EMS epidemic is now a footnote in health history, largely forgotten by a scientific and medical community that has moved on to new crises.

We will probably never know if genetic engineering was to blame for EMS. In much the same way, we may not know definitively if the gene-spliced foods on the supermarket shelves are safe. Unless there are new stringent requirements for human testing of all genetically engineered foods, there are no assurances that history will not repeat itself. It is worth noting that Canadian and American regulators do not even talk about "food safety"; they talk about "acceptable risk." It seems there are no guarantees that what we put in our mouths today will be as good for us as the apple a day once prescribed by the family dentist and doctor.

The biotechnology industry insists there is virtually no risk in transgenic foods. It claims the changes it is making to food are minuscule, so there is no more cause for concern than there would be for naturally produced foods. Those who dare to question this logic are dismissed as cranks or fear mongers.

Most critics of biotechnology tread gingerly around the question of whether genetically engineered foods are safe for human consumption. Even Jeremy Rifkin—never one to pull his punches—speaks cautiously about the cumulative impact genetic engineering may have on food already laced with chemical residues. His Pure Food Campaign does not declare globally that genetically engineered food is hazardous to human health. Instead, the lobby group deals with each new biofood individually—some are criticized for the impact they may have on the environment, others for how they will affect family farms.

Woefully little scientific assessment has been done on the impact of genetic engineering on human health. Even scientists who are fundamentally opposed to the use of biotechnology in food production cannot refer to supportive studies. Margaret Mellon of the Union for Concerned Scientists and Michael Hanson of the U.S. Consumers Association are typical when they carefully say that biofoods are "not that big a health risk." Much of the activist community does not want to be seen as alarmist. Nevertheless, history is full of examples in which "better living through chemistry" has resulted in unexpected, negative side effects. It would be illogical to blindly assume that genetic engineering, unlike many other new technologies, will be blessed with a predictable—and safe—future.

One area in which there is virtually no debate about the risks of genetic engineering involves allergies. For a long time, corporate biotechnology insisted allergens would not be transferred to test-tube foods along with spliced genes. But those assurances faltered with the release of a scientific study in March 1996 proving that proteins that can cause potentially serious allergic reactions can indeed be inadvertently transferred to new, manipulated crops through genetic engineering.

American scientists at the University of Nebraska at Lincoln and the University of Wisconsin at Madison determined that soybeans spliced with a gene from the Brazil nut to give them more nutritious protein set off a strong, potentially deadly allergic reaction in people sensitive to Brazil nuts. Pioneer Hi-Bred International had hoped to develop enhanced soybeans as an improved animal feed. Although the Brazil nut was known to cause food allergies, the seed storage protein gene that was to be fused with the soybean had not been identified as a potential allergen. In fact, earlier tests on animals had placated researchers by revealing no adverse reactions. But knowing it would be difficult to keep the soybeans from inadvertently entering the human food supply, the company decided to play it safe by commissioning human tests.

Scientists were taken aback when blood serum from eight of nine people known to have a Brazil nut allergy reacted strongly to the genetically altered soybeans. Skin-prick tests on three subjects produced an even more dramatic reaction. In the face of irrefutable proof of the soybean's allergenic properties, Pioneer Hi-Bred abandoned plans to market it. The company is now looking for another, more benign gene with the ability to produce the critical amino acid it hoped would enhance its soybeans.

Eight foods—milk, eggs, wheat, peanuts, soy, tree nuts, fish, and shellfish—cause ninety percent of food allergies. Besides these, a wide range of other foods may also cause reactions. And to further complicate things, foods often contain more than one allergenic protein. Milk, for example, contains ten to twenty allergenic proteins; most milk-allergic children react to more than one of them. Critics of biotechnology say the Brazil nut findings confirm some of their worst fears: since gene jockeys mix genes from such a wide array of species, there is no way to predict which genetically engineered foods may cause an allergic reaction. Researchers are tapping into countless organisms that have never before found their way into food. For example, a bacterium in the soil routinely lends a gene that confers herbicide tolerance to plants. Although genes from bacteria may seem innocuous, they have never before been part of the food chain. People who have managed to control their lives through strict avoidance of foods to which they are allergic may suddenly find they are allergic to brand-new foods that have been subtly altered.

According to scientific definition, true food allergies, which involve a documented reaction of the immune system, affect about two percent of North American adults and between two and eight percent of children. However, a recent study showed that about twenty-five percent of Americans thought they were allergic to certain foods. This kind of food sensitivity, along with strictly defined food allergies, is thought to be increasing as more proteins are added to commercial foods.

It is proteins that prompt some immune systems to misinterpret food as harmful and react as if they are being invaded. Every gene in food triggers the production of a protein. When the immune system produces antibodies in response to the proteins, histamine and other chemicals are released from various cells within the body. As the battle rages, these chemicals, called mediators, can cause hives, asthma, or other allergic symptoms throughout the body. Anaphylaxis, a sudden, severe, potentially life-threatening reaction, is the extreme response. Peanuts, nuts, shellfish, fish, and eggs most commonly spark this reaction. As little as one-fifth of a teaspoon of the offending food has caused death. Some severely allergic children can have a reaction if milk is splashed on their skin.

Plant allergies have their most devastating impact on new, unfamiliar consumers. For example, peanut allergies are relatively uncommon in African populations where peanuts are used as a food staple. Presumably, people with a gene for peanut allergy have been eliminated from the African gene pool by natural selection. It is when foods like peanuts are introduced to a new audience that allergies seem to flourish.

Allergenic proteins come in a variety of shapes and compositions. So far scientists have not found any shared features that would allow prediction of allergenicity. Human blood serum tests, like the ones conducted on the Pioneer Hi-Bred soybeans, are useful only when the new proteins come from known allergenic sources. However, genetic engineers may take proteins from bacteria they find in the soil, the ocean, or anywhere else, and incorporate them into human food. Since such substances have never incarnated as food before, their toxic or allergenic characteristics are uncertain, unpredictable, and untestable.

In early September 1928, Sir Alexander Fleming interrupted his holidays to stop by his laboratory at St. Mary's Hospital in London, England, to clear up some work he had left unfinished. There among the pile of petri dishes waiting to be sterilized was a plate in which an unusual fungus was growing amid staphylococci bacteria, inhibiting the bacteria's growth. This mold was penicillin—a fungus that would usher in the antibiotic age of medical science.

Fleming initially did not understand the remarkable therapeutic value of his discovery. It would be almost fifteen years before two Oxford scientists, Howard Florey and Ernst Chain, tested and proved the value of penicillin in fighting disease-causing bacteria in humans. In the following decades, scientists would set out to identify a palette of other antibiotics that could also slay bacterial dragons.

At its time, the discovery of antibiotics was considered the most significant advance in modern medicine. Finally, physicians had an arsenal to use against the stubborn microbial-borne diseases that had nearly wiped out whole populations at several points in the earth's history. By the early 1990s, we had gone way beyond penicillin, developing more than 420 antibiotics.

Today, however, we are beginning to witness the end of humankind's ability to control disease with antibiotics. Bacteria have learned how to resist the antibiotic magic bullets. Illnesses such as tuberculosis, which was once considered nearly eradicated, are again ravaging parts of the world. Pneumonia, staphylococcal infections, and sepsis are back, too, cutting a swath through the developing world. In industrialized nations, strains of pneumoccoccus, which can cause ear infections, meningitis, pneumonia, and blood infections, have become resistant to penicillin and four other antibiotics in the last few years. A strain of staphylococcus isolated in Australia was found to be resistant to thirty-one different drugs. Hospitals these days are often struck with a mutant microbe called VRE that is resistant to most commonly used antibiotics, including the most potent antibiotics in the health-care arsenal. And in late 1996, British doctors said they feared they had seen one more step in the evolution of a microbe—a veritable "superbug" that not just resisted but thrived in the very antibiotics meant to kill it.

Antibiotics have lost their potency largely through overuse. Doctors began prescribing them for just about every minor ailment. In 1995, physicians prescribed twenty-six million doses of antibiotics to Canadians. Antibiotics have become so routine that people even receive them, often at their own insistence, for viral infections, which cannot be cured by a drug aimed at aberrant bacteria. It is estimated that seventy percent of ear infections in children clear up on their own, without the ubiquitous antibiotic prescription.

The overuse of antibiotics provides an ideal breeding ground for bacteria to mutate and develop immunity to the very ammunition aimed at them. Bacteria are sexually promiscuous, spawning a new generation every twenty minutes. And remarkably, they can somehow hand over their most useful genes to other bugs. When patients stop a prescription of antibiotics early, they may be feeling better, but not all of the bacteria have been killed. Those left are able to mutate and reproduce a new generation that is resistant to the antibiotic.

Modern, industrialized agriculture has also exacerbated antibiotic resistance by plying livestock with antibiotics. Antibiotics are a routine ingredient of animal feeds, designed to spur growth and repel disease. It is considered standard procedure to give antibiotics to animals that might be stressed by intensive-confinement, factory-farming systems. One half of the world's antibiotics go to treat animals, not people. The World Health Organization identified routine use of antibiotics, particularly for growth promotion, as a critical problem.

The crisis of antibiotic resistance may worsen if the science of genetic engineering is allowed to take hold on the farm. The recent use of genetically engineered BST in U.S. dairy farms is one example. Fears that the extra antibiotic use it causes will mean that some drugs get into the milk pool are only too plausible. The industry magazine *Dairy Today* reported that in 1995, antibiotic violations in milk were up fifty percent in eight of the top ten dairy-producing states.

The danger is not limited to the milk or meat we consume. The routine practice of adding antibiotic-resistant marker genes to genetically engineered life-forms is a source of endless concern. Calgene's famous Flavr Savr tomato, for instance, sparked a long debate over its kanomycin-resistant marker gene. Kanomycin, often administered orally to patients before surgery, is not an antibiotic the medical health field can afford to lose. In 1991, sixty-six thousand Americans were prescribed the drug.

Calgene scientists insisted that the antibiotic-resistant marker gene was not transferred to microorganisms in the human digestive system. We all have organisms living inside us; science refers to them poetically as the flora in the gut. In a major review of antibiotic-resistant markers in July 1994, the United Kingdom Advisory Committee on Novel Foods essentially agreed with Calgene. It found that digestive processes degrade much of the DNA in raw foods before it is exposed to gut microorganisms. However, the committee, which was made up of independent experts who were to advise the government, warned officials not to allow live, genetically engineered microbes such as yeasts or those found in yogurt to contain antibiotic-resistant markers. Such microbes, the committee concluded, could transfer their antibiotic-resistant trait to human gut flora. The advisers also recommended that, in future, all companies proposing a test-tube food with an antibiotic-resistant marker gene "demonstrate the safety" of the genes and the "scientific need for their retention."

Despite the Flavr Savr's exoneration, some scientists continued to be anxious that the tomato might add to the ever-increasing antibiotic resistance that is confounding modern medicine. "I'm not sure you can translate what occurs in a test tube to what happens in a field," Michael Gilmore, a microbiologist at the University of Oklahoma Health Sciences Center, told the press: "Bacteria are very resourceful, and unlikely events turn up with fair frequency." And in the United Kingdom, the tomato's legacy remains. Whenever a test-tube food is presented there for consideration, scientists once again reopen the old debate about marker genes increasing antibiotic resistance.

Corporate biotechnology likes to hold up government regulators as the ultimate police force patrolling safe food. Indeed, American and Canadian governments have a commendable record ensuring the safety of the essential nutritional staple of life.

However, in this case, government regulators have adopted a passive role in the assessment of health risks. Genetic engineering alters foods so they contain proteins and other compounds that have never been part of the human diet. The only way to tell if those new foods might be allergenic or toxic is to test them vigorously. Yet Canadian and American government agencies do not require such testing, nor are labels mandated.

There are no pre-market human tests required of "novel" foods in Canada as there would be for the introduction of a new drug. For example, the federal government determined that New Leaf potatoes, with their built-in pesticide, were safe to eat on the basis of lab tests in which mice, rats, and quails were fed the potatoes or protein extracts from them. "Treatment related effects were not observed," says the decision document released by the Food Production and Inspection Branch.

In North America, both Canadian and American governments have largely delegated the responsibility for test-tube food safety to the very corporations bringing those foods forward. According to a 1996 editorial in the *New England Journal of Medicine*, the FDA's role "would appear to favor industry over consumer protection." And as one Canadian critic wryly remarked, Health Canada essentially says to the developers of new test-tube foods, "if your novel food kills people, let us know."

Even full-scale safety testing cannot guarantee one hundred percent certainty that a genetically engineered food is safe. For example, testing on volunteer human subjects for three years might not reveal longer-term effects. But at least this much caution seems the bare minimum of responsible science.

The final years of this century could be characterized as a period of food scares. Hamburger disease, chicken virus, mad cow disease—they are enough to make one yearn for the simplicity of the apple-a-day era. It is puzzling that Canadian and U.S. governments have, in essence, given the biotechnology industry carte blanche. It is using its regulatory freedom to roll out transgenic foods in what has to be seen as a giant nutritional experiment. Are the health risks so remote as to warrant these remarkably lax regulations? The story of L-tryptophan illustrates that even minor genetic alterations can be risky.

Dot Wilson has no confidence in the ability of government or industry to regulate a genetically engineered future. She shudders at the thought of her supermarket shelves swelling with products manipulated for profit, and without any labeling to let her avoid them.

These days, Wilson is struggling to find some meaning in her experience. She is an activist prepared to speak out against test-tube foods. She works on the executive of the National

EMS Network, a nonprofit group that still remembers the L-tryptophan assault on health. About one thousand Americans belong to the group, a number that is shrinking every month as more victims finally succumb to the disease.

Wilson is convinced there will be more victims of illnesses created by genetic engineering, but fears her words of caution fall on deaf ears. "There just are not enough of us. People think we are a bunch of fanatics." For now, it seems North American governments are prepared to place corporate biotechnology, with its promise of jobs and economic wealth, ahead of the Dot Wilsons of the world.

In late 1998, a postscript: L-tryptophan, repackaged, remarketed, and supposedly free of contaminants, was quietly making its way back onto U.S. health food store shelves.

6

FIELDS OF DREAMS

WITH PALPABLE IRRITATION, DEAN MOXHAM TURNS THE
page on the Manitoba Pool Elevators calendar to reveal the
image of June—a T-shirted boy and his dog cavorting under
the shade of an apple tree ablaze with blossoms. On this
June 1, 1996, the reality of life on the Portage Plains in the heart
of Canadian farm country is very different. A lingering winter
has just now loosened its grip on the landscape. Last year at
this time, Moxham's crops had been in the ground for two
weeks. This year, nearly a quarter of his fields are still too
sodden to bear the weight of a tractor.

Two days later, the feeble spring sun has warmed the soil
in a one hundred-acre field at the end of a trail dented with
muddy tire tracks. Wearing a denim jacket as a buffer against
winds left over from winter, Dean Moxham resolutely pours
tiny black canola seeds into the hopper of his seeder. Sleep-
deprived and unshaven, he will climb on the tractor, fran-
tically seeding in an attempt to get his crops in before it is
too late.

Weather is a present aggravation, not just for Moxham, but

for all farmers: spring comes too late, frost comes too early, there is too little or too much rain. The complaining farmer has become a cliché—the stuff of cartoons. But a freak storm, flood, or drought can threaten vital income and what are often paper-thin margins.

Moxham knows he can do nothing to control the weather. Like generations of farmers stretching back to the beginning of cultivation, he can only hope for Mother Nature's benevolence. But determined to gain some measure of control over the unpredictability of the living world, Moxham is borrowing from biotechnology. Although his routine is unchanged, Moxham is planting the seeds of a revolution—a genetically engineered canola that promises mastery over the weeds that would otherwise threaten to crowd his crop. He is also taking part, unknowingly, in a huge environmental experiment.

Normally, Moxham would not dream of sowing canola in this field. The earth is heavy, prone to weeds. Typically, canola has to be pampered with herbicides and coddled with the best soil. However, the seeds intended for this field are supposed to be a "new-and-improved" wonder canola designed by the multinational chemical company AgrEvo to be resistant to a herbicide it also developed—a herbicide that will kill everything that grows, except for the test-tube canola.

Moxham is sowing the seeds of the future, not because he is a particular enthusiast of things new and technological, but because he is a practical man. He says he will use any new advance, on careful assessment, if it promises to be economical. In theory, this canola will require only one spraying of AgrEvo's all-purpose weed killer. If it works, it will not translate into massive savings for Moxham, but it may offer a small financial reward—the edge a farmer needs in this challenging agricultural environment.

Even small rewards are valuable to farmers like Dean Moxham. He is the third generation in his family to work this one thousand-acre grain farm on the Manitoba prairie. But unlike his father and his grandfather before him, Dean Moxham struggles constantly with the rising costs of mechanization and chemical inputs—the essentials of modern farming. Moxham's grandfather worked the land by hand and without today's fertilizers, herbicides, and insecticides. His per-acre production was much lower than Dean's. In 1917, one farmer fed about ten people; today, a single grower sustains ten times that number.

But despite the gains in productivity the Moxhams have made over the generations, grain prices did not keep pace and their share of those prices continued to fall. According to Statistics Canada, farmers earned 2.6 percent more income in 1996 than they did in the previous year—however, all of that money was earned off the farm. In fact, fifty-two percent of the average total farm income came from off-farm employment. Dean and his young wife, Dawn, are pretty typical; both have to work off the farm to sustain the business. Dawn is a physical education teacher in the local school; Dean tends the ice each winter for the curling club in nearby Portage la Prairie.

These are no-nonsense people who will do what they have to to maintain their life on the land. Dean is not given to poetic flights about farming, but his affection for the land is clear in the way his eyes assess a kernel of grain or sweep the broad horizon. He sees himself as the keeper of the land, a guardian of the agricultural environment. There is a young Moxham on the scene now, too. And like his father before him, Dean Moxham hopes he will pass on the farm to his son: "This is what I want. This is where I want to be, and I want to keep it viable for my son."

In 1996, thousands of North American farmers like Dean Moxham stepped into the brave new world of biotechnology. They would tend the millions of acres that would be used in an experiment to assess how well the environment could tolerate genetic engineering. The fields alongside the highway gave no indication that they were planted with the latest living things created in the lab. In July, Moxham's canola would bloom with the same distinctive yellow intensity as the natural canola fields that punctuated the prairies—its origins masked by its brilliant hue.

Before 1996, biotech crops generally were confined to field trials on test sites, often tucked away behind buffers of tall crop growth. But by 1996, a flood of genetically manipulated crops were approved in North America for unconfined release and offered to farmers.

AgrEvo's Innovator canola, the one Dean Moxham was growing, was the first genetically engineered crop on the Canadian market, leading an incoming wave of plants manipulated to be used with specific herbicides. In 1995, Saskatchewan farmers had had a trial run of the crop, planting about forty thousand acres of the modified canola. The next year, the crops across the three prairie provinces swelled to 600,000 acres. By the year 2000, it is estimated that seventy-five percent of the thirteen million acres of canola crop in western Canada will be endowed with a genetically engineered immunity to herbicides.

The year 1996 was a crucial first test for genetic engineering. If corporate biotechnology was to succeed, it had to impress not just regulators and consumers, but also farmers. Agricultural producers had to be persuaded that biotechnology would help them master the natural world—without damaging the environment—and that it would be economically feasible.

Four hundred years earlier, the philosopher Francis Bacon offered a caution about dreams of mastering nature. He wrote, "If we would control nature, we must first obey her." The logic of Bacon's words resonates in these early years of the biotechnological revolution. By flouting that basic rule, genetic engineering may unleash a host of unforeseen events. Every synthetic life-form presents a potential threat to the ecosystem in which it is released. Despite the industry's assurances, biotech crops are unpredictable—they reproduce, grow, and migrate. Once released, it is impossible to recall living organisms back to the laboratory.

Over the past several hundred years, thousands of non-native organisms have been brought to North America from other regions of the globe. While most of these life-forms have adapted to their new ecosystems without major dislocation, a small number have multiplied recklessly. Gypsy moths, kudzu vine, Dutch elm disease, and purple loosestrife are all examples of living pollution that cannot be simply mopped up. In the coming decades, the biotech industry proposes to release thousands of genetically engineered products into the environment each year. While many of these organisms may prove to be benign, statistical probability suggests a percentage will be dangerous to the environment.

In 1996, corporate biotechnology was well aware that it was dealing with a desperate market. No farmer would want to harm the environment, but the financial advantage engineered crops might offer was ultimately most important. The biotech companies launched their marketing machines at farmers, on television and radio and in fields, town halls, and farm exhibitions. The language of the sales pitches was the idiom of the farmer—"productivity," "control," and "yield." "Total weed control for twenty-one bucks," the AgrEvo representative promised a group of wary producers in a meeting hall just off the TransCanada Highway. "Yields are comparable to the top varieties," the Monsanto agent told growers next to a field of blooming canola on the Canadian prairies.

There was scarcely a mention of genetic engineering in the marketing to farmers, certainly no reference to environmental impact. In one of its thirty-second TV spots, AgrEvo promoted its new herbicide-resistant canola as "the ultimate in weed control" and "the best thing to happen to canola since canola." But not one word was spoken about gene splicing or crossing a microorganism with a plant. Although it had taken many years and millions of dollars to invent these wonder crops, the industry continued to insist that engineered plants were not much different from nature's own models—just better.

However, it is farmers like Dean Moxham who, with their ledger books in hand, will determine if biotechnology truly is "better" according to their own criteria. If genetic engineering fails to deliver on its promise, the seeds of scientific progress will languish in the storeroom. Dean Moxham is typical of his farm colleagues. No brash declarations of enthusiasm here, just noncommittal caution: "I'll try it. If I don't like it, I won't try it again."

In late June, Dean Moxham's tiny canola plantlets push up through the soil to embrace the warming sun. Scattered among them is an impressive array of competing weeds—wild oats, green foxtail, millet, sow thistle, lamb's quarters. The routine for today's farmer is to eliminate every last weed with the benefit of a lengthy list of chemical herbicides.

Modern North American farmers are hugely dependent on chemicals. Fields are prepared by chemical fertilizers, then swept clean of bugs and weeds by chemical pesticides. Canadian producers use thirty-five million kilograms of farm chemicals each year. That appetite for chemical solutions makes North America the world's largest regional market for pesticide and fertilizer sales. Agrochemical purchases are expected to grow about six percent every year until at least 2001.

For his field, the choice of chemicals will be easy for Dean Moxham. He will simply spray the genetically engineered canola with its tailor-made herbicide Liberty, the trade name for glufosinate ammonium. Liberty promises to be the death ray of weed killers. In theory, it will destroy all the plants it touches in Moxham's field—except the Liberty Link Innovator canola. By having to buy only one chemical, Moxham should save about $10 an acre.

The marketers at AgrEvo, Monsanto, and the other companies driving the chemical-crops bandwagon claim these new plants are a living example of sustainable agriculture. They say farmers like Moxham will actually use fewer chemicals than they normally would. One pass of Liberty should do the job of two or more applications of other chemicals.

Not only will there be fewer chemicals, the companies claim, but the products farmers do use will leave no nasty residues in the soil to pollute groundwater or tamper with future plantings. Although for now sales of chemicals continue to climb each year, agribusiness companies say farmers are replacing older, more hazardous chemicals, like DDT, with new ones that have fewer side effects on other living things or on the soil or water. Monsanto, for example, likes to say that Roundup is no more dangerous than table salt. And it fondly notes that the Charles Darwin Institute, a group that protects endangered species, used Roundup to clear weeds that were choking off the island habitat of the Galapagos turtles.

But it is not quite accurate to suggest these new chemicals

have no effects on human health. Even Roundup's girl-next-door luster was beginning to fade in the last years of the century. In 1996, the editor of the *Journal of Pesticide Reform* wrote that "glyphosate-containing products have caused great damage in human blood cells, reduced sperm counts in male rats, and lengthened estrous cycles and increased fetal loss in female rats." In research dating back to 1988, German researchers found that glyphosate increased the level of plant estrogens of bean crops. Young children are especially susceptible to elevated levels of estrogen. Monsanto did not provide data on estrogen levels of Roundup Ready soybeans sprayed with glyphosate, although there were many scientists urging that the soybeans not be allowed into the food chain. The School of Public Health at the University of California at Berkeley found that glyphosate was the most commonly reported cause of pesticide illness among landscape workers.

Genetically engineered herbicide resistance presumes that weeds will be easily vanquished by the lethal, "take-no-prisoners" approach of full spectrum pesticides like Liberty and Roundup. But experience has shown that plants, particularly hardy weeds, show a dizzying genetic ability to mutate and develop resistance to chemicals. One after another, herbicides have lost favor as weeds develop tolerance to their active ingredients. The number of resistant weed species has grown from 48 in 1986 to 270 in 1996, of which many are cross-resistant to several active ingredients. Even the mighty Roundup was beginning to show signs of frailty. In 1996, researchers discovered an Australian ryegrass that had become immune to glyphosate's normally terminal effects. A review by Jonathan Gressel published in the journal *Resistant Pest Management* went even further; he said corn, rice, carrot, barley, chicory, and peanut had all shown some resistance to glyphosate.

Because it is impossible to stop the wind or a wandering bee, it has to be assumed that traits being engineered into crops will cross over through pollination into other plants of the same family. Almost every crop in North American agriculture has a close relative in the weed family. Canola, for example, is closely related to wild mustard. Field tests in Denmark in 1996 already showed that the genetically engineered herbicide-resistant trait crossed from a European oilseed rape, as canola is called there, into wild plants in the same family. Both were members of the *Brassica campestris* family, and the two-plant variety crossbreeds were capable of passing on the new trait in just two generations. This is how a new "superweed," immune to the toughest of herbicides, would be born.

Biotechnology companies dismiss the idea of a superweed that cannot be killed by all-purpose terminators like glyphosate or glufosinate ammonium. In 1996, Stan Prokopchuk, North American head of marketing for Hoechst, AgrEvo's parent company, said that even if such a weed were created, it could be quashed. "It would be very easily controlled with any one of the conventional herbicides being used today—the 2-4-Ds, the dicambas, the bromoxynils. So it's not as if you are going to get a weed that can't be controlled." That sounds like a recipe for more chemical use, not less—a case of institutionalizing the herbicide treadmill for the sake of what looks like short-term gains.

In fall of 1998, several reports seemed to confirm the worst fears. First, Ohio State scientist Allison Snow found that when weeds acquire herbicide resistance from genetically engineered crops, rather than becoming less fertile, as some had believed, they maintain their ability to pass on those traits. Then University of Chicago professor of ecology and evolution Joy Bergelson found that genetic engineering actually makes plants more promiscuous. Farmers often have not worried about their crop plants crossing with weeds because many plants are self-fertilizing, so their genes were considered less likely to migrate. However, Bergelson found that even plants thought to be self-fertilizing, or selfing, can outcross with closely related species, and that genetic engineering even enhanced that outcrossing. Gene-spliced, herbicide-resistant plants were able to fertilize other plants at a rate twenty times higher than normal. "It is unclear why the transgenic plants had such an abnormally high incidence of outcrossing," Bergelson said in the press release announcing the findings, "but the results demonstrate that genetic engineering can substantially increase the outcrossing in a selfing species." The specter of the superweed suddenly seemed very real.

In addition to herbicide tolerance, the next most important new trait—pest control—to be engineered into crops also poses a challenge for the environment. This is ironic, because *Bacillus thuringiensis* (Bt) has had a long and fruitful life span as the backbone of organic agriculture. It is the most important biopesticide in the world—about $60 million worth of Bt is sold each year in the United States. Used for thirty years as a pest control powder or spray by organic producers, it has no harmful impact on humans, animals, or beneficial insects and degrades quickly in sunlight. And because Bt works by producing a protein that is easily digested by people and animals, there is no concern about putting it into food.

By borrowing from organic agriculture and inserting a Bt gene into a food plant, corporate biotechnology thought it had created an incomparable convenience for farmers who want to be rid of those irritating and potentially costly bugs. The various strains of Bt can produce about a hundred Bt toxins: in corn, a Bt gene makes the plant lethal to any corn borer that ingests it; in potatoes, the target is the Colorado potato beetle. With the addition of its miracle gene, a food plant produces its own Bt and, in the case of corn, potatoes, and cotton, that substance spreads through the leaves that worms and beetles munch, but not into the corn seed or tubers that farmers harvest for market.

By using the language of organic farming, companies that produced these bug-proof plants draped themselves in the flag of "sustainable agriculture." Monsanto's self-promotion for the Bt-enhanced New Leaf potato, for example, claimed the spuds are "grown in a better way." Thanks to what the company calls "genetic modification," the environmentally friendly potatoes can be "grown naturally, with fewer pesticides, less energy and less waste."

However, it is one thing to use a spray on a plant that will quickly dissipate in the sunlight and another to insert a gene into the genetic structure of a plant. Through genetic engineering, bug-proof crops had a Bt gene introduced in every cell of the plant, and the gene was "turned on" throughout the plant's entire life.

Genetic engineers began to splice Bt genes into crops knowing bugs would quickly develop resistance to them. The industry showed flagrant disregard for the scientific advice it was given and for nature's practices. Insects are remarkably able to develop resistance to the chemicals directed at them. About five hundred species of mites and insects have already developed resistance to various modern chemicals. The National Research Council wrote in 1986, "During the early 1950s, resistance was rare, while fully susceptible populations, of insects at least, have become rare in the 1980s." For most scientists, it was not a question of "whether" Bt resistance would evolve into a problem, but a question of "when." Even the U.S. Environmental Protection Agency predicted widespread resistance by the new millennium if Bt crops were planted uniformly across large areas.

The speed with which nature seems prepared to adapt to the new Bt crops has surprised even the experts. What farmers may not know is that there are already worms, beetles, and insects that can survive Bt. Scientists have found that one in one thousand tobacco hornworms are resistant to the organism. Bruce Tabashnik at the University of Arizona at Tucson found that when diamondback moths, a major pest of cabbages and other leafy crops, acquired a single Bt resistance gene, they developed resistance to four different Bt toxins. That means a bollworm that develops resistance to the Bt gene in Bollgard cotton might also have a resistance to the Bt strain in corn. "Nothing will be gained and much can be lost if we pretend to know more about resistant management than we really do," Tabashnik wrote in "Proceedings from the National Academy of Sciences." Researchers also found that twenty-one percent of diamondback moths in an isolated lab population had the resistance gene. At one time, scientists had estimated the immunity would show up in as few as one in ten thousand insects.

When this once rarely used organic pesticide becomes a commonplace ingredient of plant life, widespread resistance to all Bt plants and sprays is sure to follow. And there goes what used to be a valuable control for organic farmers. *New Scientist* magazine felt compelled to comment in an editorial in August 1997, "It is always a tragedy when a gift from nature is squandered, where it is a river dead from pollution or a forest laid to waste for timber. Let's hope that the biotechnology industry is not about to throw away the enormous potential of a simple bacterium, *Bacillus thuringiensis*, in its haste to get to market . . . overeager gene cloners are already rushing in where cautious ecologists fear to tread. The latest research suggests that it's time to slow them down."

In recognition of the short-lived benefits of Bt, the U.S. Environmental Protection Agency required Monsanto, Novartis, and the other multinationals that wanted to introduce bug-proof plants to the marketplace to come up with resistance management plans before it would allow them to sell the new test-tube seeds. So the companies asked farmers to plant strips or buffers of unmodified plants next to a genetically altered crop. These so-called "refuges" are supposed to provide a dining table for corn borers, or potato beetles, or whichever target pest. The rationale was that these bugs would not be exposed to the Bt gene and so would have no opportunity to develop resistance to it. If they were to mate with bugs that had acquired immunity, the resistance trait, being recessive, would not be passed on to the next generation.

This strategy was pressed vigorously in the U.S. For example, Monsanto required farmers who wanted to grow cotton with built-in Bt protection against bollworms and tobacco budworms to agree to plant twenty-five acres of normal cotton for every one hundred acres of the transgenic Bt cotton. That seemed a minimum defensive move in places like Alabama where seventy-seven percent of all cotton grown in 1996 was genetically engineered with the Bt gene. The company hired a fleet of representatives specifically to visit cotton growers—forty percent of the fields on the plan were inspected. Randy Deaton, Monsanto's product manager, told *Science* magazine, "Monsanto is well aware of the potential for pests to adapt to the Bt protein." But, he added, with proper refuges, "resistance development in the bollworm can be delayed significantly."

The other key tactic in the resistance management plans was to ensure the plants would emit a high dosage of Bt throughout. When Monsanto applied to get approval for its Bollgard cotton in the U.S., it submitted lab data showing that the level of Bt endotoxin was ten to one hundred percent higher than what was needed to kill cotton bollworms and tobacco budworms. The thinking was that no insects would be able to survive the assault of the engineered pesticide.

In theory, the cotton with a built-in pesticide was a welcome addition to agriculture. In the U.S., cotton is a $50-billion-a-year crop, with many natural enemies, including the cotton bollworm, tobacco budworm, and pink bollworm. At the beginning of the growing season, farmers were sent a brochure that depicted a pesky bollworm and this bit of braggadocio: "You'll see these in your cotton and that's okay. Don't spray. Just relax. Bollgard will protect your cotton." Thousands of producers in the southern cotton belt bought the advertising line and planted Monsanto's cotton. But toward the end of the growing season, chemicals were raining down on the American cotton crop in a last-ditch effort to control a massive bollworm infestation. It seems the cotton plants did not express the pesticide gene as effectively as had been hoped. Up to half of the two million acres of Bollgard planted in the cotton belt—Texas, Louisiana, Mississippi, Alabama, and Georgia—required supplemental spraying to control bollworms.

About forty percent of Bollgard growers had to spray, though Monsanto was quick to note that other farmers had to douse their fields with pesticides four to six times. The company did not mention the fact that farmers had paid a $32-an-acre technology licensing fee that was supposed to offset the cost of spraying. Therefore, some farmers had to pay both the fee and the unexpected pesticide costs. Some Texas cotton producers were so angry they launched a legal action against Monsanto. Their argument? Bollgard just did not work.

There were dissenting opinions on whether insects could have developed resistance to Bollgard so quickly. What seemed undisputed is that the Bt produced by the crop started out high in most fields, but tapered off as the season progressed. And the expression of the Bt gene was uneven throughout the plant. One Louisiana crop consultant reported more than ninety percent control in the top of the plant and less than twenty-five percent—less than a lethal dose—in the bottom.

In their 1997 paper entitled "Return to the 'Stone-Age of Pest Management'" which they presented to the EPA, researchers Charles Benbrook and Michael Hansen concluded that Bt crops ultimately would damage the ecosystem. When Bt resistance renders the organic pesticide useless, between two and three million acres of fruit and vegetable crops will require additional chemical pesticide applications, they wrote. By their calculations, that would increase human exposure to insecticides by four to six million pounds—and on crops that are consumed by people. "We and many others felt that EPA placed too much confidence in theoretical models and heroic assumptions in initially accepting the resistance management plans for Bt cotton and corn."

In September 1997, there was a further indictment of the EPA's approval of crops with a built-in Bt pesticide. A coalition of thirty-one environmental groups and farming and scientific organizations banded together to take legal action in federal court against the EPA. They charged the agency with gross negligence, alleging that in approving the transgenic plants, the agency seriously threatened the future of organic agriculture and jeopardized the genetic variety of major food crops.

Although the amber warning lights were flashing furiously,

corporate biotechnology was still adamant that it could control the Bt vehicle bolting down the road to the future. The refuge strategy requires farmers to sacrifice part of their crop to maintain the biotech industry's efforts to stay one step ahead of the bugs. According to this logic, problems arise when farmers overuse the technology, just as overprescribing antibiotics to people can result in treatment-resistant bacteria.

It is not clear how companies or government officials will react if farmers refuse to forfeit some of their land to refuges. If the management plans are to have any chance of delaying resistance for a number of years, one hundred percent of farmers must follow the plans carefully. Even a single field not off-set by a refuge can produce a small population of bugs with resistant genes that will then spread throughout the population. Some farmers may consider it immoral to sit back and watch a refuge crop be destroyed. As one observer noted, farmers do not want to give up their crop for a refuge—they want their neighbors to do it.

The biotech industry is confident it can control the genetically manipulated life it unleashes into the ecosystem. Serious resistance problems, whether in weeds or in bugs, probably will not show up for several years. It will take several generations of crops before cross-pollination and crossbreeding result in genetically mutated weeds or pests. Much as on the health front, the environmental impact of genetic engineering in crops will become apparent only when it is too late. However, it is fair to assume there will be some adverse effects on the environment.

Corporate biotechnology likes to say thousands of field trials have taken place around the world with no ill effects. But the proponents are overstating biotechnology's record. There have been several documented examples of things going wrong. These may not seem like cases of monster-like proportions, but even a microbe or a bacterium running unchecked can have devastating repercussions.

The industry does not talk much about a certain experiment in 1989. The U.S. company Biotechnia International wanted to test a genetically engineered microorganism, *Bradyrhizobium japonica*, which it hoped would improve nitrogen fixation, thereby improving soil fertility. Yearlong field tests of soybeans coated with the modified rhizobia unexpectedly demonstrated that the genetically engineered microbes were outcompeting the indigenous strains. This was a case of lab-created life killing off natural species. This was not supposed to happen. The field tests ended with the plants and seeds being incinerated and the field being plowed over and replanted. So even when it comes to microbes for which there is an extensive historical database, genetic engineering can make unpredictable things happen.

In another case of science gone wrong, a graduate student at Oregon State University was attempting to design a genetically engineered microorganism, called *Klebsiella planticola*, that would produce ethanol from crop waste. The remaining material would be spread on fields as compost. However, the compost had an unfortunate and unexpected side effect—all the wheat plants grown in the soil where it was present died. It seems the genetically engineered organism killed the life-giving organisms in the soil. These unfortunate repercussions were discovered only through a series of detailed tests at the university. Because such tests are not part of the usual EPA testing regimen, it is quite conceivable that an approved, apparently minor genetic manipulation could strip the soil of nutrients and organisms, essentially rendering it sterile.

In fact, a very similar scenario prompted a group of unnamed EPA employees to question conventional scientific and governmental wisdom at the agency. Their 1997 report entitled *Genetic Genie* charged their employer with "failing to assess the risks associated with the massive release—hundreds of thousands of pounds over several million acres—of a new living organism that cannot be contained or eradicated." The scientific mavericks were referring to what many might have considered an innocent manipulation—a bacterium called *Rhizobium melitoli RMBPC-2* was designed to act as a soil inoculant, a means to induce critical nitrate formation and increase yields in alfalfa and other legumes.

The scientists said the new bacterium was not even given a risk-benefit analysis. They suggested the effectiveness of the rhizobium was questionable, that it "could permanently reduce crop yields from the land on which it is applied." By taking the unusual step of releasing a report critical of their own agency, the whistle-blowers hoped to shock the EPA into stepping back from an expected decision. The report said, "The EPA currently lacks a sound process to assess the risks these organisms may pose to human health and North American ecosystems, yet the Agency proposes to abandon its authority to regulate whole classes of genetically engineered creatures." (In September 1997, the EPA did approve limited commercialization of the microbial seed inoculant, saying a natural version had been used for a hundred years and this genetically engineered rendition had been field tested for four years. Although the agency acknowledged there were some uncertainties, it ruled RMBPC-2 posed "a low level of risk to health and to the environment.")

Another unexpected environmental implication: In 1994, scientists at Michigan State University inserted pieces of genes from plant viruses to make virus-resistant plants. They found instead that the added genes can recombine with natural plant viruses to produce wholly new viruses at a rate much higher than previously reported or expected by experts at the EPA and the U.S. Department of Agriculture. The investigators concluded with a carefully phrased suggestion: "RNA recombination should be considered when analyzing the risks posed by virus-resistant transgenic plants." Other scientists were more insistent; the Union for Concerned Scientists called for a moratorium on the commercialization of virus-resistant crops.

However, there are indications that the next big trend in corporate biotechnology will be crops that are resistant to plant viruses. A crookneck squash was the first of this wave of edible progress in the United States. The squash, developed by Asgrow, received the green light in 1994 and was marketed as baby food. In addition, the U.S. has either already approved or is about to approve virus-resistant beet, cucumber, lettuce, melon, pepper, potato, sunflower, tomato, and watermelon.

Despite the experimental setbacks, North America continues to be the primary testing ground for the worldwide environmental experiment in genetic engineering. Since genetically engineered crops first began being tested in 1984, the U.S. has topped the list of countries to approve field trials; Canada is a close second. Most of the trials in Canada were carried out by multinational companies that did their laboratory research elsewhere but chose Canadian soil for their testing ground. For example, herbicide-resistant canola was developed in labs in the U.S. and Europe, but tested in Canada. A proponent would say that is because canola is routinely grown in Canada; an opponent might note that other countries were not willing to allow field tests.

A review of field trials from 1986 to 1996 by the International

Service for the Acquisition of Agri-Biotech Applications showed North America was much more prepared than Europe to approve biotechnology experiments in the open air. During that period, Canada and the U.S. hosted nearly four times as many tests—2476—as the entire European Union, a particularly striking imbalance considering that Europe is a major food-producing region. It seems other nations are somewhat more anxious than Canada and the U.S. about possible environmental disasters.

Using its own calculations, the U.S. Animal and Plant Health Inspection Service (APHIS) documented even more field tests of new agricultural products. From 1987 to the end of 1997, APHIS records show there were 3315 field trials at 14,154 sites. Applicants for field testing must provide information about the plant, including all new genes and gene products, its origin, the purpose of the test, the experimental design, and the precautions to be taken to prevent the escape of pollen, plants, or plant parts from the test site. Candidates for crop approval are expected to monitor the trials themselves and report back to the government.

In an effort to speed up the procedure for companies, APHIS has also moved to deregulate the biotech business by allowing field tests to take place with simple "notification." About eighty-six percent of field tests are currently conducted without the review that was required before 1993. Deregulation allows field-tested organisms that have unknown potential for plant pest risk to enter the marketplace with the most cursory of reviews. In 1996 and 1997, APHIS approved fourteen new products in seven crop areas under these rules. They included Northrup-King's insect-resistant corn, DuPont's herbicide-resistant cotton, and Monsanto's Colorado beetle-resistant potato.

At one time APHIS expected its personnel to check each site, but that obligation is disappearing under deregulation. In Canada, there never was a system of spot checks or inspections by government officials. The overriding assumption is that the companies or agencies doing the trials will act responsibly.

In some parts of Europe, where resistance to biotechnology is strongest, test plots are routinely destroyed. In Germany in 1995, when the locations of five test plots were revealed, activists demolished the plants. On other occasions, protesters set up what they called "resistance camps," complete with solar power, near the field sites. Residents of neighboring small towns and villages demonstrated their support with gifts of food and supplies. In the U.K. in 1998, a community action called "Genetix Snowball" saw more and more people rise up to destroy any field sites the government approved. Hostilities escalated to the point that companies appealed to the government to keep the location of test plots secret.

In Canada, corporate biotechnology has already won that battle. The location of field trials is not revealed—Agriculture Canada says this is to protect them from activists. But it is difficult to imagine a Greenpeace-type assault taking place in the broad, unpopulated stretches of Saskatchewan farm country, far from any population centers and journalists. Local farmers likely would be unconcerned—even blasé—about what is going on in the plot down the road behind the buffer strip.

The self-policing policy continues once corporations apply for full-use registration of their genetically engineered crops. Before approval, companies are required to show the likelihood of their plants crossing with wild relatives, their potential impact on pests or other non-target organisms, and other implications for the natural ecosystem. But regulators rely on the information presented to them, without doing their own studies or tests. And once the green light is given to new crops, Canadian and American regulators simply ask to be informed of any problems.

Government research to assess the risk of genetic engineering is sporadic at best. In the U.S., it is becoming more acceptable for scientists to question the risks of biotechnology. The U.S. Department of Agriculture, for example, began to dedicate the equivalent of one percent of its biotech budget to risk assessment studies. In Canada, risk assessment research of biotechnology is not well funded and, essentially, does not exist. If mistakes are discovered, they are shared with a small scientific community, not the public or the media.

The flaws in the regulatory system became evident in Canada in the spring of 1997, when a mix-up required the recall of a huge quantity of two of Monsanto's Roundup Ready canolas. About sixty thousand bags of seed, enough to grow 600,000 acres of canola, had to be pulled back from seed dealers and farmers just two weeks before they were destined to go in the ground—because they were carrying the wrong gene. Two southern Alberta farmers had to dig up the crop they had just planted.

In this case, wrong—and unapproved—genetic material had got into the canola seeds by mistake. Monsanto had been given approval for gene line #73; somehow gene line #200 showed up instead. Canadian authorities did not catch the mistake. Monsanto and Limagrain Canada Seeds, the company that multiplied the seed, initiated the recall themselves. It seems the two firms had been working with two genes containing the herbicide-resistant trait before they decided to take only one of them through the full regulatory process to obtain environmental, livestock feed, and human food approvals.

Monsanto had been boasting that as many as a million acres

of its herbicide-tolerant canola would be planted in Canada in the spring of 1997. The recall would cut that projection by at least two-thirds. In the rush to market, both the industry scientists and government regulators had failed both farmers and the public. It is impossible to say whether the unapproved canola would have been dangerous to the environment or to human health. However, the incident reflects badly on an industry that is at a stage where everything should be double or triple checked.

Over the summer of 1996, the sun considerately delivered growing warmth to Dean Moxham's fields. With just the right combination of moisture and heat, the Innovator canola plants rose proudly toward the sky, their seed pods filled with the kernels that would later produce the precious oil for which canola is known. They undulated gently in the summer breeze —a uniform blanket of color, unmarred by weed patches. In the corners of the field that the chemical sprayer had missed was evidence of the ragged weed growth that would have spotted this acreage had it not been for the Liberty herbicide.

Dean Moxham had a passing moment of hesitation as he prepared his combine for the fall harvest. He hardly wanted to be party to a trend that might be dangerous to human health or to the environment. But he reassured himself that his genetically engineered crop had been reviewed and approved by the Canadian government. "The precautions Canada takes are good precautions. I think that consumers will get a good-quality product out of this."

What he would harvest from his field would not be destined for the European market—consumer concern there had stymied regulatory approval of engineered canola. Instead, the oil crushed from Moxham's canola seeds would be delivered to North American food processors and supermarket shelves, where there was little opposition.

Dean Moxham's appreciation for the engineered canola would depend almost entirely on what it did for his pocketbook. It was sold to him and other Canadian farmers as the ultimate in easy and economical weed control. And on that score, it succeeded. Any signs of herbicide-resistant "superweeds" would take a few years to show up. Now the test was how much the crop yielded compared to a garden-variety canola Moxham had also planted.

When the canola was in the bin, Moxham was able to do his productivity calculations. The herbicide-resistant canola had underperformed, delivering about thirty-two bushels for every acre. The conventional canola was more productive, about forty bushels an acre. Biotechnology was supposed to deliver higher yields to cash-strapped farmers. That was supposed to offset any concerns about possible environmental impact. It did not deliver for Dean Moxham in 1996.

Although there were reports of increased productivity from farmers across the continent, many, like Moxham, did not benefit from biotechnology's much-touted returns. The following year in the American south, cotton farmers were saddled with stunted crops. Monsanto's Bollgard insect-resistant cotton had already failed to perform for some producers; in 1997, herbicide-resistant Roundup Ready cotton also did not totally deliver on its promise of productivity. Toward the end of summer, after a second pass of Roundup, cotton bolls on some of the 600,000 acres of the gene-spliced crop began to droop and fall off. Monsanto had a difficult time explaining how the damage occurred in a crop engineered with biotechnology's favorite trait. The company insisted the losses happened in only a very small portion of the crop. Researchers at the

Center for Ethics and Toxics in California reported in October 1997, "We tried to speak to a Monsanto scientist to ask why crop failures are occurring and were told that the information is not available. The U.S. government does not require this type of reporting, leaving the public and the farming community alike in the dark about the true cause of the problem." Beyond the possible implications for the environment, it was beginning to seem like the technology might not even work.

It is tempting to believe we can get the irritants of farming under control. An exhibit at the Epcot Center in Florida's Disney World imagines a high-tech agriculture where all the variables are controlled: plants are held up by mesh rather than messy dirt; nutrients are supplied at precise intervals by an automated flow-through system; air is filtered and sterilized to prevent the introduction of insects and disease.

This perfect world is, and will continue to be, a fantasy. Biotechnology's attempts to create it are doomed because, as Francis Bacon said centuries ago, nature is ultimately in charge —it will simply mutate and adjust to human efforts to create life. Our exercise in attempting to master nature may, in fact, backfire in the elimination of many natural species. We may soon come to a point where all the crops in the fields are artificial, the flowers in our garden are genetically engineered for color, and the trees in the forest are manipulated to grow faster and produce more wood. Jeremy Rifkin asks, "Do we want our children to grow up in a world where the genetic codes of plants, animals, and humans are interchangeable and living things are programmed as engineered products with no greater intrinsic value than autos or microwave ovens?"

Many people fear the consequences of genetic engineering will be much more than just aesthetic. Mae Wan-Ho writes,

"The large scale release of transgenic organisms is much worse than nuclear weapons or radioactive nuclear wastes, as genes can replicate indefinitely, spread and recombine. There may yet be time enough to stop the industry's dream turning into a nightmare, if we act now, before the critical genetic 'meltdown' is reached."

Corporate biotechnology is using the desperate financial situation of today's beleaguered farming community to sell its products. It is a question of short-term gain for long-term pain. There is already ample evidence to suggest that the release of genetically engineered crops into the environment has been premature and ill-advised. These crops may promise convenience and efficiency for farmers, but that is unlikely to last. A return to more toxic and hazardous products, within just a few years, seems inevitable. Of course, biotech corporations can always devote their research energies to finding the next solution to the side effects of their gene splicing. There will always be business in trying to stay ahead of the bugs and the weeds and the other furies of Mother Nature.

7

ANIMALS AS COMMODITY

BABE, THE PORCINE STAR OF THE HOLLYWOOD FILM OF THE same name, is the ultimate in 1990s feel-good, family fantasy. Babe never grows fat and porky. His voice chirrups with a perpetual childlike innocence. He lives in an old-fashioned farmyard, with ducks and roosters and talking sheep. He is smart enough to beat the border collies at their herding skills and endearing enough to appeal to the plaid-shirted farmer who, thankfully, has no particular taste for pork chops.

Of course, the life of a real pig on the brink of the new millennium is very different from his celluloid incarnation. The chilling life cycle of the modern pig could never be filmed for the delight of city-raised children weaned on fantasies of "Old McDonald's Farm."

The real-life Babe would likely be conceived through artificial insemination according to a meticulous recipe of porcine genes designed for modern human tastes. He would never snuggle against his mother's girth, even in the days just after his birth; infrared lights would be provided in place of the sow's warmth. He might suckle at her teats, but the bars of the so-called farrowing crate would keep her at bay to ensure her clumsy bulk would not accidentally crush the valuable piglet commodity. After three weeks, our modern Babe would bid adieu to the puzzling teats and move in with some one to two thousand other pigs in a massive barn of concrete and steel and automated feeding and watering systems. He would probably never touch straw in his short, five-month life, never mind a blade of grass. His only glimpse of sunlight would occur when he was loaded onto a truck for the next barn in his fattening cycle or filed up the chute into the slaughterhouse.

This is the true story of modern livestock production—a procedure designed to ensure maximum weight gain with lowest possible costs. Today's hogs grow faster and are leaner, more feed efficient, and comparatively cheaper to produce than the pigs of thirty years ago. This type of "factory farming" produces a lean pork chop for the modern, fat-conscious consumer. In the drive to produce what the industry affectionately calls "the other white meat," little thought is given to the psychological well-being of the animal. This factory farm livestock has no latitude to behave like hogs. This is the business of growing pork, not pigs.

Modern agriculture, with the tacit agreement of society, treats food animals as unseen commodities to be used for human consumption. Factory farming is an industrial process that applies the philosophy and practices of mass production to animal farming. And it does so very well: in Canada, about 450 million animals are slaughtered each year. Animals are not considered sentient beings, but rather the means to an end—eggs, meat, leather, etc.

By all measures, industrial manufacturing styles, along with improvements to feeds, barn systems, and reproductive technologies, have been remarkably efficient. For example, in 1951,

800,000 cows produced milk for all of Canada; in 1991, even with a significantly increased human population, that number dropped to 443,000.

Science deserves much of the credit for the shift to industrialized livestock production systems. The development of sophisticated reproductive technologies in particular has been a key factor. Artificial insemination, freezing of sperm, multiple ovulation, and embryo transfer are all routinely used as a means of sidestepping the painfully slow breeding prescribed by nature.

In the breeding systems defined by science, males of the species are viewed as sperm donors; females as vessels. These days, a significant number of registered pure-bred dairy cattle are derived through embryo transfer. Scientists are working to ensure cows do not have to wait until puberty to become mothers—eggs are taken from heifers as young as five months old, fertilized in vitro, and transferred to surrogate mothers. Cows and sows do not even need to be alive to be mothers in today's modern farmyard. Animals about to go to slaughter are super-ovulated and their eggs are harvested after their death.

The culmination of science's role in reproduction surely has to be cloning—essentially doing away with the last remnants of natural procreation. The idea of cloning became an international cause célèbre in February 1997, when news broke of the birth of a Dorset lamb at the Roslin Institute, a research farm and lab near Edinburgh, Scotland. *Business Week*'s "Biotech Century" was "suddenly upon us, not like a lion, but in the guise of a lamb." The lamb, Dolly, was a clone or an exact genetic copy of an adult ewe. She had no father and her mother simply contributed cells from her udder for the experiment. The DNA was taken from one of her mother's cells and fused with an egg cell from which the DNA had been stripped.

The egg was prodded to grow with an electric shock and inserted into the womb of another sheep. Although scientists had known before how to clone copies of a donor cell taken from an early embryo, all efforts to clone mammals from older cells had consistently failed—that is, until Dolly. The new technology would enable researchers to identify an adult animal with attractive traits and select it for copying. In theory, this would enable science to clone a dairy cow that produced copious amounts of milk, or a basketball player with the skills and genetic make-up of Michael Jordan.

For years, scientists had successfully cloned other animals, albeit through a different technique and without much fanfare. These clones were constructed with DNA from fetal cells, rather than cells from an adult. Genetic handiwork at the University of Guelph and at a private company in Alberta produced a small herd of cattle. In the early 1990s, the encouragement of the British milk board led to the creation of about one thousand cloned cows. And in 1993, the *New York Times* reported seventeen human embryos were cloned in a number of experiments. Those embryos were destroyed before they became full-fledged human clones, but the experiments proved it can be done.

After Dolly came Polly, then Molly, and then a whole host of cloned farmyard creatures, most accompanied by cute names and "baby" photos of young, identical copies. But the technology was advancing quickly, and perhaps ominously. Polly, also created by the Scottish Roslin Institute, was not just a clone, she was also a cross between human and sheep. She was grown from DNA taken from a lamb and then altered with a human gene. Polly has no discernible human features, but her genetic "humanity" means her blood will contain rare proteins, blood-clotting factors, and important biochemicals. Then a commercial laboratory managed to produce the world's first two identical monkeys, taking the cloning experiment uncomfortably close to human cloning. And then, underscoring the fact that this was a commercial race, an American company stepped from the shadows to announce it had found a way to mass-produce clones. The technique, it said, worked with either fetal or adult cells.

The announcement of Dolly's birth sparked near hysteria from a public no doubt picturing the incarnation of *The Boys from Brazil*. The Roslin scientists seemed puzzled by the reaction. After all, they said, they had no intention of using the technology that produced Dolly to produce human clones. Of course, that is exactly what their experiment showed could be done. If a complicated farm animal could be cloned, so could a human. U.S. President Bill Clinton asked for a national commission to review what he called the "troubling" implications of cloning. France's farm minister mused openly about farmyards transformed by six-legged chickens and eight-footed sheep. And right around the world, it seemed people were darkly predicting the imminent arrival of armies of Hitlers or labs of Einsteins.

Although political leaders around the world quickly attempted to limit the progression to human cloning, within months it became clear there would be no stopping science— or those with questionable aims. Chicago scientist Richard Sears told public radio in January 1998, regarding his plans to set up a clinic to produce cloned children, "We are going to become one with God. We are going to have almost as much knowledge, as much power as God." In late 1998, he announced he would clone himself. And a religious cult, the Raelian group, which maintains extraterrestrials brought the first life to earth, indicated it wanted to offer cloning services to its four thousand members. It announced it would set up a clinic in a country that did not have constraints on human cloning, and said it would begin cloning humans by the year 2000, though it would begin its work by cloning pets for a fee.

The awareness of cloned life suddenly focused attention on the question of whether limits should be put on experimentation with animal life. We are told it took 277 attempts to create Dolly. "They killed a lot of embryos and made a lot of malformed sheep," University of Pennsylvania bioethicist Arthur Caplan told *Business Week*. The scientist who pioneered the Dolly-style breeding acknowledged that commercial success of the program might be doomed because so many of the lambs are born abnormally large and die after birth. A lamb born at twice the normal size threatens the well-being of both mother and offspring. Animal welfare organizations had no doubts about where they stood on the question of cloning. Joyce D'Silvia, director of Compassion in World Farming, told the London *Sunday Times*, "We believe this can cause great suffering to the animals in terms of painful births and caesarean operations. It should be banned." The scientific perspective remained pragmatic. Alan Colman, the research director of PPL Therapeutics, the commercial arm of the Roslin Institute, suggested scientists should consider bigger sheep to act as surrogate mothers.

Evidence that cloning efforts could lead to animal harm was leaking out from the closed doors of research laboratories. A South African "supercow," which scientists wanted to clone for her ability to produce more than thirty gallons of milk a day, died after an experiment went wrong. The cow's angry owner, Ludwig van Deventer, told *Reuters*, "The scientists made a bugger up." From the scientific perspective all was not lost, because researchers were able to harvest some of the cow's eggs before she died.

Cloning, embryo transfer, multiple ovulation, and the other scientific means of animal husbandry seem otherworldly. Yet these strides in modern genetics have been achieved without breaking open the genome or the genetic map of the animal. Biotechnology's ability to mix and match genes from different species offers agriculture and science a new opportunity for enormous advances in the development of improved livestock. Or, from another perspective, genetic engineering will exacerbate the trend to confinement factory farming that has accelerated in the last three decades.

As in the development of crop plants, genetic engineering allows scientists to create new, improved meat and milk animals without the cumbersome and time-consuming practice of natural breeding. And, not surprisingly, the industry's focus is the development of commercially acceptable animal products.

The first and obvious market for genetic engineering in animals is a consuming public that has become obsessed with fat. Chicken meat sales have increased and egg sales have fallen over the past two decades with a new focus on low-fat, low-cholesterol foods. Genetic engineers are busy trying to create new life that will answer modern consumer tastes. In an effort to make pork more lean, scientists have already experimented with inserting a human gene into the pig's genome—humans, after all, are leaner than pigs. If people want chickens with big white breasts, gene splicers are going to find a gene that will endow the birds with huge, malformed breasts. The birds will simply have to be slaughtered before their legs can no longer hold their weight.

Much like biotechnology's efforts in the plant world, its research in the animal kingdom is directed at financially strapped farmers. Industrialized factory farming has increased the stress of animals, which is often manifested in increased disease. Much of current gene-splicing research is aimed at engineering animals that can withstand horrendous conditions, such as making chickens less sensitive so they will not peck each other to death. As smart creatures that can bristle under the confines of modern farming, pigs sometimes develop a stress condition that makes their meat unpalatable. If pigs are engineered to be less intelligent, they will tolerate their limited lives more readily.

These moves are applauded by many who endorse the idea of industrialized farm systems. Genetically engineered, extra-hardy animals will mean savings for farmers in the handling of animals with vaccines or antibacterial agents, improved health of the livestock, and less risk to consumers of drug residue in their diets. The issue of whether farm systems can be adapted to raise livestock more humanely rarely seems to come up in North America. In countries like Sweden, where there is a strong animal welfare movement, battery cages for hens have already been outlawed, as have full confinement barns for hogs.

Canada is a leader in the biotechnological development of new livestock vaccines and tests that ironically both improve animal health and allow factory farm systems to continue unabated. Scientists at the University of Toronto and the University of Guelph identified the gene that causes porcine stress syndrome (PSS). The genetic test for this gene is used worldwide to eliminate susceptible hogs. However, some observers have noted that problems could be solved more simply and humanely through improved handling and housing of the animals.

Similarily, the Saskatoon-based company Biostar genetically engineered two vaccines to control shipping fever pneumonia, which usually strikes calves in transport to feedlots. Shipping fever costs Canadian livestock producers close to $1 billion a year. It could be argued that a more logical, albeit low-tech solution, might be to avoid stressing and crowding the calves in the first place.

So far, the international biotech industry has not dipped deeply into its box of tricks to create transgenic livestock and poultry animals. Although genetically engineered foods like canola, soybeans, and potatoes are already in the marketplace, none of the new test-tube foods involve manipulated animals.

Scientists have already succeeded in inserting human genes into mice, cattle, sheep, pigs, and salmon. However, the development of transgenic animals is lengthy and very expensive. Typically, only a small portion of animals included in an experimental group successfully express the desired gene. Corporate biotechnology has also come to understand what seems obvious to many—consumers may accept a gene-spliced canola plant, but a pig with a human gene somehow crosses the line. That surely is one of the reasons why commercial energy and money have been put into manipulation of plants and microbes, rather than animals for slaughter.

The one exception to this rule is aquaculture. In 1982, only a handful of Canadian scientists worked in the field of fish. By 1991, that number had increased to more than sixty. The consumer appetite for fish rose proportionately during the same period, as did the development of fish farming in Canada. At the West Vancouver fisheries lab where scientists are growing giant salmon in the hope of satisfying new consumer tastes, researchers acknowledge that the animals sometimes display misshapen lumps of calcium and seem not to be able to swim as well as normal fish. Whether they are experiencing discomfort or pain, we can only guess.

The use of biotechnology in the animal kingdom forces society to ask how far it is prepared to go for its convenience and appetites. Cows crippled by bovine somatotropin? Slow-swimming fish? Clones of big-breasted chickens?

Polls show that consumer support for genetically engineered meat animals is low. The area in which there is most likely to be support for animal biotechnology is biomedical research. In this field, animals are not so much housed in a factory as they are factories themselves. Gene splicing is creating "bioreactors"—animals with an added human gene so that they will express valuable proteins for medicines in their milk or blood. Such medicines are usually culled from human blood or painstakingly grown in laboratory cell cultures that can produce just minute amounts of the drugs in a day. Goat, sheep, pig, or cow bioreactors can churn out many times those amounts. Dolly and her successors were cloned with the thought that they or clones like them could produce drugs for humans.

For example, in the early 1990s, Dutch researchers succeeded in inserting the human lactoferrin gene into a bull. Lactoferrin in human breast milk is a good source of iron for babies, promoting natural immunity. Herman-the-bull's assignment was to pass the trait on to his female offspring so they would be capable of producing milk containing lactoferrin—an obvious boon to mothers who cannot breast-feed. However, animal rights activists created enough concern about Herman's security that he was transferred to a pasture in California to live out his days.

By the late 1990s, news reports of commercial advances were becoming nearly routine. At Genzyme Transgenics Corporation in Massachusetts, goats were designed to produce human antithrombin III, a protein that controls blood clotting. In Scotland, the folks at PPL Therapeutics and the Roslin Institute produced transgenic sheep, which in turn produced human alpha-1-antitrypsin, a protein that is hoped will be of help to cystic-fibrosis patients. In Maryland, designer pigs were generating human blood products such as Factor VIII and fibrinogen in their milk. And in Ste. Anne, Quebec, Nexia Biotechnologies produced a dwarf sheep that would ultimately produce proteins in its milk to bolster the immune systems of transplant recipients and reduce the side effects of chemotherapy. As we step into the next century, there will be more and more news about cloned animals producing biomedical products for human beings.

Although these drug bioreactors are four-footed farm animals, they are not likely to be the backbone of the future farm. They are among the most valuable animals in the world, and their lives will be played out in secure, high-tech facilities, provided with the best of feed and veterinary care.

The appeal of living bioreactor systems is that proteins or drugs can be extracted without sacrificing the animals. But other so-called animal factories are being designed expressly for the purpose of sacrificing animals for the sake of human lives. In the mid-1990s, at least four biotechnology companies were working to develop pigs with organs that would be suitable for transplant into humans.

Before the advent of biotechnology, cross-species transplants or xenotransplantation were impossible because the human body was quick to reject organs from other animals. Such transplants inflame the proteins of the human immune system, prompting hyperacute rejection of the foreign organs. Now, all of the companies in the race for scientific headlines are developing pigs that are engineered with human genes designed to camouflage the foreign nature of their organs.

Pigs are considered the most likely donors because their organs can be matched to human size and they are easy to breed. Early experiments had focused on primates, but animal rights organizations were particularly appalled at the idea of harvesting organs from higher-life forms. And scientists expressed concerns that new disease viruses, like primate AIDS, could be passed on to human recipients. This potential hazard prompted the FDA in 1997 to put a hold on all clinical trials of porcine donor organs, tissues, and cells. However it was not a global ban, and transplant trials continued for people with Parkinson's and Huntington's diseases.

In 1997, British scientists found a virus called porcine endogenous retrovirus (PERV) scattered throughout pigs' genetic makeup. Their research suggested that pig organs used for xenotransplantation would introduce new, possibly deadly viruses into the human population. In August 1998, *The Lancet* carried a cautionary report from a German group at Hanover Medical School that found PERV in three breeds of pigs from twelve sites across Europe, and in every sample of skin, liver, lung, and endothelial cells taken from those pigs. Cultivation of those cells with human embryonic kidney cells led to the infection of the human cells—seemingly clear evidence that a virus in pigs could move to humans. Counterbalancing that report was another from the Centers for Disease Control in the U.S. concerning ten patients in late-stage, insulin-dependent diabetes who received insulin-secreting islets from fetal pig tissue. Five patients survived with the pig cells and showed no sign of PERV infection.

The strongest argument for xenotransplantation is the scarcity of available human donor organs. In the U.S., there are about sixty thousand patients on the nation's official organ transplant list, but there are only enough organs to do eighteen thousand transplants a year. About three thousand people die every year while waiting their turn. This undersupply of human organs is a powerful motivation for financial investment in the xenotransplantation race. Major pharmaceutical and medical-device companies have already made significant investments in the competing companies, and others are looking to jump in. The investors foresee business on a scale of more than $1 billion by the year 2000, climbing to much more than that within a few years. Analysts are predicting each pig organ will be worth about $10,000.

A letter to the editor in *The Lancet* in April 1997 began, "It is a common assumption that patients with end-stage organ failure will be enthusiastic participants in xenotransplantation programs." However, it continued, Australian research showed that among 113 patients with chronic renal failure, only forty-eight percent believed it was appropriate to breed animals to provide organs for human beings.

Although transplants into humans had not yet taken place at the time of this writing, cross-species transplants had occurred. Researchers from the U.S. biotech company Nextran reported that pig hearts, engineered to resist rejection, had survived for thirty hours after they had been attached to the necks of baboons. Pig hearts without the benefit of genetic engineering were rejected in sixty to ninety minutes.

In fall of 1996, the British company Imutran stunned the world by declaring it would be able to transport pigs' organs into human recipients within the year. The company predicted that xenotransplantation could become commonplace by 2005. Richard Nicholson, editor of the *Bulletin of Medical Ethics*, accused Imutran of making "widely optimistic claims about its work." Later in 1996, Imutran was bought by Sandoz, and since then Sandoz merged with Ciba-Geigy to form Novartis. Xenotransplantation was evidently a game with big stakes, for big players. James Murray, professor of animal sciences and veterinary medicine at U.C. Davis commented, "It's really a hard slog. That's why most work is being done by pharmaceutical companies which see it as a big pot of gold."

In response to Imutran's bold declarations, the British government ruled that no animal-to-human transplants would proceed until further research was conducted. The U.S. responded with guidelines that included everything from the breeding of transgenic animals to the makeup of transplant teams. In Canada, where the University of Western Ontario, in London, has carried out a number of experiments that apparently are designed to culminate in baboon-to-human transplants, the government called interested parties together for a forum in November 1997.

In early 1998, a New York-based lobby of scientists, health-care professionals, and public interest groups set up the Campaign for Responsible Transplantation. The campaign was formed to counter what it called the irresponsible rush to transplant animals organs into people. It said the health-care field would be better off promoting other transplant methods that did not risk human health with deadly animal viruses. Representing the campaign, Alix Fano said, "Putting an animal organ into an immune-suppressed transplant patient could open a Pandora's box of new, fatal, infectious agents."

For now, genetic engineering of animals has little impact on the environment or human health, essentially because the research is largely confined to the laboratory. It is most unlikely that modified goats developed for their human-enhanced milk would escape and breed with natural goats, creating a new, uncontrolled species. And it is improbable that scientists would allow valuable transgenic animals to slip into the food system. There are greater concerns about the development of transgenic fish, a technology that is relatively advanced. If these super-fish are offered to farmers, how will they be contained so they do not slip out to mate with wild fish? And what are the consequences on the ecological environment in the event of unplanned escapes?

The manipulation of animal life to produce more attractive foods or new medical products may not provoke immediate concerns about human health or the state of the environment, but it cuts to the heart of our beliefs about our relationship with other living creatures with whom we share the earth. There is a tangle of scientific, philosophical, religious, economic, and political issues tied up in the question of whether it is right or wise for humans to create new species of animals. The issue is especially contentious when biotechnology proposes to one-up the natural world by developing new creatures that serve only a human purpose.

Little guidance can be taken from government. There are no regulations in Canada ruling how animals are to be treated once they arrive on the farm. The use of laboratory animals is governed only by a set of guidelines administered by a quasi-governmental agency, the Council on Animal Care. Essentially, individual research organizations are expected to set up their own animal-care committees and follow common-sense procedures, usually with regard to housekeeping matters such as the size of cages, the need to feed and water the animals, and the maintenance of appropriate humidity and temperature controls. The concept of "necessary suffering" is considered a legitimate component of research, and therefore beyond regulation.

In 1993, 2.3 million animals were used by Canadian research, teaching, and testing institutions. Biotechnology is expected to increase the number of animals used in experiments. The first major rise in the use of lab animals in Britain in years was attributed to that country's biotechnology industry. Transgenic mice are used so frequently in Canada that their sperm are being frozen for future propagation. Yet neither Canada's federal guidelines nor provincial laws specifically address the issue of genetic engineering. For example, there is no requirement that transgenic animals be euthanized if they experience pain or suffering, nor is there a procedure outlined on how to dispose of transgenic animals.

In February 1996, the Canadian Council on Animal Care raised hopes when it released draft guidelines on transgenic animals. However, the guidelines merely suggested that provisions governing animals produced through genetic engineering be the same as those for other animals; in other words, that the animal-care committees of individual research institutions be charged with keeping an eye on things.

Responding to the draft guidelines, the Canadian Federation of Humane Societies expressed the disappointment of the animal welfare community, noting that the proposals did not allow for any kind of public input. The federation continued: "The guidelines assume the commercialisation and use of transgenic animals is given as a generalised, current and acceptable practice."

Animals are an integral part of virtually every aspect of biotechnology's transformation of agriculture. They are used not only as food, but also as essential components of the development of new pharmaceuticals. Yet, they are routinely ignored in any discussions of the industry.

Invariably, when genetic engineers talk about the challenges of creating new animals, they are concerned with practical, not ethical, questions. When scientists consider putting a human growth hormone gene in a pig with the anticipation of making the hog leaner, they are focused on how to insert the gene or how to grow a transgenic embryo, not whether it may cause the animal pain or trauma. The biotech industry's failure to recognize the intrinsic rights and interests of animals further institutionalizes the idea that animals are mere tools for human use.

Manipulation of farm animals by natural means to enhance productivity and efficiency has already resulted in an escalation of animal suffering and disease. Antibiotics and other drugs have become routine on today's factory farms. But biotechnology raises the bar to unseen heights. Transgenic manipulation between species can produce far more profound changes in animals than has ever before been possible. Now, animals can be treated as mere matter to be altered at will. Already efforts to create new life have resulted in animals born frail, sickly, and sterile, their organs and bones unable to support freakish weight gain. What new horrors await laboratory animals when the sky is truly the limit?

Biotechnology's application to animals poses some fundamental ethical questions. Bioethicist Arthur Schafer says people have to assess the risk/benefit ratio on the basis of the value they give animal life. Animal rights activists, for example, view animals as just as valuable as human life. On the opposite end of the scale, some people regard animals as objects to be used for human service. How you would view a twenty-first century barn with identical copies of one sheep, cow, chicken, or pig, selected for the ideal cut of its meat, depends very much on the value you put on the existence of those animals. For many people, the ethical questions probably lie in the middle of the two extremes. Shafer suggests that people ask themselves at what point they believe that the suffering and death of an animal is worthwhile. Is harm and suffering to a sentient creature worth a better cut of meat? Is it worth a new human drug? Or is it worth giving a human being a new organ and a new chance at life? And finally, in assessing the risks and benefits of biotechnology on animal life, consumers should ask themselves if the manipulation is truly necessary.

It is difficult to predict what life will be like for a twenty-first century Babe. His genes may be manipulated to give him increased resistance to disease or to ensure that when he gets to the slaughterhouse, he will offer up the perfect pork chop. Or perhaps his genome will be dumbed-down with a gene from another animal that will desensitize him to his life in concrete and steel. Or maybe he will make the ultimate sacrifice—donating his blood or even his organs for implantation into his scientific masters.

8

THE PRICE OF PROGRESS?

From the bow of the ferry, Salt Spring Island shimmers lush and verdant through the fingers of mist that rise off the gray waters of the Strait of Georgia. The island is an elusive retreat, an isolated and forgiving escape from the world of urbanization, mechanization, and globalization. At 180 kilometers square —the largest in the Gulf Islands chain off of Canada's west coast—Salt Spring is home to craftsy dope-smokers, wealthy retirees, corporate and professional dropouts, and some of the country's best-known artists.

At the turn of the century, Salt Spring Island was the center of a thriving apple industry. With a long growing season, mild temperatures, and not too much rain, the climate on the tiny island was perfect for growing fruit. With some fourteen thousand fruit trees, it was considered the leading fruit orchard area in British Columbia.

At that time, more than seven thousand apple varieties were available in the U.S. They ranged in color from near white to near black; some were best in storage for winter, others were ideal for pies; there was the citrus tang of the Lemon Pippin and the hint of pineapple in Ananas Reinette.

Today, the misshapen, overgrown branches of the abandoned apple orchards stand as mute testimony to the apple business that has long since vanished from Salt Spring Island. The small orchards on an island accessible only by ferry could not compete in the world of modern agribusiness. Today, the Grimes Golden apple that put B.C. fruit on the world's culinary map cannot be found in a Canadian supermarket. These days, new, "improved" varieties like McIntosh, Spartan, and Golden Delicious are mass-produced by huge, more easily accessible orchards, waxed to a glossy finish, labeled with their corporate stickers, and delivered to markets across North America.

These apples have attained their approved status with grocers because they are uniform in size, not prone to bruising, and easily shipped. Taste and nutrition are not the key considerations in the new world order. The Wealthy apple, for example, though prolific and juicy, did not ripen all at one time, so was deemed unsuitable for mass production. The Rural Advancement Fund International found it would take ten McIntosh apples to match the level of vitamin C in a single Wegner apple. The Wegner, however, cannot be found in a typical supermarket.

It should be no surprise that a move to turn back the pace of "progress" is happening on Salt Spring Island. The diminutive mixed farms where a handful of sheep graze on gentle hills are a clue that this place is out of step with what we think of as modern agriculture. There is a community of people here who believe that traditional farming actually might be better. Dan Jason runs Salt Spring Seeds, the largest heritage seed operation on the continent. Governments collect what they deem to be valuable seeds in gene banks, but it is up to people like Jason to gather, trade, save, and grow out the seeds of plant varieties that are otherwise not popular in modern farming and gardening. His hand-drawn catalog lists page after page of bean varieties and thirty-two kinds of garlic. He takes pride in preserving what would otherwise be lost in the path of modern agriculture. "You have a case where people are too old to carry on. They've been growing what they call the Aunt Jean bean—something that's been passed down in the family. They mail it to me and ask me to grow it."

Mike McCormick is the curator of the "Preservation Orchard," a project of the Heritage Seed Program, a volunteer organization that strives to maintain heirloom plant varieties by trading seeds between members. The orchard is a virtual living museum of rare fruit varieties—320 types of apples, pears, cherries, and plums. It is a reflection of what the island, and agriculture, may have looked like a century ago. "There was a purging at one time of all green apples," McCormick recounts. "So they were left with red apples that were shiny and had a snap in the night. Those were the three breeding categories for what would be planted in the next 20 years. What they gained was an economically higher production apple with more marketing appeal. What we lost, I don't know."

For thousands of years, farming meant scratching life out of the soil, tending plants and animals that would one day grace the soup pot. An eye was always cast toward the sky, in apprehension of the next natural calamity. Of grim necessity, farming families were in tune with the rhythm of the seasons and accustomed to the vagaries of nature.

That changed in the mid-1960s when the so-called "Green Revolution" transformed agriculture into big business. Although nature still wreaks havoc from time to time, farming in the developed world now takes its cue from industry and manufacturing rather than the traditional roots of agriculture. The

Green Revolution spawned new hybrids—virtual miracle crops —that used nutrients more efficiently, prompting high yields at low nitrogen levels. Coupled with new mechanization and chemical fertilizers and pesticides, the revolution sparked a new, hyperproductive agriculture. It essentially tripled yields of corn, rice, and wheat from 1950 to 1980. In my grandfather's day, a farm family, with plenty of kids to handle the weeding, could work 160 acres; now, through the development of chemicals and equipment, a single farmer can handle one thousand acres or more. When we think of modern agriculture, we imagine a sea of neat, uniform crops, unmarred by weeds, stretching to the horizon and tended by huge, monolithic machines.

Many argue that biotechnology is the next logical step in agricultural "progress"—they call it the "Double Green Revolution." After all, the new technology allows scientists to more effectively increase short-term productivity by engineering efficiency right into the genetic code of a species. But with its focus on designer foods and crops, biotechnology is not likely to replicate the massive yield improvements achieved by the post-war developments. Indeed, there are indications that biotechnology may exacerbate what is wrong with agriculture's transformation into an industry.

In today's agriculture, crops are selected according to an industrial model—not just for their productivity, but also for their ease of handling and processing. Machine harvesting these days requires crops to ripen at the same time and grow to the same height. The Campbell Soup Company, for example, wants its tomatoes to be all the same size for easy, automated processing.

Modern agriculture's focus on easy handling along with high yields has urged farmers in the industrialized world into the widespread cultivation of a small number of popular crops. For example, only a few crop varieties are grown on the Canadian prairies, and only a few types of apples are available in the local supermarket. In the push for progress, many of the traditional crops, or landraces, that were grown by our agricultural forebears were abandoned.

"The unsustainability of modern agriculture is in part a measure of its inability to tolerate diversity. Both genetic and ecological uniformity—the same crops of fields sown horizon to horizon without interruption—demand costly and often dangerous or futile reliance on chemicals to protect crops from pests or diseases that are rapidly spreading and evolving," writes the Worldwatch Institute in its 1992 State of the World report *Conserving Biological Diversity.*

This agricultural homogenization is quickly eroding the world's storehouse of food crop varieties. This has become such a critical concern that the variety of life on earth has been given a name—biodiversity. Approximately three-quarters of the biodiversity in the world's twenty key food crops has been lost in the past fifty years. About ninety-seven percent of vegetable varieties that used to be on the U.S. Department of Agriculture list eighty years ago are now considered extinct. Not a single variety of native broccoli still exists in the U.S. Between four and six thousand plant and animal species disappear from the earth each year, many under the farmer's plow and the force of his resolve to reshape nature. If the pace of agricultural progress continues as it has during the past five decades, as many as twenty percent of the species on earth will be driven to extinction in the next fifty years.

Species began disappearing much more rapidly once human beings showed up. The current rate of human-caused extinctions for mammals, for example, is estimated to be one hundred times greater than the average shown by the fossil record; for birds, it is about one thousand times greater.

Beyond the basic ethical and spiritual appreciation for the diversity of life, there are some very pragmatic reasons why the loss of plant and animal species, even that of a lowly plant or a pesky insect, is risky. Of the top 150 prescription drugs in the U.S., 118 were originally derived from plants, fungi, and other species. For example, cyclosporin, an important suppressor of immune responses, was derived from an obscure fungus in Norway. It is impossible to say if the cure for cancer may have been lost in the extinction of what some might have dismissed as an unproductive plant.

It has long been understood that overbreeding and over-hybridization can be dangerous. Every plant and animal breeder knows that attempts to streamline the efficiency of species or to satisfy whimsical tastes can result in more lucrative but weaker strains and breeds. The pushed-in noses that characterize boxers and bulldogs have given those breeds respiratory problems. Multicolored hybrid roses are unlikely to survive some Canadian winters. Today's turkeys have huge breasts to supply the holiday dinner table, but they are unable to have sex naturally.

Reliance on a few super strains or breeds also increases vulnerability to disease. Biodiversity is a survival mechanism. It ensures that each species will have enough genetic variety to effectively adapt to changing environments. By eliminating unprofitable or inefficient strains, we undermine the adaptive capacity of life. Monocultures, the widespread planting of a single crop, make our food sources vulnerable to new diseases, pest infestation, and climate change.

The Irish potato famine of the nineteenth century is the classic lesson of the perils of relying on just one variety of food.

About two million people died over five years as the staple of the Irish poor—essentially, one type of potato—was decimated. Modern industrialized agriculture seems to have ignored the teachings of the past, subtly encouraging today's farmers to depend on an increasingly narrow range of crops. Not long ago, American corn farmers were hit with a devastating blight that silently wiped out fifteen percent of the nation's corn crop. "Most Americans don't know how close we came to being a food importing nation during the 1970 southern corn blight," Steve Eberhart, director of the National Seed Storage Laboratory, told *National Geographic* magazine in 1991.

In the realm of animal breeding, Holstein cows dominate the dairy industry because of their superior milk yield. But Holsteins also demand specialized feeds, an array of technological support systems, and continuous monitoring. So we have a more productive cow, but one too frail to survive a northern winter outside. And in a search for the ultimate cow, the industrial model has led to widespread inbreeding. Of the half a million Holstein cows in Canada, seventy-five percent of them are being artificially bred with the semen of just a dozen or so bulls who have proven themselves as successful procreators of high-yielding offspring.

Many scientists and critics see the loss of biodiversity through farming to be critical to human existence. "To simplify the environment as we have done with agriculture is to destroy the complex interrelationships that hold the natural world together. Reducing the diversity of life, we narrow our options for the future and render our own survival more precarious," says Arran Stephens, founder of the organic group Nature's Path. Cary Fowley and Pat Mooney write in their book *Shattering: Food, Politics and the Loss of Genetic Diversity*, "The diversity of plants is the underlying factor controlling the diversity of other organisms, and thus, the stability of the world ecosystem. On these grounds alone, the conservation of the plant world is ultimately a matter of survival for the human race."

In addition to hastening the industrialization of agriculture, biotechnology also proposes to create new life-forms that may push out natural species. Life created in a laboratory may well be the ultimate in genetic pollution. Many ecologists fear that genetically engineered organisms could function as exotic species often do—multiplying rapidly and without constraint in the absence of natural control from predators and competitors. And those invading alien species could obliterate native, natural life. By virtue of their space-age genes, some genetically engineered plants and animals will inevitably spread like a cancer, overpowering wild species in the way that introduced exotic species have created problems in North America.

Ironically, most of the world's biodiversity—about seventy percent—exists in the world's poorest countries. One small Philippine volcano contains more woody plant species than can be found in the vast forests of Canada. One small Panamanian island offers more floral diversity than all of the United Kingdom. The United States is known as the breadbasket of the world, yet only one of the major crops harvested there—the sunflower—is native to the continent. All fifteen of the U.S. food crops worth $1 billion or more depend on genetic diversity from other countries. Corn, potatoes, and tomatoes came from Latin America; rice and sugar from Indochina; soybeans and oranges from China; wheat, barley, grapes, and apples from Asia.

The wealth of biodiversity in otherwise poor countries is now at risk. Farmers in the developing world are often eager to mimic the practices of their more affluent counterparts in industrialized countries. Where they can afford the cost of the inputs—the hybrid seeds, the equipment, and the pesticides—

they abandon the old landraces, often in favor of a single variety. In the process, they bulldoze virgin forests and clear and terrace vulnerable hillsides. High-yield varieties of wheat such as Maxipack and Sonalika have already been sown over seventy percent of traditional wheat lands in Saudi Arabia and Lebanon. In Indonesia, the Philippines, and Vietnam, sixty percent of the fourteen million hectares of rice land are planted with one variety.

The ledger of loss does not stop there. Family farms are also on the endangered species list. In a side effect of post-war industrialization, the more productive agriculture held down North American commodity prices. From 1947 to 1997, prices for wheat, corn, and barley rose thirty-five percent, sixty-nine percent, and three percent, respectively. In comparison, a postage stamp cost 966 percent more over that same period, the cost of a tractor increased by 481 percent, and it cost 13,000 percent more to bear a child in a hospital.

Farmers who had welcomed the technical advances of the Green Revolution soon found they had to cultivate larger areas and spend more on chemicals and equipment if they hoped to maintain their operations. Many discovered they could not manage the economics and opted for bankruptcy or early retirement. Census statistics show that fewer than two percent of Americans now live on a farm. Farm families account for such a small proportion of the population, they no longer make up their own census category. In contrast, about seventy percent of Americans choose to live in cities and suburbs, far from where food is produced.

Family farms have disappeared along with plant and animal species in the wake of industrialized agriculture. In 1940, nine million people lived on American farms; by the mid-1990s, that number had shrunk to about two million. And observers say that even that number is inflated by people looking for tax advantages—the real number of farmers in the U.S. is closer to 500,000.

The loss of farm populations in North America has transformed rural life. Today, huge expanses of the American Midwest are essentially empty breadths of land. We can travel miles down a dusty gravel road, flanked by perfectly uniform fields of corn, and never see a single house. The fabric of rural life has been irrevocably torn, as small-town churches, schools, and banks have closed.

Farming was once the preserve of the independent-minded pioneer. According to American mythology, a farmer did not allow his life to be ruled by a time clock; a farmer would decide on his own what he wanted to plant and how he wanted to tend it. Life was sustained by a supportive community. Seeds were a thing farm families simply shared.

The Green Revolution began to wrest some of that independence from the American farmer by developing new hybrids that had to be purchased each spring. Gone was the congenial, sharing system of the past. Commercial biotechnology proposes to deliver an even bigger blow to the fabled farm independence. Under the current version of corporate biotechnology, the farmer is no longer in charge of his universe.

The biotechnology establishment insists no industry values biodiversity as much as it does. The business can claim to be creating new species, but more importantly, gene jockeys value genetic diversity because they are constantly in search of genes that may give their inventions commercially profitable traits. It is on this biodiversity front that the new technological science is facing what may be its greatest challenge.

Developing countries have often seen researchers from the industrialized world descend on them to collect seeds, only to discover later that the genetic material from landraces is being patented by pharmaceutical or seed companies that will profit handsomely. From the perspective of the developing countries, their natural biodiversity is being plundered. There has been next to no recognition, never mind recompense, for genes that developing countries thought were their own. What corporate biotechnology calls "appreciation for biodiversity," the developing world calls "biopiracy."

The developing world is fighting back. It wants a piece of the monetary benefits that corporations from the industrialized world seem to enjoy—millions of dollars in royalties for the use of native species and genes. One-half of the known plant species in Brazil, one of the countries with the richest biodiversity, have been patented by large multinationals. In response, the state of Acre in Brazil announced it would restrict researchers and scientists from what it calls the "illegal trade in modern colonialism"—the dealing in genes. One nongovernmental organization was found trading painkillers with six Indian tribes in Acre in exchange for species of plants with medicinal properties. The plants were then sold to international pharmaceutical companies. In the future, bioresearchers will have to take out special licenses before they go harvesting for genes. And if they find something profitable, they will have to pay royalties to the native community.

In 1989, Costa Rica took control of its own valuable biodiversity by establishing an agency, the Instituto Nacional de Biodiversidad (INBio), to gather new sources of chemicals, genes, enzymes, and microorganisms from its diverse tropical forests and market them for commercial biotechnological purposes. In essence, Costa Rica decided biodiversity was a resource to be exploited. INBio struck a deal with the U.S. pharmaceutical giant Merck & Co. under which INBio agreed to send the company chemical substances that might be used in therapeutics. Merck agreed to pay the agency a $1 million fee and royalties on the profits of any new drugs. Eight similar agreements followed.

The value of biodiversity was recognized when the majority of nations attending the Earth Summit in Rio de Janeiro in 1992 signed the Convention on Biodiversity. Article 19 of that convention made mention of an "advanced, informed agreement in the field of safe transfer, handling, and use of any living modified organism resulting from biotechnology." Attempts to define what that means were called the "biosafety protocol." Toward the end of the decade it seemed that "biosafety protocol" was being developed as a clear assault on biotechnology and the countries promoting it.

Because the protocol falls under the jurisdiction of the United Nations Environment Program, environmental organizations tend to be taking the lead role in the discussions. They consider the commercial transfer, handling, and use not just of seed, but of any genetically modified food or feed to be subject to their regulatory scrutiny. That means a shipment of wheat or corn or canola might be considered a living modified organism even though it was not intended for seed, but for consumption. It further means that exporting companies would have to get express consent before they ship.

The biotechnology industry views these protocol discussions warily. It argued that getting explicit approval to ship to each individual country could add millions to R&D costs. Bill Leask, vice president of the Canadian Seed Trade Association, who sits on an advisory working group to the protocol, took it one step further. He told the *Ag Biotech Bulletin* in July 1997,

"I have come to the conclusion that it could effectively shut down the research and development of genetically modified crops in Canada."

The biosafety protocol was escalating into a focal point of friction between developing and industrialized countries. Having refused to sign the Convention on Biological Diversity, the U.S. was not a full participant in the negotiations. However, APHIS and other federal agencies were said to be working "to ensure the appropriate policies are agreed upon to guarantee the safe international use and development of new products derived through biotechnology."

Biotechnology proponents, like the U.S., protested that test-tube foods were safe and already overregulated. Developing countries, however, led by Malaysia and India, persevered even in the face of significant lobbying by the corporate industry. The decision to continue discussion on the creation of a biosafety protocol was hailed as a major victory for the developing world. "The sincerity of developed countries to provide adequate safety regulations in respect of a technology which they have introduced and are subjecting the developing world to, will be judged in the coming months," Gurdial Nijar, a Malaysian lawyer, reported in the newsletter *Third World Network*.

The developing world was clearly in a combative mood by the late 1990s, its sights trained on corporate biotechnology. It had succeeded in linking what it viewed as a threat from biotechnology to its attempts to protect biodiversity. It was beginning to seem as if the biotech industry's biggest challenge might ultimately come from an unexpected source whose power had always been discounted—the developing world.

In the United States and Canada, on the other hand, there seems to be surprising acceptance of the conditions that have forced the extinction of thousands of species and sent many of our farmers into early retirement. There are government-sponsored gene banks around the globe to save precious seeds that might have otherwise disappeared entirely. But like museums or zoos, the gene and seed storage banks are no replacement for diversity that lives and thrives in the ecosystem. It is curious that in this commercial era that celebrates choice, most consumers do not seem to care that there are fewer options in the produce aisles. And most farmers have stoically stood by while progress decimated their way of life.

The protests to agricultural progress come quietly from places like Salt Spring Island, where alternative approaches to agriculture thrive among the abandoned orchards. Nongovernment organizations like Unitarian Service Committee Canada (USC) have gone to the island to explore how the past can be revitalized. USC's interest in biodiversity was born from its aid work in developing countries.

Mike McCormick, who lovingly planted the "Preservation Orchard," has no delusions about what he is doing. He may return some of the diversity that Salt Spring Island enjoyed a century ago, but he knows his efforts won't slow the pace of progress off the island. "This is a grassroots survival program rather than taking on General Motors of the fruit industry," he explains. "We're just saving a little of what has been lost."

9

OLD MCDONALD HAD A PHARM

LUNCH IS IN ONE OF THOSE FAUX BRITISH PUBS THAT HAVE sprung up in strip malls across North America. The menu offers Thai lime, Italian tomato, and Indian curry, defiantly out of keeping with the Coronation Street decor, the typical fare of the fusion-friendly 1990s. In an obstinately uncosmopolitan move, I order a cheeseburger and fries.

A group of test-tube food promoters from Canada's self-described independent Food Biotechnology Centre has come for a meal and an opportunity to advance the cause of biotechnology. Although the professor and the public relations specialist have opted for soups and salads, Milly Ryan-Harshman, the dietitian, absolves me of nutritional guilt by choosing a fat-infused helping of shepherd's pie. There are no admonitions, no cautions, no advice. She bears no resemblance to the strict diet disciples who used to appear in my grade 4 health class in the 1960s to preach the gospel of the Canada Food Guide. Somehow that disciplinary message sunk in—even this rushed meal today will include those four key food groups.

One day soon, Ryan-Harshman says as she glances at my plate, biotechnology will create french fries with the health benefits of broccoli. Her profession is well aware that may be exactly what it takes if North Americans are to eat healthfully. In these last years of the century, Americans have the worst diets in the world. Nearly forty percent of the average consumer's daily caloric intake is made up of fat; eleven percent of Americans eat no fruits or vegetables in an average day. Only one percent of American children between the ages of two and nineteen eat a diet that contains proper amounts of all food groups.

Canadians have no reason to be smug. In the past two decades, the average Canadian's intake of red meat may have fallen by ten percent, but high-fat cheese consumption has doubled. Most Canadians drink less milk than they used to and have switched to skim, one, and two percent, but they consume fifty percent more cream than they used to.

Both the American Dietetic Association and Dieticians of Canada have grown weary of trying to convince North Americans to stay clear of fat and fast food. Both organizations now believe biotechnology may be the answer. They endorse the new science as a way to produce "safe, nutritious, healthful, abundant and tasty food." Modern nutritionists accept the biotech gospel that there is no need to label genetically engineered food, that gene splicing is no different from the breeding that has developed agriculture over thousands of years. And instead of forcing those with a diet modeled on Homer Simpson to adjust to the rigors of five fruits and vegetables a day, Ryan-Harshman says biotechnology will adapt foods to the tastes of modern consumers.

A time when french fries are not really french fries is one that many of us might appreciate. Although North American diets are abysmal, there is a contradictory and growing interest in health and nutrition. As baby boomers in the developed world lurch toward their fifties, there is a frantic search for a dietary fountain of youth. Thousands of foods on supermarket shelves now proclaim their "low fat" or "reduced salt" status. Americans are huge consumers of dietary supplements —they spend about $2.5 billion a year on vitamins and other supplements, whether vitamin E to prevent heart attacks or megadoses of vitamin C to combat the common cold. Since 1993, the numbers of natural food stores in the U.S. have jumped by fourteen percent a year; in the same period, supermarkets grew by only 3.3 percent. Bookstores are a mirror of the health-conscious trend—the best-sellers are titles like *Heinerman's Encyclopaedia of Juices, Teas and Tonics.* *Maclean's* magazine in Canada put the obsession with "eating right" on its front cover in October 1997.

For centuries, human beings have consumed foods not just for their taste and bulk, but for their purported healing properties. In 400 B.C., Hippocrates wrote, "let food be your medicine and medicine be your food." Today, Grandma's cold-busting chicken soup may still be the stuff of folklore, but science has confirmed there is a logic to this diet therapy: chromium in broccoli may save us from Type II diabetes; the calcium pectate in carrots may lower cholesterol levels; oat-based products that contain beta-glucan, a soluble fiber, are proven to reduce blood cholesterol; red wine in moderation may hinder cardiovascular disease; ginseng root may have medical benefits for the heart, liver, spleen, lungs, and kidneys, in addition to increasing learning skills, short-term memory, and energy; and flaxseed's lignan and alpha linolenic acid are believed to reduce the risk of heart disease and cancers.

Ryan-Harshman says this is where biotechnology enters the stage. Nature has always defined a limitation to healthful foods.

Genetic engineering will broaden the menu of healing foods by permitting the genes of one food to be inserted into another. That is how the diabetes-fighting gene from broccoli could be transferred to a fried potato.

Science will take foods from folklore to the lab to the grocery store as "functional foods." The market in the U.S. for these healing, medicine-foods is huge—estimated to be $250 billion a year. In the future, the choice for a dinner out may not be "Shall we go Chinese or Italian?" but rather "Shall we reduce our risk of colon cancer or lower our blood pressure?" And all North Americans, even those with a taste for burgers and fries, may be eating healthfully.

For now, genetically engineered functional foods remain only wishful thinking, but agribusiness has recognized their market potential. These are, after all, the ultimate designer foods. Monsanto hopes to release a potato in 2002 that will absorb less fat when fried. French fries from these new, engineered potatoes may not be as good for you as broccoli, but they will not clog your arteries. The company is also planning to release several canola and soybean oils early in the new millennium that could be used as margarine replacements, with no trans-fatty acids to increase cholesterol.

Research elsewhere is designed to produce garlic cloves with more allicin, which may help lower cholesterol, and strawberries with increased levels of ellagic acid, which may reduce the risk of cancer. Scientists in Edmonton are trying to isolate the beta-glucan component in oats that lowers cholesterol so it can be mixed into other foods. Other researchers are attempting to create a beta-glucan that could be available in the dairy case as a yogurt.

In the European Union, a program known as the Project

of Technological Priority allocated millions of dollars to laboratory teams to research functional foods. In July 1997, a team from Egham, outside London, reported it had genetically engineered tomatoes with four times the normal levels of beta-carotene and twice the normal levels of lycopene—tomatoes it hoped would help prevent heart disease and cancer. Researchers anticipate the nutritionally boosted tomatoes will be "more acceptable to Europeans frightened by the idea of transgenic food." Teams in Spain and Germany are working with peppers, and elsewhere in Europe, scientists are experimenting with the creation of rice rich in beta-carotene.

Genetic engineering may grant foods some new, valuable properties, but it is not simple to modify foods without affecting other characteristics. For example, some product development tests show that beta-carotene can impart an "eggy" flavor to foods; minerals can deliver a chalky, dry taste; vitamins are not heat stable; and dietary fiber needs flavor masking.

Although functional foods are not yet ready for the field, there is all kinds of optimism in the farming community about lucrative new crops. In anticipation of a hopeful rural future, observers have already coined a new name. The future farm will be a "pharm," producing functional foods and biopharmaceuticals on agricultural land.

Terry Sharrer is the agricultural curator of the Smithsonian Institution in Washington, D.C., and a bit of a futurologist. He predicts the demand for healing foods and drugs will transform farming and the rural way of life in the new millennium. "We are looking at the virtual reinvention of agriculture," he recently told the Virginia Farm Bureau Federation. "I don't imagine that the principal plants and animals farmers will raise a generation from now even exist today."

The biggest challenge for functional foods is establishing a well-balanced legislative structure that will encourage the development of foods with legitimate value and discourage the faddish foods that may win attention through unsubstantiated claims. Throughout time, snake-oil salesmen have marketed cures without the proper scientific research to back up their claims. Many consumers may remember the recent beta-carotene about-face. First, there was much publicity about beta-carotene preventing lung cancer. Then, a 1994 Finnish study of twenty-nine thousand older men who smoked showed the opposite—in fact, beta-carotene supplements actually increased the risk of lung cancer.

Japan is leading the way in legislating health claims by recognizing functional foods as an alternative to drugs. Under a 1991 law, foods that are deemed to have healthful properties are officially recognized as Foods for Specified Health Use (FOSHU). It is not easy to get a FOSHU certificate; manufacturers have to go through a complicated three-stage process. However, by the late 1990s, dozens of functional foods had appeared on Japanese supermarket shelves. They included tuna containing docosahexaenolic acid, a substance thought to improve learning function, sharpen memory, reduce cholesterol, and suppress allergies; and soft drinks with added bifidobacteria to improve the condition of the gastrointestinal system.

Legislation is not nearly as straightforward in North America. For starters, the term "functional food" has no legal status in the U.S. or Canada. Laws prohibit health claims on foods, forcing manufacturers to promulgate their claims through the unregulated media or word of mouth. It is no surprise that some food processors attempt to make grandiose claims about the health benefits of their foods. One manufacturer recently violated truth-in-advertising standards by claiming his fiber-enriched fruit juice could help lower cholesterol and reduce the risk of coronary heart disease. U.S. government regulators stepped in, ruling the advertisements exaggerated the drink's likely health benefits. Otherwise, consumers have been on their own when it comes to separating the hype from the healthful in the world of alternative dietary supplements. There is raw thymus, shark cartilage, Siberian ginseng, vitamins C and E, or beta-carotene for those worried about cancer. Overweight? Try "herbal phen-fen," "dieter's tea," or "Diet Pep" pills. Impotent? There is yohimbe, royal jelly, vitamin E, ginseng, or amino-acid supplements when Viagra is not at hand.

Functional foods have the potential to be of enormous benefit to health-conscious consumers, but only if they are advertised honestly and regulated carefully. The hype behind alternative remedies offers an uncomfortable look into a future in which genetically engineered functional foods are not adequately legislated. Examples of natural remedies gone wrong are not uncommon. Remember, L-tryptophan was promoted as a surefire cure for insomnia. Over the past few years, twenty people in the U.S. died and hundreds of others suffered from dizziness, tremors, headaches, heart attacks, and strokes after taking ephedra, also known as Ma Huang. Those folks turned to the nutritional supplement because they wanted to lose weight, boost their energy, and build muscles. Authorities also point to liver toxicity from *Acorus calamus*, kidney damage from *Magnolia officinalia*, and acute hepatitis from Shou Wu Chih.

PR Watch, a newsletter that engages in public interest reporting on the public affairs industry, described the alternative remedies business as a giant, $4-billion-a-year industry that worked hard to create an image of itself as a homespun, back-to-nature, rebellious option to the nasty, conventional medical system. Yet, at the same time, it was marketing products made of raw cattle parts—spleen, lymph nodes, bone marrow, pituitary glands—under healthful-sounding names like "Raw Adrenal" and "Pituitary Caps." Although there was no direct indication of their harm, scientists had identified all of the ingredients in these products as being possible sources for transmissible spongiform encephalopathy—mad cow disease.

It was just one example of an industry that was overselling health. Bruce Silverglade, director of legal affairs for the Center for Science in the Public Interest told *PR Watch* in 1997, "People should have the right to try any type of health care that they choose. But what we're talking about is whether the manufacturers have the right to hype supplements on the basis of unreliable scientific information or downright false claims."

The U.S. approved the 1994 Dietary Supplement Health and Education Act, clearing the way for the alternative industry to continue making health claims without scientific backing. In 1998, it was still very different in Canada. According to the Food and Drugs Act, whatever Canadians ingest is registered as either a food or a drug. By virtue of their familiarity, foods are essentially unregulated. Drugs go through a rigorous approval process designed to assess their safety and their claims of health benefits. Nutritional supplements or herbal remedies—the bottles of capsules and infusions you find in the health food store—fall into the gray zone. The sales clerk may enthuse about them, but the supplement makers cannot legally claim that their goods have a particular benefit.

Consumers seeking the fountain of youth have been doubly frustrated by what they see as Health Canada's overzealous crackdown on the distribution of "illegal" health food supplements that are readily available south of the border. DHEA is the most broadly used nutritional supplement of the 1990s, but in Canada it is regulated as a drug and is available only by prescription. Potential Canadian purchasers who read or hear about DHEA's apparent energy boosting and weight loss attributes are frustrated with its limited distribution in this country.

Because of considerable pressure from Canadian consumers looking for greater access to herbal remedies, in 1997 Canada's Health Minister Allan Rock called for a public review into how health food supplements should be regulated. How the government decides to regulate—or deregulate—dietary supplements may offer an indication for the future of functional foods in Canada.

In addition to creating healthful whole foods, the new science of biotechnology hopes to take boosted nutrition one step further. Scientists hope to train farm crops and animals, with a little help from genetic engineering, to produce valuable drugs. The technology to create biopharmaceuticals or nutraceuticals, as they are called, is still experimental. However, industry experts believe the biopharmaceutical industry—the linking of plant and animal science to human health—has the potential to surpass both the prescription and the over-the-counter pharmaceutical industries.

With some ten thousand pharmaceutically important human proteins, the prospects for many new, high-value commodities are quite real. Corporate multinational giants, like Novartis and Monsanto, are responding to the evolving market by restructuring their operations to merge their agricultural and drug interests into new "life sciences" business strategies. Bayer and Bristol Mayer are pouring money into research.

Nearly one-quarter of all prescribed drugs in the last years of this century contains plant extracts or active ingredients obtained from or modeled on plant substances. Some of our best-known medicines fit into this category—aspirin is a synthetic version of a traditional pain remedy derived from the bark of willow trees. According to consumer polls, using transgenic plants for pharmaceutical "pharming" is the most ethically acceptable of all of the developments in agricultural biotechnology.

Although no foods or drugs developed through biotechnology were available by 1998, research had brought medical and agricultural science to the brink of change. In 1997, Wisconsin's Agracetus began trials treating cancer patients with human antibodies grown in mutant corn. If the remedy works as intended, the antibodies will stick to tumor cells and deliver radioscopes to kill them. SemBioSys, a Calgary-based company working on a technique for implanting human protein genes into oilseed plants like canola, recently received a $17 million infusion of capital from Dow Elanco. With this extra cash, drugs from canola oil are one step closer to the marketplace. In 1998, trials were also already underway into potatoes engineered with a vaccine that would prevent childhood diarrhea.

Cargill and ADM, two grain industry giants, are investing in natural vitamin E extraction technology, using corn, soybeans, and wheat. Petoseed, a major seed supplier, is focusing research on pharmaceutical uses for peppers and carrots. And at John Hopkins University, field trials are underway on broccoli boosted with sulforaphane, which may help to prevent breast cancer. Researchers at the university are so convinced of the prospects for nutraceuticals that they set up a new Chemoprotection Laboratory to link human and plant research. In Canada, there was so much optimism about the biopharmaceutical business that the federal government established a $3 million nutraceutical innovation center in Portage la Prairie, Manitoba.

Because tobacco is easily genetically engineered, the "evil weed" may enjoy a metamorphosis into a healthful substance as science reclaims it as a factory for biopharmaceuticals.

Researchers have manipulated tobacco plants so they produce Compound Q, an antiviral compound used to treat AIDS patients. Cooperative research in Canada has succeeded in producing transgenic tobacco containing human genes to control blood clotting, proteins vital to human organ transplant work, and a vaccine useful against a virus called CMV, which is dangerous to people with weak immune systems. The Plant Biotechnology company of California is testing an anti-tooth-decay mouthwash made with antibodies extracted from transgenic tobacco plants.

Research developing modified animals with valuable drug qualities is continuing around the world. Dolly, the cloned sheep in Scotland, was produced with the thought that others like her could be created to express valuable biopharmaceuticals. Enzon, a New Jersey company, has asked the FDA for permission to market its blood products derived from cows. Genzyme Transgenics of Massachusetts hopes to chemically test goats that produce cancer antibodies in their milk, not their meat. And PPL of Edinburgh plans to develop a human protein used to treat emphysema in transgenic sheep.

The advantage cited in using plants or animals to grow drugs is the reduced cost. It can cost $50 million to build a physical plant to produce pharmaceuticals from tissue culture. By comparison, once research and development are complete, growing the drug-producing crops or milking the animals is relatively inexpensive—perhaps only a tenth of the cost of a physical manufacturing plant. Of course, it is difficult to say whether consumers will benefit from the reduced cost. Insulin, for example, is now produced through genetic engineering—a much cheaper process than harvesting insulin from slaughtered hogs. Yet most diabetes patients say they have not seen a drop in the price of insulin at the drugstore.

Of course, only small amounts of drugs are needed in comparison to food, so biopharmaceuticals will never be grown over large areas like standard crops. Agracetus, the company testing antibodies grown in engineered corn, admitted it could supply the entire U.S. cancer market, tens of thousands of patients, with drugs grown in a single thirty-acre field. And the Dollys of the transgenic animal kingdom will likely still be pampered in the research barns of life sciences and biopharmaceutical companies. Pharming will likely represent a diversification of the agrifood economy that will grant some farmers access to niche markets. But despite the enthusiasm of people like the Smithsonion's Terry Sharrer, pharming is unlikely to give the beleaguered family farm a new lease on life.

It will, however, reshape the food and pharmaceutical industries. In the next century, a tomato may not simply be just a tomato. Or a cow the source of milk. Or an order of french fries the route to unnecessary fat. Of all the developments in genetic engineering in food, pharming is probably the easiest to justify. But it is necessary once again to ask those fundamental questions about benefits and risks. Is the benefit of a french fry with the attributes of broccoli worth the potential environmental damage of a new, engineered plant? Are the benefits of lactoferrin in milk worth the possible pain and suffering of a goat engineered with a human gene? No matter how it is used, gene splicing still carries the possibility of long-term health and environmental risks.

There is no doubt that food and nutrition will become more complex in the new millennium. Although dietitians today still urge consumers to eat a healthy diet, Ryan-Harshman thinks the new food future will offer everyone a path to healthy food, even those with a weakness for burgers and fries.

10

THE UNIVERSITY BRAIN DRAIN

ANN CLARK ARRIVED AT THE UNIVERSITY OF CALIFORNIA'S
Davis campus in the early 1970s filled with the innocent enthusiasm of youth and of the times. Those were the years of student activism and social energy, the language of Kent State and
Vietnam. U.C. Davis, known for its agricultural university, was
a treed, gracious college town in the heart of California's tomato
country. City born and bred, Clark came to Davis to realize her
girlhood dream of becoming a veterinarian.

But in her third year of pre-vet, she became fascinated by
a study on how plants, animals, and people live together. A
course in population ecology convinced her she could make
a difference. She abandoned thoughts of veterinary medicine,
focusing instead on a masters in agronomy, specifically on how
plants interact with one another. "I was going to save the
world," she says.

Universities like Davis would be the birthplace of biotechnology, and the source of much of its continuing inspiration.
Academic researchers here were among the first to recognize

the commercial potential of the new science. Davis professor of genetics Raymond Valentine, for example, would go on to launch the biotechnology company Calgene. However, in the early 1970s, that was all in the future. Most of the research that Ann Clark saw and participated in at the College of Agriculture and Environmental Sciences was field-based—attempts to develop better crops and animals through conventional breeding, and examinations of how different plants and ecosystems responded to one another in the external environment.

In those days, the pure pursuit of knowledge defined academic study. University-based agriculture schools were certainly more pragmatic than the departments of quantum physics or nineteenth-century Russian literature. As part of the U.S. land-grant structure, which developed universities in every state, the school here was designed to serve the American farmer. However, although the agriculture students might have labored under the California sun, they and their teachers were engaged in a process of higher learning.

At that time, agriculture was not a proprietary science, regulated by intellectual property rights and by huge agribusiness interests. Rather it was a fundamental and egalitarian way of life practiced by society. Throughout the history of agriculture, farmers had selected the best of their crops and animals and, through trial and error, had domesticated varieties and breeds useful to society. Each producer was essentially an agricultural scientist. It was only a hundred years ago that plant and animal breeding was handed over to universities and extension research stations. Scientific researchers assumed the task of studying the fundamental nature of plants, animals, soils, environments, markets, and the application of that knowledge to food production and processing. However, the ultimate ethic was the free exchange of information.

The agricultural scientists at Davis believed they were charged with the task of developing new knowledge for the benefit of the public good. It was those values that propelled Clark into the academic life. Fueled by a passion to understand plant growth, she went on to complete a Ph.D. in crop production and physiology at Iowa State University. Her open, direct manner of speaking made Clark a natural and popular teacher. She came to Canada in 1979 to take a position as assistant professor at the University of Alberta, moving on to the University of Guelph's Department of Crop Science in 1983.

The University of Guelph might be considered the Canadian equivalent to the University of California, Davis. With some sixteen thousand students, it defines the community of Guelph. Much like the tomato country around Davis, Guelph is in the heart of southern Ontario's farm belt, an hour's drive from Toronto, an hour and a half from Niagara Falls. In its annual survey of post-secondary educational institutions, the Canadian newsmagazine *Maclean's* consistently rated Guelph as the first or second best comprehensive university in the country.

However, by the late 1990s, the university was suffering from enormous funding cutbacks. On a per-capita basis, Ontario universities received less funding from their provincial masters than did schools in any other Canadian province. In November 1995, the province announced a fifteen percent reduction in support—the largest ever post-secondary cut in Ontario. For 1996–97, it would mean a $20 million slice to Guelph's budget, with significant reductions in staff and faculty and increasing pressure on research.

Aggravating the situation at that time were huge financing cuts—fifteen percent over three years—from Ottawa's granting agencies, notably the National Sciences and Engineering

Research Council and the National Research Council. As a nation, Canada spends a smaller proportion of its GNP on research than any other industrialized country—about half of what the U.S. and Japan spend, about the same as Greece and Albania. In Canada, science is the responsibility of a minister of state, not even a full-fledged minister.

Since it became an official university in 1965, Guelph had earned its reputation as one of the most research-intensive universities in Canada. The grim financial scenario threatened to undermine that status. The university had grown from its roots as an agricultural research and teaching arm for the province of Ontario, so it had always been pragmatically minded. At the end of a yearlong review of its structure and services, the university determined it would have to become still more pragmatic. In its 1995 "Power to Change" mission statement, the University of Guelph acknowledged it would have to develop "alternative funding sources through innovative partnerships" if it hoped to maintain its research base.

"Innovative partnerships" was a euphemism for the private sector. Although the university described itself as "a research-intensive, learner-centred university" whose core value was "the pursuit of truth," private businesses would become the essential funding agencies for research at the College of Agriculture —particularly in the field of biotechnology. And to underscore its endorsement of the private sector's role in public research, the university also became a partner in Guelph University Alumni Research and Development (GUARD), an agency supported by $10 million in investment capital, designed to commercialize the inventions and discoveries of university scientists.

Wayne March, director of research services at the university, says the institution had no choice but to be very aggressive in its attempts to find support in the private sector. In the late 1970s, about three percent of the university's research was financed by business. By the late 1990s, the proportion of corporate support had reached about fifteen percent. But Marsh insists that "private industry does not dictate the research." For example, the university's research policies say that while "proprietal research" is allowed, researchers at the public institution may not conduct "confidential research." From an outsider's perspective, that may seem like splitting hairs.

Probably no part of the university's agriculture program has been shaped more by private funding than the Department of Crop Science. A cynic might say the division could be more aptly renamed the department of biotechnology. In fact, in 1998, Crop Science was amalgamated with Horticultural Science, the Horticultural Research Institute of Ontario, and a brand-new division of plant biotechnology. "The strongest reason for creating the merger was to bring together a critical mass of plant scientists, particularly in biotechnology, so they could work together, share facilities, share expensive equipment, share ideas and create improvements that all of plant agriculture can share," said Crop Science chair David Hume in announcing the merger.

Faculty members in the original Crop Science department were central in the 1980s in the development of Allelix, one of Canada's first successful biotech firms, whose agricultural division has since been sold to Pioneer Hi-Bred. Wally Beversdorf was the chair of Crop Science until he was recruited in the mid-1990s to become the international head of research at Ciba Seeds, a company that would become part of Novartis, the world's largest life sciences firm.

Today, at least five of the fifteen professors in Crop Science work full time with genetic engineering and another five use recombinant DNA technology in their varietal breeding work.

Lab-based biotechnology work—funded through partnerships with business—is standard fare in the Department of Crop Science. Hume says the department is a reflection of what is happening at the university: "It looks a lot more like University of Guelph Inc."

For example, in 1997, Crop Science researchers were working to develop a corn genetically manipulated to be immune to fusarium, an improved winter-hardy alfalfa, and forage crops that would grant protection to the animals grazing on them. At least two research projects were virtually service jobs for the private sector: one molecular geneticist was essentially working for Monsanto to insert the company's Roundup Ready gene into several varieties of soybeans that are favored in the Ontario marketplace; another research team, bankrolled by a private vineyard, was attempting to engineer greater cold tolerance into several grape varieties grown in the Niagara peninsula. Hume says this work is designed to create "useful" products, "competitive in the marketplace." One current project that does involve basic research is the effort to create chemicals in plants to immunize grazing animals. If it works, Hume adds gleefully, "companies will be falling all over one another to get a piece of that."

Ann Clark is a member of the faculty of Crop Science. As a pasture agronomist, she is definitely not a member of the biotechnology club. Her supporters describe her as outspoken, honest, and a good teacher. Her detractors say she is poorly informed and not a team player.

She is critical of genetic engineering and the new high-tech molecular genetics approach to agriculture, arguing it continues the financially crippling and environmentally damaging reliance on chemical-based farming. She says there are often basic management techniques that could solve a farming problem—it is simply more fashionable to opt for modern biotechnology. For example, careful rotation of crops in fields would limit the growth of weeds just as easily as the development of herbicide-resistant crops designed to be planted year after year in the same fields. Clark also says there has not been enough research to determine how genetically engineered plants will react in differing environments, and whether biotechnology will create future disasters. Anticipating the worst under the auspices of the new science, Clark comments, "I don't want my son to ask me in ten years why I allowed this to happen."

In comparison to genetic engineering, Clark's research interests are decidedly low-tech. Her focus is on "management-intensive grazing," which does not require a farmer to purchase expensive chemicals or expertise. By its nature, pasture management research is nonproprietary, and thus unlikely to interest biotechnology companies producing herbicides or new, genetically engineered seeds. She is more involved in seeking common management solutions to problems than in breaking open the genetic structure of an alfalfa plant. For example, she might be inclined to examine whether cattle should be moved from a pasture daily or weekly to encourage the best fattening of the animals and the health of the land. However, funding for that kind of research is hard to find. Instead, Clark has set up a consulting company, and dipping into her 1970s idealism, she directs the proceeds from that work to her research.

She laments the loss of the public research that used to define what universities did. Much of the work her colleagues are engaged in today is designed not to create crops and products for the public good but to grant private sector companies a vehicle to develop proprietary, profit-making products. "Ethically, these industrial partnerships are a very questionable thing," she says.

As part of work she did for the faculty association's status of women committee, Clark conducted a survey examining what happened to the female Ph.D. graduates of 1990. She suspected they might not have gotten jobs as good as the men. But what she found was even more shocking: forty-five percent of the graduates worked in biotechnology, twenty-five percent in more conventional breeding, and the rest in everything else—weed science, tillage and rotations, agronomy and pasture management. "We have become 'a department of biotechnology, breeding, and others'."

Like Clark, David Hume also talks about "the public good." However, he sees genetic engineering as just one more tool to help researchers develop suitable crop varieties. He believes the work of modern gene jockeys is not much different from the extension field stations that were strung along Canada one hundred years ago to advise farmers. However, genetic engineering offers a unique opportunity to solve problems that otherwise have stumped plant breeders—for example, fusarium blight in wheat or corn, he says, will never be resolved through traditional methods. Hume says the overriding question university scientists must ask themselves before they launch their biotech research is: "Is the social fabric of the country going to be better?"

Hume admits the university research environment has changed greatly since the 1970s. These days, he acknowledges, university researchers have to think "more entrepreneurially." Hume spends much of his time signing contracts, not just with private research funders, but for access to research information protected by patents. "But as far as I am concerned," he says pragmatically, "that is the way things are."

At the senior levels of university management, there are few regrets about the practical requirements of research today and the concomitant dependence on corporate dollars. According to Wayne Marsh, the old-fashioned university with its focus on knowledge for the public good could be interpreted as "a kind of utopia where people do research that nobody cares about. It could be argued that the relationship with the private sector is good for the country." Jobs and economic activity are the by-product, he says—and, of course, the university gets money, too.

This businesslike approach to research is sanctioned by the Canadian government. The National Biotechnology Advisory Committee's 1998 report takes pride in the new focus of academia. "University scientists are becoming more and more receptive to the idea of business links, and are learning that the business of biotechnology is different from research."

In the United States, university research life has also changed— although that change cannot be attributed to funding cutbacks. In the early 1980s, the American government concluded public money had to be spent if the United States was to maintain its competitive position in the world biotech market against challengers like Japan. Federal support for public research from the National Science Foundation, the Department of Agriculture, the Food and Drug Administration, and the Agency for International Development, among other agencies, has not fallen appreciably since, even though aid has not kept pace with inflation.

In May 1996, the U.S. Department of Agriculture put out a report that reaffirmed its commitment to agricultural research. However, *Agricultural Research and Development: Public and Private Investments Under Alternative Markets and Institutions* notes that federal expenditures had not grown in real terms since the mid-1970s. As much as thirty percent of current expenditures are used to maintain current productivity levels. "From society's point of view, there has been underinvestment in agricultural research," the report said.

The report also concluded that there has been a noticeable shift to corporate financing of public research. Private industry spent at least $3.4 billion on food and agricultural research in 1992, compared with $2.9 billion in the public sector. More than forty percent of private R&D was earmarked for product development, compared with less than seven percent of public agricultural research. One can assume that imbalance has increased even more over the years as biotechnology hit its commercial stride.

The USDA gave voice to the growing concern that research might be skewed to areas that interest the private sector. The report stated: "Specifically, public research programs could be disproportionately leveraged towards the needs of private industry rather than for the broader interests of farmers or consumers. For instance, a firm may give a grant to a university department if specified research is carried out."

Even ten years ago, says Lawrence Busch, a professor of sociology of agricultural research policy at the University of Michigan, universities were loath to accept private funding. By the last years of this century, that reluctance seems to have been replaced by a corporate pragmatism that reflects the growing political, economic, and social clout of the business sector. Busch estimates that two-thirds of all research conducted in the U.S. twenty-five years ago was carried out by public institutions such as universities, the private sector doing only a third. By the mid-1990s, that proportion had reversed.

The new lab-created foods being introduced to the American marketplace were essentially all products of private sector development—except for one entry, which was so unusual it attracted special note from the Animal and Plant Health Inspection Service. A virus-resistant papaya, approved in 1996, had been created by researchers at Cornell University, the University of Hawaii, and the USDA. It was the only academic entry to have been considered by the federal regulator—and, of course, it involved a plant that would not attract a lot of commercial attention.

Corporate financing in universities threatens to alter the shape of the U.S. carefully designed agricultural research system. When President Lincoln founded the Department of Agriculture in 1862, he called it "the People's Department." Of course, at that time sixty percent of Americans were farmers. Soon after, universities like the University of California, Davis were established in every state with public funds to research, develop, and implement advances in agriculture to help local farmers and rural communities. They were called land-grant schools.

Land-grant universities and their agricultural experiment stations could do a lot today to help improve the economic well-being of rural communities and to protect the family farm from extinction. Instead, the emphasis on genetic engineering seems designed to hasten the demise of rural farm communities. Research into pigs with human genes or crops immune to proprietal herbicides hardly seems what was intended in 1862 when the land-grant institutions were established.

Although statistics are difficult to find, it is generally acknowledged that the corporate sector has had significant influence on land-grant universities and their agricultural experiment stations. Wally Huffman, agricultural economist at Iowa State University, says that in 1980, nine percent of the work at experiment stations was funded by the private sector; in 1995, it was up to fourteen percent. The USDA report *Agricultural Research and Development* says the private sector paid for sixty percent of the agricultural research happening in the U.S. in 1996; however, it only did fifty-four percent of the work itself—the extra six percent largely fell to the agricultural experiment stations.

In 1984, observers estimated that nearly half of the companies in the biotechnology business supported university research. It is probable that number has increased significantly. Also in 1984, researchers reported in Science magazine that the corporate sector spent $120 million in university biotech labs, about twenty percent of its total investment in R&D. That can be compared to about three to four percent a year spent by other industries on university research.

The corporate sector seems to view academia as a source for new ideas and innovative techniques and a vehicle to conduct basic research. Biotechnology companies rely largely on university scientists to do the basic research work for them. Once the research takes on hints of leading to a new product, the companies step in with funding or take over the work themselves. Support for the university research environment gives the private sector a window on the technology without requiring huge investments in equipment, time, and personnel.

Lawrence Busch says the shift in funding comes with some significant costs. With corporate biotechnology calling the shots, research tends to be conducted primarily on the big, potentially profitable U.S. crops—corn, soybeans, cotton, and wheat. With the exception of wheat, all of these crops have been genetically engineered already. With funding from Monsanto, Agriculture Canada researchers in Winnipeg are working on cracking the wheat genome and creating a Roundup Ready variety. Busch says work on an improved cauliflower or bean sprout seems most unlikely. The virus-resistant papaya, proudly announced by APHIS, is truly an anomaly. Busch writes in his book *Plants, Power and Politics* that it is unclear who will do the breeding for minor crops in the future.

Additionally, the new emphasis on private financing will encourage the concentration of scientific biotechnology research in just a few well-heeled states. In the days before biotechnology, every state could afford a conventional plant breeding program—in fact, they were compelled to do so through the land-grant university program. However, not every state will be able to afford a comprehensive plant biotechnology program. A survey of land-grant institutions in 1988 indicated start-up funds for each faculty member in biotechnology were as high as $25,000, almost twice that of agricultural faculty in other areas. The state agricultural experiment stations reported it cost at least $100,000 a year for each biotech project. And starting salaries for trained genetic engineers were significantly higher than for other academics. The web of agricultural research that had been designed to address the needs of local farmers across the country was being skewed by biotechnology.

Private sector support also seems to be affecting the traditional open, collegial relationships between scientists. When corporate secrecy is preeminent, the information flow between scientists is obviously inhibited. Researchers must often delay public discussion of their work or its results until it has been reviewed by the grantor or a patent has been issued. Busch writes that even some scientists with public funding feel inhibited in talking about their work or their research ideas, fearing a company might beat them to it. It is difficult to predict the effects of such restriction of communication, but scientists themselves view increasing secrecy as very harmful to the scientific enterprise.

There is plenty of evidence that the aims of the public interest and private corporations operate at cross purposes. As one example, the Ontario soybean marketing board spent $100,000 to finance research into the development of low-linolenic acid soybean varieties at the agricultural college in Ridgetown, Ontario. Because the school, in turn, sold the exclusive worldwide marketing rights for the gene to Pioneer Hi-Bred in 1996, Canadian farmers would not immediately benefit from the research the marketing board had financed. Indeed, they would only see the new soybean varieties if and when the U.S. company chose to bring them to Canada.

Biotechnology also seems to be accelerating a shift, which began in the 1920s, of varietal breeding from the public to the private sector. It may seem quaintly old-fashioned now, but until 1923, the USDA regularly distributed free seeds, collected from around the world, to farmers who wanted to test them on their farms. Today, varietal seed propagation is essentially the commercial territory of large seed and agribusiness companies with the finances to play the biotechnology game.

Most important is the fact that universities once dedicated to free knowledge are increasingly conducting research for the benefit of the corporate sector. One effect is that when private patents are issued for work done in universities, the public ends up paying twice—once in taxes for the institution and again for the biotech products.

The vast sums of money available from the corporate sector are forcing a lot of academics to review their values. The question must be asked: Do they, as scientists, pursue biotechnological research and development to further scientific knowledge or for missions of public good? Or do they do so with the hope that discoveries will ultimately produce rewards in the form of grants, gifts, or fame?

In January 1998, researchers in Toronto published a review in the *New England Journal of Medicine* that offers some clues as to what influence corporate funding may have on scientists. The researchers examined a medical controversy over calcium-channel blockers that are used to treat high blood pressure and heart disease. In 1995, the National Heart, Lung and Blood Institute warned doctors that such blockers could increase the risk of heart attack deaths. In examining seventy articles on channel blockers, the researchers found that one hundred percent of the scientists who wrote articles in support of the controversial drugs had financial arrangements with pharmaceutical manufacturers. Only forty-three percent of those critical of channel blockers had a corporate connection. "Financial ties" were defined as funds for travel, speech honorariums, research grants, educational programs, or direct employment compensation. Only in two of the seventy articles did the authors divulge their connections to corporations.

Today, university academics have learned to adopt a commercial sensibility their predecessors never knew. They know how to write research proposals that will earn them funding from companies working in the life sciences. They know they are best off pursuing research in the major crops that may earn them the attention of the private sector. Efforts to build a better banana are fated to obscurity, or at best to scraps from the public sector.

The diversion of scarce research resources has a consequence. Rather than looking at the cropping malfunctions that cause agricultural problems, biotechnology-based university research attempts to fix the symptoms. "To a hammer, everything looks like a tack, and to a community that sees genetics as the root cause of agricultural problems, genetic engineering may seem like the best—or perhaps—the only solution," said the 1997 report from the Organic Farming Research Foundation, *Searching for the 'O-Word.'* The organic research organization found that only thirty-four of three thousand projects in 1996 funded by the USDA, accounting for about $1.5 million of a $1.8 billion budget, could be identified as pertaining to organic farming.

Ann Clark says the focus on problem solving, rather than problem avoidance, has directed university efforts away from farmers themselves. "We have redefined the agricultural community as a few large pharmaceutical companies."

The idealism that brought Clark to university life has faded now. She is in her forties—her academic prime. But the shift to fashionable biotechnology research at the University of Guelph, as at other educational institutions, means there are few opportunities for her. She is willing to speak out against biotechnology because she feels she has nothing to lose—she knows she will get none of the perks that are doled out in the university community. She is not interested in the glamor of gene manipulation, in winning commendations from the corporate sector, or in seeing her name on a patent. At least now she is beginning to find that others in the department share her views, albeit quietly—not yet prepared to publicly take an unpopular stand. But more importantly, she says the focus on molecular biology has detracted from basic research that might have been useful to farmers. "The biggest long-term legacy of biotechnology is the loss of a generation of scientists and their focus on the real problems of agriculture."

There has been some recent positive news from the Canadian government. Perhaps as affirmation of the role of research, the fifteen percent that had been cut from NSERC and NRC budgets was reinstated in 1998. And Ottawa established an

$800 million Canadian Fund for Innovation—the only rub is, no surprise here, researchers have to come up with private funds to match whatever they may get from the government. It seems government believes the corporate sector has a clear role to play in the research, and perhaps regulation, of biotechnology.

11

TAKING CARE OF BUSINESS

THE EARLY MORNING SUNLIGHT IS JUST BEGINNING TO slant through the arched windows in the ballroom of the Bessborough Hotel in Saskatoon as Saskatchewan Premier Roy Romanow scrambles to his feet. On this day in June 1996 it is his assignment to address about seven hundred scientists and biotechnology industrialists from as far away as Australia and Indonesia who are attending the first international agricultural biotechnology conference to be held in North America. Most have no idea how the government of Saskatchewan fits into the biotechnology picture, but Romanow is relishing his moment on the international stage. He offers them what has become the biotech mantra: "With less arable land and more people to feed, ag biotech offers a vehicle to meet the needs of the world. It's a perfect example of mankind's inquiring mind and desire to provide for the people of this world."

Romanow is reflecting the typical language and attitudes of just about every government in North America. As the leader of a New Democratic Party government, Romanow is not usually inclined to promote big business. But in this case it is perhaps understandable. After all, Saskatoon is Canada's rags-to-riches biotech fairy tale. A short time ago, Saskatoon was a small, isolated, prairie city in a "have-not" province; now it can claim to be one of the world's five biggest centers of agricultural biotechnology.

Governments across North America are the promoters of biotechnology ... and at the same time, are the regulators. This apparent conflict of interest is not without repercussions. Most consumers assume that their governments are working hard to ensure their food is safe. Indeed, politicians like to say, "Canada has one of the safest food systems in the world." But consumers may not know that governments on this continent conduct only the most cursory policing of genetically manipulated crops and animals. They are much busier promoting the new technology.

In political circles across North America, the biotechnology industry is viewed as a business of choice. It is a sector housed in office buildings, not in industrial plants that pollute the air with smoke or the rivers with effluent. The workers in this business wear lab coats, not hard hats; they belong to professional associations, not unions. Biotechnology is perceived as modern and sexy, a step into the brave new knowledge-based world. And it claims a noble purpose to boot—feeding a growing and hungry world.

Many consumers may think they do not have to analyze the risks and benefits of biotechnology—because the government is doing it for them. However, although the Canadian government promotes genetic engineering in food, it takes no responsibility for assessing the benefits to farmers of any new, modified crop variety. Its responsibility ends with assessing efficacy. That is, the question is not "Do we need another herbicide-resistant crop?" but "Does it work in the way it claims to?"

The lure of economic gain is propelling the biotech world forward at a frantic pace—a pace so fast governments have a difficult time keeping up. Before new biotech foods are grown, manufactured, or imported to either Canada or the U.S., they have to be approved by a patchwork of government departments. The Animal and Plant Health Inspection Service (APHIS), a division of the Department of Agriculture, is the lead agency in the U.S., although both the Environmental Protection Agency and the Food and Drug Agency also have roles to play in the consideration of test-tube foods. In Canada, the Food Safety Inspection Agency, staffed largely with former Department of Agriculture officials, coordinates the approval process, with input from Health Canada and Environment Canada.

When the new Canadian Food Inspection Agency (CFIA) was first established on April 1, 1997, it had two goals, according to the Minister of Agriculture and Agri-Food—"consumer protection and the promotion of Canadian trade and commerce." The aim was to set up a "national, flexible system based on harmonised standards." "Harmonized standards" apparently means the new agency would do its best to conform to U.S. trade requirements. A "flexible system" sounds ominously like a regulatory system that does not operate according to rules. Neither phrase would appear to inspire much public confidence about food safety.

The Ram's Horn newsletter, which bills itself as an analysis of food systems, assessed flowcharts accompanying the Agricultural Biotechnology Regulatory Information Manual, published by the Agricultural Biotechnology Coordination Office of Agriculture Canada (the precursor to CFIA) in 1995. It wryly noted that the flowcharts showed that, "all paths lead to commercialisation, regardless of how the questions are answered along the way." The assumption is that every product will be approved, said the newsletter. In fact, it concluded that there are no standards by which to measure failure.

Agriculture and Agri-Food Canada was an early proponent of biotechnology and continues to be a consistent and uncritical advocate for the technology. Although the government department was folded into the new CFIA, its promotional publication, *Biotechnology in Agriculture—Science for Better Living*, was still being distributed in early 1997. According to government, biotechnology means "better quality and greater selection" and offers wondrous "improved crops . . . enhanced food products . . . better, healthier animals." The language of material produced by the government is rife with terms that corporate biotechnology would applaud—"better," "improved," "enhanced."

Other government departments are just as enthusiastic. Even the National Research Council, once Canada's primary research vehicle, became the sponsor of the biannual Industrial Biotechnology Conference—a session billed as an opportunity for businesspeople to "network" and "biopartner." The NRC seemed to have no hesitation about abandoning pure research for a more pragmatic role. In its promotional material it wrote: "NRC is taking a more aggressive entrepreneurial approach to technology transfer and is playing a key role in the development of an innovative knowledge-based economy."

The language of government when it comes to the business of biotechnology is expansive. It has interpreted its regulatory responsibilities in a much more narrow fashion. The Canadian regulatory system does not require, nor does it perform, much independent research into the claims made by those applying for approvals. It says food safety can be defined as "the level of acceptable risk." Just what is "acceptable risk" has not been determined.

The tone for the regulatory processes in North America was set in 1992 when the FDA determined recombinant DNA was not a food additive. On that basis, foods produced through genetic engineering are considered essentially the same as natural foods as long as they do not incorporate an allergenic substance or differ significantly in composition from known foods. Natural foods are not tested for safety or nutritional value. Instead, their place on the North American dinner table had been established by centuries of consumption. The principle of "substantial equivalence" means that manipulated foods are examined according to an inspection of the final product, not the process that created it. For example, as long as a genetically engineered, herbicide-resistant sugar beet seems like a sugar beet derived from a natural harvest, it is considered on the basis of a rudimentary review of information provided by the company bringing the sugar beet forward.

Since its detailed review of the Flavr Savr tomato, the FDA has not found it necessary to conduct comprehensive scientific reviews of foods derived from bioengineering. Instead, the FDA expects developers to consult with the agency on safety and regulatory questions. Special reviews are only required when specific safety issues are raised—for example, if a potential allergen, like a peanut gene, were to be inserted into a tomato, or if a known toxicant were to be used.

The approach is very different in Europe, where the regulatory structure focuses on the process through which food is produced, not the final product. And in Japan, all foods and crops produced with recombinant DNA are carefully reviewed.

Bioethicist Arthur Schafer says North America's more liberal approach is a reflection of our societal views. Consumers here see regulations as cumbersome and unnecessary impediments to progress and individual freedom. "The willingness to regulate, the willingness to take collective action for the public interest and the willingness to move slowly and cautiously does not appear prudent in North American society," he says. In comparison, European cultures accept that their governments will undertake the job of policing and preventing fraud. "They view government as a more positive vehicle for creating a better society," Schafer said in an interview. "The view here is that big government is bad government." Although Canadians once viewed themselves as different from their counterparts south of the border, the essential cultural value of both societies today is that commercial values should dominate and that the individual liberty of the consumer is the only one that really counts.

It is no wonder in a society where commercial values matter that Canada and the U.S. accept the logic that "overregulation" compromises the competitiveness of the industry. In the U.S., the government dealt with perceived overregulation in 1993 when APHIS decided to allow field tests to take place with simple "notification." Canada's move to deregulation has been more clandestine.

Michele Brill-Edwards worked as the senior physician responsible for the regulation of prescription drugs in Health Canada's Health Protection Branch for fifteen years. Her demeanor suggests the civil servant she was until she quit government in 1996. Soft-spoken and kindly, it is almost a shock when she says bluntly that she quit because she could no longer tolerate the profit motive overtaking public safety concerns.

Brill-Edwards says that unlike the American process, where there has been a political and public debate on deregulation, the Canadian administration has chosen to deregulate its system quietly and without discussion. "It has been almost a silent process, where we left the laws on the books. We didn't tell anybody that the safety net was disappearing. We just stopped enforcing the regulations so gradually. Companies now know they can get away with more and more safety shortcuts."

One move to deregulation did attract media attention. In 1997, the government quietly served notice that it intended to close six food laboratories dealing with nutrition, food additives, and food toxins and eliminate 123 positions in Health Canada, saving about $6 million a year. Ottawa's plan was to contract out a lot of the work that had been done in-house. However, about seventy-five scientists from the Food Directorate at the Health Protection Branch were so alarmed they blew the whistle on the government. They signed a petition, marked "urgent and important," and delivered it to the health minister's office. The government scientists warned that the cuts would have "disastrous health and economic implications" and would transfer responsibility for food and drug research into the hands of manufacturers. "Scientific research is neither a luxury nor an afterthought that follows policy development but is, in fact, the essential underpinning for sound policy and standard setting." The government scientists were not alone in their concern. Dennis Fitzpatrick, head of the department of foods and nutrition at the University of Manitoba said in a letter to the prime minister that shutting down the labs was "a worst nightmare come true."

Health Minister Allan Rock responded quickly. He announced a moratorium on his planned cuts, saying, "Safe food is key to the health and safety of Canadians. I have listened to a number of groups, from both the consumer and scientific arenas, and they have expressed a number of concerns regarding cuts to the food program. I will not allow financial considerations to jeopardise the safety of food products used by Canadians.

Brill-Edwards says the threatened cuts were just one public

example of the kind of deregulation that has insidiously been happening at Health Canada. Although she did not work with the unit that considered genetically engineered foods, she said the tone in the department is the same throughout. "The new model for all regulation is voluntary compliance. It is absolute insanity. But it is what the industry wants." Her point was underscored when six scientists at the Bureau of Veterinary Drugs claimed unfair labor practices by alleging they had been pressured to approve bovine somatotropin and other animal drugs they believed posed a health risk to humans. The pressure does not necessarily come from malfeasance, says Brill-Edwards, but from the government's willingness to take chances in the hope of producing benefit. "There is a belief in government that biotechnology is the goose that laid the golden egg—that industry knows what it is doing."

Despite the evidence of looser regulation, the biotech industry claims that Canadian regulation of it is still too tough. In their annual review of the biotech industry, management consultants Ernst & Young identify Canada's "complex regulatory environment" as the hurdle to growth. Turnaround time for the necessary government approvals in Canada, they say, is longer than that in the U.S. or Europe—particularly in the agriculture field. It is perhaps a predictable complaint; right from its birth, the biotechnology industry has demanded more "efficient"—meaning easier—regulation.

Industry complaints seem churlish when you consider how much effort Canada puts into promoting the biotechnology business. Canada likes to brag about the breadth and competitiveness of its biotechnology industry. According to some overzealous estimates, there were more than seven hundred Canadian biotechnology companies by the mid-1990s, employing twenty-five thousand workers. But in reality, by the end of this century the "industry" in Canada was largely a figment of wishful thinking: small, dispersed, poorly financed, and hardly a player in the global marketplace. Biotechnology in Canada was largely confined to the nucleus of a biomedical industry in Quebec and the agricultural efforts in Saskatoon.

Despite the promotional support of government, biotechnology began comparably slowly in Canada, largely because of the lack of venture capital and entrepreneurial spirit that characterized the American business. In the late 1980s, there were few true biotech companies in Canada—just mere stirrings in Quebec and Saskatoon. The fruits of the biotech industry came to the Canadian marketplace in 1996. That was the year genetically engineered crops were first made available to farmers, and test-tube foods first appeared on grocery store shelves. However, the Canadian government, provincial jurisdictions, and industry lobby associations could claim no role in that arrival. None of these genetically engineered foods or seeds were produced by the Canadian industry but rather by multinational giants like Monsanto, AgrEvo, and Novartis.

Although the industry was still small, Ernst & Young identified 1996 as its coming of age. In the fourth of a series of reviews of the country's would-be biotech business, Ernst & Young described the industry's growth from 1994 to 1996 as "impressive." The report counted 224 companies in the country that did most or all of their work in biotechnology, up from the 121 identified in their 1994 survey. The report also noted industry revenues had increased from $353 million to $1.1 billion in those two years. But measured by total revenue, the Canadian biotechnology industry was still tiny next to that in the U.S., only 5.6 percent the size of that on the other side of the border. That figure was up from 2.9 percent in 1994, but it lags well behind the conventional rule of thumb that Canadian economic activity should be ten percent that of the U.S.

The disproportion comes because Canadian companies are so small. In 1995, Ottawa's own Canadian Biotechnology Advisory Committee found fifty-eight percent of companies had fewer than twenty-five employees. Today, larger companies with more than 135 workers make up just eleven percent of the industry. In comparison, thirty-one percent of the U.S. industry is comprised of large or "top-tier companies"—those with more than three hundred employees.

The one big exception is Saskatoon, Canada's biotech star. There, the high-tech jobs and the economic benefits that politicians like to dream about are a reality. Agricultural biotechnology is the city's number one growth industry, with fourteen hundred people working in nearly a hundred different government organizations and private companies. Saskatoon's agriculture biotech companies generated about $30 million in sales in 1996; those sales are expected to reach $300 million by the turn of the century. The University of Saskatchewan's Innovation Place research park is home to Canadian offices and subsidiaries of some of the world's largest biotechnology companies, like Monsanto and AgrEvo. The federal government's Western Economic Diversification program has concluded that Saskatoon's agriculture biotechnology is the only "internationally-competitive technology cluster in Western Canada." City councillor and bioindustry spokesman Peter McCann is only half-joking when he remarks: "This is a very good time to buy land in Saskatoon."

Saskatoon's success is particularly noteworthy when you consider it happened in an environment otherwise afflicted with economic malaise. The once-vibrant agricultural industry that shaped the province of Saskatchewan has been shrinking, along with farm revenues. Many of the small towns that once supported a thriving rural way of life disappeared from the map as services and facilities were concentrated in larger centers. For years, thousands of people—often the young and well-educated—have left the province for greener pastures elsewhere. From 1990 to 1996, the population of just under one million lost twenty-nine thousand people to other provinces.

This isolated city in a have-not province transformed itself from farm center for an agricultural breadbasket to a key supplier for the global biotech supermarket by following a relatively basic recipe—take a core group of scientists and leaven it with a generous dollop of government money. Saskatchewan had been well equipped with a strong community of agricultural research scientists long before there was any talk of biotechnology. With its work on the development of crops and animal veterinary medicine, the University of Saskatchewan, established just two years after the province joined Confederation, was the biggest and most significant agricultural research school on the Canadian prairies. Agriculture Canada had a research station in Saskatoon, as did the National Research Council. This is where rust-resistant wheat was developed. And it was here, in the 1960s, that Keith Downey and other plant breeders transformed the lowly rapeseed plant into lucrative canola.

The decision to turn Saskatoon into a center for biotechnology was a very deliberate one, which was supported by a series of provincial governments of differing political stripes. In 1980, Allan Blakeney's NDP administration joined forces with the university in Saskatoon to develop a research park at the campus. Innovation Place began with just two buildings, five companies, and an amorphous desire to attract technology, whether in aerospace, communications, fisheries, electronics, or other fields. The strategy became more focused in 1984 when a study team commissioned by the Conservative Premier Grant Devine reported that agricultural biotechnology was the next big thing in technology and a natural fit for a city that had been defined by farming.

It may have seemed a natural fit, but banks and lending institutions were reluctant to provide start-up money for fledgling biotech companies because of the high cost of technology equipment and the slow rate of return. Devine's government stepped in to help. It established Ag-West Biotech, a nonprofit agency with $9 million to use as equity or loans for biotechnology companies. The agency proceeded to kick-start what was then an embryonic industry.

Murray McLaughlin, a Dow Elanco executive recruited to lead the Ag-West effort, wanted to do more than finance local, homegrown companies. He traveled the world to advance Saskatoon as a center of international biotechnology. He had to begin with the basics; he says he was regularly asked: "Where is Saskatoon?" and "How do you say Saskatchewan?"

Key international companies soon began to arrive in Saskatoon: American Cyanamid, Monsanto, Plant Genetic Systems, Limagrain, Pioneer Hi-Bred. The provincial government, now under the direction of the New Democrats, continued to finance biotechnology through a myriad of agencies and departments. And it convinced the federal government to be just as generous to Saskatchewan biotechnology. (It did not hurt that the then federal agriculture minister, Ralph Goodale, had grown up in Regina, Saskatchewan.) For example, in 1995, the two governments co-signed a joint agreement to set up the Agri-Food Innovation Fund—a fund that would see $91 million spent in Saskatchewan by the year 2000.

By 1998, the Innovation Place research park had become

a business incubator, home to ninety-four agriculture biotech companies and organizations. Frantic efforts are being made to make room for more. An expansion is underway to build a new multitenant office building—the twentieth structure at the research park—and a massive addition to the greenhouse and laboratory facilities. And McLaughlin says that geography and pronunciation lessons are no longer required. "We don't have to take a hind seat on the research and science base at all here in Saskatoon or in Canada. Now, as soon as you mention Saskatoon, people just say, oh, that's the world-leading centre in ag biotechnology."

Saskatchewan's biotech business expanded by 286 percent from 1991 to 1993. In comparison, Ontario saw its industry grow by a mere six percent in the same period. The fact that a "have-not" province was home to the majority of the country's agriculture biotech business clearly rankled Canada's largest and most prosperous province. In 1994, the Biotech Council of Ontario appointed a study team to draft an industrial strategy to help deliver the industry the province felt it deserved. Lorne Meikle, the head of the study team, tartly noted in the Research Money newsletter: "Saskatchewan has been successful in luring away some Ontario based biotechnology firms and it seems like Romanow has a purse with no bottom to it."

Indeed Saskatchewan government agencies spent large amounts of taxpayers' money to entice players they felt were key to their strategic industrial policy, including offers of funding to large, multinational corporations. For example, in 1997, Ag-West Biotech and the federal Department of Western Economic Diversification contributed $400,000 to Mycogen Corporation, to persuade the U.S. company to establish a microspore culture laboratory for canola research at Innovation

Place. Mycogen, recently purchased by Dow Elanco, was hardly in desperate need of financial incentives, but accepted them anyway.

When Hoechst, Europe's largest chemical firm, wanted to set up its North American headquarters in Regina, the federal Department of Western Economic Diversification handed over $1.6 million. The money was earmarked for a "project" to help Hoechst develop crop varieties tolerant to a nonselective herbicide—a project that would ultimately earn the company millions in profits. Little of the earning would come back to governments. And farmers would be required to pay extra for a new technology that their taxes had already bankrolled.

In 1985, Plant Genetic Systems, based in Ghent, Belgium, attracted international attention when it produced the world's first transgenic bug-proof plant. Ag-West brought PGS to Saskatoon with the promise of about $1 million. (In 1996, PGS was purchased by AgrEvo, the partnership between Hoechst and Schering. So AgrEvo benefited from at least $2.6 million from Canadian taxpayers.)

Government spending on biotechnology is rarely challenged in Saskatchewan's media or in the legislature. The science of engineering new life seems to have the full support of the province's residents, many of whom grew up on the farm and can appreciate the value of crop and animal research. Only in a province where there was unwavering public support could a series of governments, of competing political stripes, finance so significant a biotech industry. To resilient prairie residents faced with a dwindling population and eroding industrial base, the new high-tech enterprise must have seemed like a beacon of hope.

It has been difficult for other governments to duplicate Saskatchewan's unwavering political and financial commitment to the business. Despite its own fiscal limitations, the provincial government says it spent at least $31 million in grants, loans, and equity investments from 1984 to 1996. This support is exactly what it takes to curry favor with the large multinationals that dominate the biotechnology business. However, contributions to a controversial industry, anywhere other than Saskatchewan, are difficult to rationalize when health care, social services, and arts institutions are routinely asked to make do with less.

Canada's federal government officially embraced biotechnology in the early 1980s by declaring it a "strategic technology essential to Canada's future international competitiveness." In 1983, the words were given form with the release of the first National Biotechnology Strategy, the appointment of an advisory committee, and the establishment of a system of research and development networks across the country.

However, by the late 1990s, it was beginning to seem as if Canada would never truly become internationally competitive in biotechnology. Ernst & Young's review said that although Canada has considerable research capabilities, scientists unfamiliar with the business terrain often do not have the skills to translate innovation into commercial products. As a result, the industry suffers from a lack of management talent. "There are few skilled Canadian managers who have experienced the life-cycle of development of a biotech company, forcing companies to look elsewhere for proven talent," the review concluded.

Except for the core group in Saskatoon, the Canadian agriculture biotech business also seems to be scattered across the country. In the United States, fifty-seven percent of employment is generated by nineteen industry "clusters." In Canada, Jim Stewart of KPMG management consultants said in an interview that only Saskatoon, with forty percent of the country's agri-culture biotech companies, can be considered a world-class, high-tech cluster.

Armed with their own lobby organizations, regions and sectors sometimes seem to work at cross purposes to one another, competing for business and profile. In the U.S., the national Biotechnology Industry Organization (BIO) speaks with one, very effective voice. The Ernst & Young report says: "To date, Canada has benefited from both local and national associations but none has the impact of BIO, which lobbies governments at all levels for increased government funding and changes to taxation and export policy."

However, it seems the greatest obstacle to the realization of a globally competitive Canadian biotechnology industry is the financial constraints of the 1990s. It takes money to build a high-tech industry and that is something governments do not have. Ernst & Young noted that the U.S. spent $4.6 billion in assistance and incentives for biotechnology firms in 1992. In contrast, Canadian governments were far behind, offering only $175 million in the same year.

Not only is it difficult for provincial or federal jurisdictions to compete for the affections of multinational companies, the cuts to government spending leave homegrown compa-nies scrambling to find alternative sources of funding. For fledgling biotechnology firms, nothing is more persistently daunting than finding capital at reasonable rates. For most small companies, the only option is to build alliances with other companies, which, these days, often translates into Canadian companies looking to the U.S. for funding.

The Canadian stock market is often not an option; Canadian biotech firms generally access public equity markets only when they are moving into product trials or commercialization.

Although successful Saskatoon companies like Philom Bios and Biostar have achieved some international reputation, in 1998 they were still privately held companies. Not one Canadian firm working to develop biotech foods and crops was publicly traded on the country's stock exchanges in the late 1990s.

If fate is kind to these firms, they will find themselves swallowed up by larger companies based in other countries. In Canadian biotechnology, that is an ironic measure of accomplishment. Allelix still stands as the ultimate example of both Canadian limitations and Canadian success. The Ontario-based company was created in 1983 through $90 million in capital from John Labatt Ltd., the Canadian Development Corp., and the Ontario government. It was one of the country's first and most noteworthy forays into biotechnology. However, rather than take the canola hybrids it was working on to market, it sold out in 1990 to Pioneer Hi-Bred International. What was once a thriving enterprise employing more than two hundred people became a tiny research branch in the Canadian hinterland.

The Allelix story is a cautionary tale for Canada's efforts at biotechnology. Industry observers agree the true test of the new technology sector will be its success in commercialization. As biotech companies move from the research stage to the marketing of products, entrepreneurial and business skills— expertise that seems to be in short supply in Canada—play a more important role. If Canadian companies continue to sell out when they succeed, Canada will lose the jobs it so eagerly courted, and Canadian farmers and consumers will have to buy back technologies that were originally developed in Canada.

In the spring of 1997, the federal government and the Industrial Biotechnology Association of Canada initiated a program to help companies develop the business skills needed to take biotechnology products to market. The Ontario government announced the creation of GUARD, a corporation set up to commercialize technologies developed by University of Guelph researchers and others and to act as a bridge between the university and the business community. The brochure announcing the corporation's arrival stated the obvious: "Canadians are said to be among the best in the world at developing new technologies ... but among the worst at turning them into jobs. Because so few Canadian companies have experience moving research out of the lab and into the marketplace, new technologies are often snatched out from under us by foreign companies."

Even in Saskatoon there was a nagging anxiety that its much-heralded research cluster may not evolve past its role as a branch plant with research capabilities for multinational corporations. At some point in the future there may be more frustration than satisfaction when scientists at public research labs in Saskatoon recall the part they played in helping AgrEvo or Monsanto develop the latest genetically engineered canola hybrid. "We have to start moving from the research and development phase into commercialization," said Murray McLaughlin. "We've seen a little bit of commercialization now. Now the real phase, I think, as we move into the next century is the commercialization side."

Nonetheless, toward the last years of this millennium, Canadian biotechnology was far from being any kind of force in the stock market, never mind the commercial marketplace. As genetically engineered foods began appearing on grocery store shelves and manipulated plants began sprouting in farmers' fields, Canada's biotechnology "industry" largely remained an expensive dream, far from delivering much-touted jobs and economic benefits. Even Saskatoon, the symbolic icon of success, is in danger of being typecast as a research cluster, rather than a production center.

In the late 1990s, Canadian consumers were much more concerned with food safety than with the development of a new industry. They had seen news reports of young people developing fatal Creutzfeld-Jakob disease from eating British hamburgers and of bags of dead or nearly dead chickens along the roads as Hong Kong attempted to vanquish a devastating chicken flu. Closer to home were reports of toxic hamburger, poultry tainted with salmonella, and grapes irrigated with fecal-contaminated water. Consumers wanted to be able to trust their governments to stop any genetically engineered food from delivering the same kind of harm.

By mid-1998, there was a growing acknowledgement in both industry and government that not all consumers automatically bought the biotechnology line. The federal government, for example, released a new biotechnology strategy in fall of 1998 to replace the one first drafted in 1983. Five months of cross-country consultations convinced the committee developing the strategy that public discussion was necessary. It urged government to create an arm's length advisory committee made up of experts in science, ethics, the environment, and other spheres affected by biotechnology. However, the strategy's vision statement was still adamantly boosterish: "To enhance the quality of life of Canadians in terms of health, safety and the environment, and social and economic development by positioning Canada as a responsible world leader in biotechnology."

Although its purpose was to encourage growth of the sector, the 1998 report from the National Biotechnology Advisory Committee entitled *Leading in the Next Millennium* urged the government "to undertake a national project to engage all Canadians in a dialogue about biotechnology." It quoted a survey conducted for the Food and Consumer Products Manufacturers of Canada: "more than credentials, consumers want reassurances about the character of the firms with which they do business and the people who represent them."

Other signs of change: The business lobby group the Industrial Biotechnology Association of Canada established an ethics committee to begin examining broader ethical issues. On the farm front, in a letter to the editor of *Ontario Farmer*, a producer wondered if it was appropriate for an industry association, the Ontario Federation of Agriculture, "to shed its advocacy role for farmers and instead mollycoddle the life sciences companies with fluffy rhetoric and big warm hugs."

Michele Brill-Edwards acknowledges that consumers are slowly becoming more aware of the potential consequences of biotechnology. But, she says, they have not yet realized that their government has virtually no regulations in force to protect them from harm—that they are at the mercy of the global biotechnology industry. She says people tend to think that the regulatory failures that led to the horrors of damaged silicone breast implants and HIV or hepatitis C infections from tainted blood are just fluke accidents. "They believe those are glitches to an otherwise well-functioning system," she says. "They don't understand that they are the predictable outcome of a weakening system." And in a soft but authoritative voice, she offers grim advice to consumers about those who produce and regulate genetically engineering food: "Don't trust them. Period."

12

MAD COWS AND ENGLISHMEN

JUNE 1997. IN THE BROAD STRETCHES OF THE AMERICAN Midwest, the soybean pods are beginning to swell, bristly and bulgy. In a few months, they will turn a dusty red-ocher—the signal for the start of the harvest. The beans will be crushed into oil and meal and then absorbed matter-of-factly into the North American diet. Apparently there will be no thought, no hesitation, no concern about whether they might have been altered in a laboratory with a gene from another organism. To Americans and Canadians, it seems to matter little if genetic engineering had a hand in the production of these beans.

Across the Atlantic, things are different in the mercantile city of Amsterdam, where the newly established industry lobby group that represents 540 biotechnology companies and organizations is holding its first general congress at the RAI Centre. It is a private meeting; there has been no effort to attract the press. In fact, on the advice of its public relations consultants, EuropaBio has been careful to avoid a "media-centered" event that might invite the protest of environmental groups. If it is not careful, the PR advisers warned the industry group, "EuropaBio will set the table and Greenpeace will have eaten the lunch."

Yet, despite all the deliberate care, the meeting does attract unexpected, and unwelcome, attention from Greenpeace. In North America, such a session would not spark more than a listless protest from a handful of students. In Amsterdam, environmental activists from across Europe arrive in a lumbering semitrailer truck. With the flourish Greenpeace "actions" are famous for, they dump ten tons of soybeans in a heap on the boulevard in front of the conference center. This flagrant display of littering is Greenpeace's very visible objection to the import of genetically engineered, herbicide-resistant soybeans into Europe. Test-tube foods—according to Greenpeace and what seems to be the majority of European consumers—have no place in the food supply.

Other countries have also balked at the test-tube diet North America's corporate biotechnology hopes to export around the world. Japanese retailers collected one million signatures in 1997 demanding labeling of genetically engineered foods. And by late 1998, the government was considering providing those labels. Brazil banned both the production and importation of genetically engineered soybeans, even though that cut off the supply from the U.S., the primary source for soybean imports in the past. But nowhere is the response against genetic engineering as vigorous and determined as in Europe.

Why would Monsanto's Roundup Ready soybeans provoke such a different reaction in Europe and North America? The two continents share similar lifestyles born of an affluent, industrialized, free-market economic system. Immigrants from European countries form the backbone of an ethnically diverse North America. And trade continues to bind the two continental economies.

However, Europe is undeniably distinct from North America. Despite an ever-growing urban population, Europe has not lost its connection to the land. Farmers are still regarded highly, and play an essential role in the mythology, economy, and culture of even the most urbanized European country. When farmers in France object to a reduction in government subsidies, their protest—complete with livestock and trucks—is welcomed in the streets of Paris. The taste and quality of food are paramount in the heartland of gastronomy. And although there are supermarkets everywhere, many Europeans—whether in Germany or Italy—prefer to pick up something fresh for dinner at the neighborhood bakery or butcher shop.

The natural environment is revered in Europe, in history and culture. Perhaps its loss through centuries of cultivation and the demands of an ever-growing population has made it all that more dear. Chernobyl was seen as an assault on Western European centers; acid rain throughout the early 1980s was an affront to the well-tended forests of Europe. Climate change and global warming are intensely moral issues in Europe. It is no surprise there is a widespread appreciation for environmental activism here. The green movement, which might provoke derision in North America, is rewarded in Europe with seats in the houses of political power—a clear indication of influence.

But perhaps most importantly, according to bioethicist Arthur Schafer, Europeans have a sense of community that eludes North Americans. They are willing to give up some personal freedom for a regulated structure they feel will protect them. "They view government as a more positive vehicle for creating a better society." Although North Americans believe their governments will protect them from harm, they do not want cumbersome regulation and rules that might stymie individual effort or financial reward. They believe in a commercial culture and are willing to export it.

European emotions are inflamed when it comes to any kind of tinkering with their food or their environment. That in itself might have triggered the protest that led to the ten-ton heap of soybeans in central Amsterdam. But the huge explosion of opposition to test-tube foods was likely set off by a single event: the biggest food scare ever to strike the continent, a scare that undermined the foundation of the British diet—toxic beef.

In the mid-1980s, cows across Britain began to display the symptoms of a disturbing new disease—a nervous disorder, always fatal and impossible to treat. The sick cows began to stagger, drool, grind their teeth, and show an unusual aggression toward other animals. When their brains were examined after death, they were pitted with channels, much like a sponge. The disease was identified as a variety of a class of diseases called "transmissible spongiform encephalopathies." This new cow version was dubbed bovine spongiform encephalopathy (BSE) or, in everyday language, mad cow disease.

Scientists finally determined that the bovine epidemic sprang from human-caused animal cannibalism—the feeding of ground-up animals to other animals. In the 1980s, industrial agriculture began to "render" or boil up parts of animals not fit for human consumption into a stew of cheap protein. The rendered protein was pressed into feed that promoted significant weight gain and milk production in animals raised in factory farms that were then becoming popular. It seems that sheep with "scrapie," another transmissible spongiform encephalopathy, had been rendered into feed that was offered to cattle. It is assumed that sick cows, in turn, were rendered and ended up in livestock feeding troughs.

By 1990, mad cow disease had developed from an obscure veterinary curiosity to an epidemic affecting 120,000 animals. The long incubation period of the disease—as much as eight years in cattle—suggested countless other infected but undiagnosed animals may have gone to slaughter for human consumption.

At the same time, people began dying from what scientists referred to as new variant Creutzfeld-Jakob disease. CJD is a rare disease that normally strikes the old, destroying the brains of the victims with microscopic spongelike holes, very similar in appearance to those in BSE-struck bovines. However, in this "new variant" incarnation, otherwise healthy people—some of them teenagers—were inexplicably incapacitated by a voracious, untreatable, and always fatal illness.

The appearance of devastating disease in both cattle and humans prompted speculation that the mad cow epidemic was passing from bovines into humans eating meat from infected animals. One professor, Richard Lacey of Leeds University, went so far as to warn that England "could lose a whole generation of people." The scare was exacerbated when Sir Bernard Tomlinson, the country's leading neurologist, appeared on a British Broadcasting Corporation program to declare he feared a link between mad cow disease and CJD. "I would not eat beefburgers or meat pies under any circumstances because of the unknown effects on humans," he declared.

Consumers in greater and greater numbers heeded that advice and began to avoid what had been the longtime staple of the British diet. Pressure from concerned parents drove hundreds of schools to drop beef from their menus. The Four Seasons Hotel in London stopped serving beef, and hospitals expressed unease about feeding it to their patients. The beef market fell off dramatically with each new suggestion that mad cow disease might jump from cows to humans. By the early 1990s, it had already plummeted by twenty-five percent.

Through it all, farmers, their organizations, and the government clung to the official stand—there was no scientific proof that the mysterious disease had made the transition from cows to people. Any contrary suggestions were dismissed as far-fetched and ridiculous, and the scientists who made them were out of date or bogus. They launched a carefully synchronized scientific information campaign, designed to reassure an anxious public. The government's advisory committee insisted cattle would be a "dead end host" for mad cow disease. The Institute of Food Science and Technology, an association of food industry advisers, issued what it called an independent, objective statement decrying "experts and perceived experts" responsible for alarming the public.

Perhaps in recognition of the industry's contributions to the economy, the government continued to insist that British beef was perfectly safe. In December 1995, Agriculture Minister Angela Browning told reporters her government's stance was "ultra-precautionary" and she accused the media of an "unprincipled" effort to "whip this up to a frenzy of public alarm where there is simply nothing there." Other government ministers did their part, posing for the media cameras with smiles on their faces and hamburgers in hand. Even then Prime Minister John Major got in on the act. "There is no scientific evidence that BSE can be transmitted to humans," he told the British House of Commons. The safety of beef, he said, "was not in question."

However, there was no sign of that kind of bravado from government ministers who appeared on the front bench of the House of Commons on March 20, 1996. A shamefaced Health Minister Stephen Dorrell, who had long insisted BSE posed no risk to humans, rose to publicly concede that mad cow disease was "the most likely explanation at present" for "ten cases of CJD in people aged under 42."

Overnight, the British beef market collapsed. Europe responded by banning all imports of British beef. The appetite for red meat fell off throughout Europe, especially in France and Germany. People ate pork, poultry, fish, and even horse meat—anything but beef. The industry was dealt another blow late in 1997 when a government advisory body said it had identified a risk of BSE getting into the food chain through the bundles of nerve cells attached to the skeletal structure. Prime Minister Tony Blair decided to take the cautious route by banning the sale of all beef on the bone. So much for T-bone steaks and prime rib roasts. It was not clear either what bones, if any, could be used for the production of gelatin.

The British beef industry and the culture that revolved around the Sunday roast were decimated. No exports of British beef cattle or meat were allowed. More than 1.7 million cows, heifers, steers, and bulls over the age of thirty months were slaughtered. The rendering procedures that had allowed infected sheep and cows to enter the feed system were stopped.

Slowly there were signs that the defensive front line was holding. In the peak years of 1992 and 1993, three thousand new BSE cases were registered each month; by 1997, that number was down to five hundred. However, there were deep scars on the British spirit. Britons, and their neighbors in Europe, had stepped into a universe where they no longer could feel assured their food was safe. Because of the long incubation period, people feared they might have acquired CJD years before and not know it. By late 1998, the death toll stood at twenty-nine.

Canada's Michele Brill-Edwards said the mad cow–CJD

disaster was an inevitable result of the deregulation of the feed system that had taken place in the 1970s under Margaret Thatcher's government. Consumers unfortunately learned the hard way that they could not trust the assurances of their regulators and their politicians.

In the process of confronting their fundamental fears, British consumers began to assume greater responsibility for the safety of their food. The mad cow scare had taught them that the principle of buyer beware applied even to food. Although meat sales were still down significantly by 1998, about fifty percent of the beef on the shelves was "identity preserved." That means butcher shops routinely offered consumers a virtual history of a cut of beef, based on such criteria as ethical production or free-range feeding.

Britain joined Europe in its appetite for organic food. The U.K. had long been the trailblazer among European nations for high-tech, intensive farming. But by the late 1990s, England's demand for organic food, growing at about twenty percent a year, was far exceeding supply. It was unfamiliar territory for Britain—fully seventy percent of the organic produce had to be imported.

There was a further psychological repercussion, which extended all across Europe. The mad cow crisis undermined public confidence in the authority of government. That lack of confidence was revealed in a survey of sixteen thousand Europeans conducted by the London School of Economics and the Science Museum in fall of 1996, six months after the confirmation of the bovine-human connection. Participants were asked if they thought they could trust their governments to deliver safe genetically engineered food. Ninety percent said no. Less than thirty percent thought the biotech industry could do the job. Even the European Union received few votes of confidence. Instead, respondents said they wanted to take the matter all the way to the top, to the World Health Organization.

Monsanto would be the first company to feel the wrath of consumers who had lost their fundamental confidence in the safety of food. Tom McDermott, head of European public relations for the company, was charged with the difficult task of paving the way for the introduction of genetically engineered soybeans. He ruefully told the press in January 1998, "We are on the heels of a major European-wide food scare, and it has undermined the authority of the government to protect people from food danger. The mad cow crisis is probably the most significant factor."

When the first shipment of Roundup Ready soybeans from the 1996 U.S. harvest arrived in Hamburg, Germany, in November on the freighter *Ideal Progress*, Europeans were well primed to be skeptical. When the Greenpeace activists who tried to stop the freighter's progress said, "They say it's safe. But how can we trust them?" they were preaching to the converted.

The European Commission, the executive body of the European Union, had already given Monsanto the green light to bring its manipulated soybeans to the continent. Many scientists agreed they posed no particular hazard to the environment or to human health. And, of course, these were pretty ordinary looking soybeans that would be pressed, ground up, and essentially disappear into margarine, chocolate, and pancake mix. But no matter how innocuous the beans seemed, European consumers had learned a painful lesson. If beef could kill you, couldn't a genetically engineered soybean also do the job? One thing was sure—they felt you could not trust the industry or government assurances. Soybeans, genetically engineered and grown in the United States, were to become the primary line of resistance against a coming wave of biotechnology crops—the focus of countless protests.

Had it not been for the BSE scare, Europe's reaction to the innocent-looking beans might have been surprising. It is not as if Europeans are backward, superstitious people, wary of new technologies. Some of the world's biggest pharmaceutical and chemical companies, such as Bayer, BASF, and Hoechst, are headquartered in Europe. The techniques of biotechnology are surely being used in those corporate labs. Europe was also where Dolly—the first mammal to be cloned from an adult cell—was created.

In its study *Benchmarking the Competitiveness of Biotechnology*, a group at the University of Sussex expressed high hopes for the new science. It predicted biotechnology would become a key engine of future growth in Europe, creating three million jobs. The study estimated the potential market for biotechnology-related products within the European Union would be $280 billion by 2005. In 1997, the U.K., home to mad cows, had the largest biotechnology industry in Europe with about two hundred companies listed. Germany, Holland, France, and Sweden were the other industry leaders. However, almost all this activity was focused on the pharmaceutical and medical health fields. European consumers had made their feelings clear about gene-spliced food, so efforts in the agricultural area lagged well behind the established and supported industry in the United States.

The political leaders of the European Union tried to stimulate a competitive biotechnology industry by funding work at 130 labs across the continent. However, all the research efforts were aimed at producing functional foods, like tomatoes with boosted beta-carotene. Researchers hoped the souped-up vegetables would be acceptable to Europeans otherwise frightened by the idea of transgenic food.

However, Europe had always countered pressure from the global biotechnology industry. After Monsanto introduced bovine growth hormone to the United States in 1994, the European Union defiantly banned the milk booster, determining there would be no sale on its turf before 2000. Despite persistent industry lobbying for more than a decade, Europe refused to allow patents on living organisms until it finally bent under the pressure in late 1997.

However, consumers across Europe were not prepared to yield to industry or government initiatives. *Nature* magazine reported that a poll in the spring of 1997 showed that although Europeans were anxious about the impact biotechnology might have on their health and the environment, their primary concern was the morality issue: Was it right to change natural food into something else? The magazine suggested that public relations teams and civil servants might be wasting their time attempting to win consumers over with scientific proof about safety.

The 1996 London School of Economics and the Science Museum survey had also revealed public concern about the moral aspects of genetic engineering. Britons in particular were troubled about the ethics of altering life. About sixty percent of respondents said they believed farm animals should only be bred traditionally. And in a wholesale indictment of the biotech industry, most of those surveyed thought genetic engineering for any reason was unnecessary.

The voice of the people reverberated across Europe. In Austria, a record 1.2 million citizens, representing twenty percent of the electorate, signed a people's petition to ban test-tube foods, as well as the deliberate release of genetically engineered organisms and the patenting of life. Genetically modified foods were also rejected by a laypeople's consultation in Norway and, according to an activist group survey, by ninety-five percent of consumers in Germany.

The ultimate insult for Europeans was that gene-spliced foods—Roundup Ready soybeans, for example—were not labeled. The soybeans were grown on American farms, collected, and mixed in with conventional soybeans in silos and co-op warehouses. The industry argued that any effort to keep genetically engineered soybeans separate would cost millions —a cost that would be borne by consumers.

Consumer distaste for genetic engineering had a direct impact on Europe's grocery sector. Instead of standing in solidarity with biotechnology companies, grocers seemed prepared to listen to their customers. EuroCommerce, the association for hundreds of retailers and commerce groups in twenty countries, set the tone in 1996 by urging importing governments and companies to advance cautiously. Hans Kroner, the secretary general of the retail association, pleaded with Monsanto to segregate its Roundup Ready soybeans: "I am telling the American exporters to please in this season, if you are wise, don't ship these soybeans to Europe because you may trigger a lasting reaction."

The opposition to test-tube foods created a vibrant alternative business sector. There was work for companies, like TNO Nutrition in the Netherlands, that claimed to be able to identify processed foods that contain even trace amounts of genetically modified organisms. Processors like Unilever and Nestlé Deutschland pledged not to use genetically modified soybeans. The British supermarket chains ASDA and Iceland announced they would ban unlabeled, genetically modified foods despite a European Union agreement to allow their import. And in November 1997, U.K. retailers said they would voluntarily label all products containing genetically engineered soybeans and corn if the European Union did not impose its own rules.

The anxiety over test-tube foods continued to generate stories for the nightly news. About five hundred tons of Switzerland's best-known chocolate bar, Toblerone, were pulled off store shelves when a routine check revealed they contained genetically engineered soybeans. Much to the laughter of observers, no genetically engineered foods were served in the U.K. House of Commons—a decision made by the catering manager, not the politicians. Several inmates at U.K. penal institutions argued they were entitled to a diet free of test-tube foods. And a young woman was arrested in a London supermarket for sticking labels on several packets of frozen food warning that they could contain genetically manipulated organisms.

In an effort to satisfy the appetite for natural produce, European companies were turning to soybeans and corn that could be verified as free of genetic engineering. An Austrian broker, in cooperation with Greenpeace, guaranteed the delivery of one million tons of natural soybeans for a five-year period, to be sold around Europe. South American soybean production rose by nearly twelve percent in 1997, partly to meet European demand for natural soybeans. Ontario soybean farmers who abided by special identity-preserved rules benefited from increased prices and guaranteed sales. Kim Cooper, marketing specialist for Ontario's soybean marketing board, told *Farm and Country*, "We had to keep telling processors that we're a small country. There is no way we can supply all the soybeans they want."

If corporate biotechnology is irritated by the North American regulatory system, it must be absolutely exasperated by the tangled European legal procedures and the ever-changing political climate. Although efforts have been made to apply a consistent law across Europe, they have been regularly derailed by political land mines. In theory, all genetically engineered foods or food ingredients must be assessed by the same Europe-wide standards. However, the European Union's regulatory procedure is so complicated and fraught with political sinkholes that by early 1998, only two genetically modified organisms (GMOs) had been legally cleared for import. These were Monsanto's Roundup Ready soybeans and Ciba-Geigy's (now Novartis) herbicide-tolerant and Bt-infused corn. However, as both Monsanto and Ciba-Geigy came to learn, legal approval from the European Commission did not guarantee support from European countries, consumers, or environmental activists.

European Commission directive 90/220 outlines the conditions altered crops must meet to receive environmental approval. Under the directive, a GMO is defined as "an organism in which genetic material had been altered in a way that does not occur naturally by mating and/or natural recombination." Like North American regulations, the rules here refer to "substantial equivalence." However, European regulators interpret that phrase in accordance with the process of creation, rather than the appearance of the product. On that basis, even though Roundup Ready soybeans look and act like natural soybeans, they are not "essentially equivalent."

In May 1997, the commission approved a set of "novel food" guidelines that were to complement directive 90/220. These guidelines were to define when and how GMOs would be considered safe for human health. The corporate industry was pleased at what seemed to be a step toward cohesion. AgrEvo filed paperwork on its herbicide-resistant canola the day after the novel food guidelines were announced. However, according to Margaret Gadsby, regulatory director for the company in North America, there were no procedures to go with the guidelines. By early 1998, after two growing seasons in North America, the AgrEvo application was still stuck somewhere in the regulatory process. (The regulatory hurdles were cleared later in the year.)

If a company wants to grow or sell a genetically modified crop in Europe, it must first apply to a single country as a sponsor. That country then brings the application forward to the European Commission, which makes a ruling, with input from the Council of Ministers, the European Parliament, and the fifteen member countries. At least, that is how things are supposed to work, but in Europe, rules, procedures, laws, and attitudes seem to change week by week.

Ciba-Geigy's experience with its glufosinate ammonium herbicide-tolerant, Bt-infused corn is typical of what happens in this ever-changing political environment. France first sponsored the company's application, which was endorsed by the European Commission in March 1995. But when the application was passed on to member countries for ratification, Denmark, Sweden, Britain, and Austria refused it and several other countries abstained. The European Parliament took its turn, voting by an overwhelming 402 to 2 majority to censure the commission's authorization of the transgenic corn, calling for imports to be suspended while the authorization was reexamined.

Although it had originally sponsored the application, France then banned all French farmers from cultivating genetically engineered corn. This was a blow to corporate biotechnology, especially since France was Europe's largest corn producer, harvesting a record crop in 1997 of sixteen million tons. But the news was welcomed by France's Corn Producers Organisation, which said that "a crisis on the level of mad cow was to be feared." However, the ban prompted Axel Kahn, the head of the independent Biomolecular Genetics Commission in France, which had reviewed and blessed the corn, to resign in indignation, saying the scientific evidence clearly indicated the manipulated corn was absolutely harmless. Late in 1997, there was yet another about-face—this time, the government urged farmers to plant genetically engineered crops so France would not lose its competitive position in the global marketplace. Through all of these ups and downs, Ciba-Geigy technically had full legal approval to import its corn.

Although the law granted the European Commission authority for GMOs, individual countries chaffed at the imposition of rules from the European Union's executive body. Italy, Austria, and Luxembourg invoked Article 16 of the directive, which allowed them to ban GMOs entirely for three months on the basis that they might "constitute a risk to human health or the environment," and "the effects of such releases on the environment may be irreversible." By 1998, the European Commission was still trying to figure out how to get the renegade countries to comply.

As difficult as it was for products that had been approved, there was even less tolerance for GMOs that had not yet been approved but found their way into the system. For example, Monsanto had been issued a permit by the Dutch Ministry of the Environment to conduct trials of Roundup Ready sugar beets. However, the company did not have the necessary EU approvals to market the product. In November 1997, Monsanto inadvertently shipped about two tons of the beets from a test farm to a refining plant, where they were mixed in with normal sugar. Monsanto took responsibility for the mistake and notified the Dutch food group CSM before the sugar was marketed.

The company had to isolate and seal about ten thousand tons of sugar, and the government launched an inquiry.

In the late 1990s, the European Union strained to find the appropriate balance between consumer attitudes, industry lobbying, and member countries who refused to follow the rules. For a time, the commission was thinking about requiring importing companies to separate genetically modified crops from conventional grains. Corporate biotechnology blanched at the idea. For one growing season, the Canadian canola industry had segregated its biotech versions from the conventional varieties. The cost of maintaining contracts for farmers and separate handling and distribution services topped $4 million. It was an experience the canola industry would embrace only once—it argued it was simply too expensive. The biotechnology industry argued that similar segregation systems in every crop would be costly and unnecessary. As AgrEvo's Margaret Gadsby put it, "The whole food production system would come to a grinding halt." In the summer of 1997, the lobby persevered and the E.U. commission agreed to shelve the segregation proposal.

Instead, the commission argued, the next best way to appease consumers was to label all grains and all processed products that might contain organisms created in the laboratory. In the London School of Economics and Science Museum poll, about seventy-four percent of respondents said they wanted labeling of modified food. In 1997, the European Commission changed its mind twice and finally adopted guidelines making labeling compulsory for all novel foods. However, beyond the public relations problem, the mechanics of labeling proved to be more difficult than the commission had originally anticipated. When would foods be labeled as containing GMOs—when they were one hundred percent GMOs? Fifty percent? Twenty percent? How would those levels be established? Who would do the testing?

The European labeling rules took effect September 1, 1998. According to the law, food manufacturers had to label all products containing any genetically modified food. The directive was seen as an important step in boosting consumer confidence. But it included a loophole on which activist organizations zeroed in. Companies had to state whether genetically modified soy or corn had been used in their foodstuffs, but the regulation exempted foods that contained soy and corn oil derivatives, such as the thickening agent lecithin, which make up ninety percent of soy products.

The EU said fourteen hundred products would be labeled, but thousands would escape the labeling requirement. Friends of the Earth campaigner Adrian Bebb told *The Guardian*: "Shoppers are being conned by politicians into believe that this labelling will help them avoid genetically engineered foods. It won't." According to *The Guardian* of September 1, the rules were a mishmash. "[T]he consumer should not feel reassured with the new genetically modified labelling regime. It is a curate's egg, designed by European governments to not inconvenience the powerful food barons and landowners, while at the same time recognising that there is much public disquiet. . . . As always in this political climate, it seems the corporate interests have triumphed and the consumer has been fobbed off."

The seemingly innocuous soybeans mechanically plucked from midwestern American fields represent one of the United States' biggest farm exports to Europe. But perhaps most importantly, they are a bellwether for future agricultural trade between the U.S. and Europe.

Monsanto's Roundup Ready soybeans were mixed with

natural beans—to the naked eye, it was impossible to tell if the soybeans in the hold of a freighter were genetically altered or not. Even in the face of protests from the European Union, Monsanto stubbornly maintained its right to mix its test-tube soybeans with nature's own. And it pursued its plans for a $1 million advertising campaign designed to tell Europeans they were being selfish in denying people access to the new technology.

The industry was clearly growing more and more frustrated by demands from European authorities. AgrEvo's Margaret Gadsby warned that continued lack of support in Europe would lead multinational firms to look to friendlier nations. "If Europe does not give the go-ahead, then damn Europe," she said.

In the American marketplace, Monsanto, AgrEvo, and Novartis are vigorous competitors, invoking patents law and court procedures in their cutthroat struggle for corporate domination. In Europe, these competitors are prepared to work in parallel for their common aim—unfettered access to the European marketplace. The biotechnology companies wrote a joint letter to U.S. President Clinton before the G7 summit meetings in Denver in 1997, asking him to use his influence with the leaders of the world's other powerful countries.

The U.S. government followed up with public shows of confidence in the industry. For example, in fall of 1997, Agriculture Secretary Dan Glickman appeared before the forty-four-nation International Grains Council meeting in London to launch a hard-nosed assault on countries that dared to restrict the sale of genetically modified foods. "As long as these products prove safe, we will not tolerate their segregation," he said. "Truth is truth. Science is science."

The dispute escalated as claims and counterclaims flew back and forth across the Atlantic. The U.S. saw European efforts to label genetically modified foods as equivalent to a non-trade tariff barrier. Traveling through South America, Glickman said: "We strongly oppose efforts to have mandatory labelling and or segregation of genetically engineered products. It would make it virtually impossible to sell any tangible commodity, like wheat or corn or soybeans." If there was no satisfactory resolution to the dispute, the United States said it would ask the World Trade Organization to adjudicate the argument. After all, $4.5 billion in potential agricultural exports was at stake.

For its part, Europe dug in its heels in the face of what it described as U.S. imperialism. In the past, Europe had accused the U.S. of trying to control commerce beyond its borders; for example, by imposing sanctions against countries that trade with Iran, Libya, or Cuba. This time, the British Retail Consortium and eight other trade associations threw down the gauntlet. In spring of 1997, they signed an open letter to the U.S. grain industry warning that several members of the European Union would require complete segregation of genetically engineered crops if the U.S. did not act voluntarily.

By 1998, it was clear the impasse would not be easily resolved. Despite considerable pressure from the biotechnology establishment, European consumers and their governments resolutely held their position.

The confrontation had an impact on Canada as well. In 1996, the first year of the biotech harvest, the Canadian government thought it would take only a few months to convince European regulators to allow genetically engineered canola into Europe. Canada's segregation of its canola that year was largely designed to appease Japan, Canada's biggest canola customer, with a market of two million tons a year. At the beginning of the growing season, Japan had not approved modified canola seed, meal, or oil for import. When it did so later in the year, Canada assumed Europe would follow soon after.

That meant that, in 1997, Canadian authorities abandoned their expensive segregation system. And because full approvals had not been won for all engineered canola varieties by the end of 1998, no Canadian canola was sold to the European Union. In 1995, Canada sold $425 million worth of natural canola to Europe; when it introduced genetically engineered canola but kept it separate, total sales dropped to $180 million; in 1997, when transgenic and natural canolas were mixed, sales plummeted to zero. By refusing to segregate their produce, Canadian canola producers wrote off Europe as a market.

Looking at the canola experience, the Flax Council of Canada said it would continue to segregate conventionally produced flax from any future varieties that might be genetically engineered. About eighty percent of the one million tons of flax produced in Canada go to export markets—most of them to Europe.

The government of Canada, which has otherwise followed the American lead on the biotechnology front, was not ready to take sides in what was developing as a U.S.–Europe trade dispute. Agriculture Canada's trade specialist Charles Craddoch told the *Western Producer* that Canada would not join the U.S. in objecting to an EU move to require labeling of all GMOs, including engineered corn and soybeans. "From our point of view," he said, "this is a labelling issue. We decide what labels to use here and they can do the same."

Even EuropaBio, the corporate lobby organization that Greenpeace drew attention to in the summer of 1997, understood it had to soft sell its message to the European market. Its first news releases and presentations to the media were replete with references to the ethical considerations of genetic engineering. Using language rarely heard from corporate biotechnology in North America, EuropaBio talked about opening up a dialogue on ethical questions raised by the use of modern biotechnologies. Well coached by the Burson Marsteller group, the world's largest public relations firm and the one that managed the fallout from several huge disasters including the Bhopal Union Carbide toxic chemical explosion, EuropaBio announced politically palatable positions on human cloning, animal welfare, protection of medical information, consumer information for food products, and conservation of genetic diversity.

A full-scale trade war over food casts a looming shadow over relations between Europe and North America in the waning years of this century. How a number of potential political pitfalls are negotiated will determine the future of international trade in test-tube foods. One thing seems very clear: The attitudes of European consumers are unlikely to change no matter how soothing the party line from North American corporate biotechnology. The gulf between European and North American attitudes is symbolically as wide as the Atlantic.

The mad cow disease scare generated a fierce distrust of regulatory agencies in European consumers—one they are not likely to shed quickly. The language British consumers heard from scientists and government representatives trying to quell public fears about the outbreak sounded identical to what is being said today about test-tube foods.

Meanwhile, North American consumers demonstrate what seems to be unshakeable confidence and trust in their regulatory systems. Even while the British beef market disintegrated and the U.K. government proposed the extermination of millions of British cattle, a U.S. survey showed that a majority of Americans believed their administration was taking appropriate measures to prevent such a disaster from happening on their home ground.

Until 1997, what the U.S. administration actually did was monitor the situation in Britain. Although consumers seemed to think that was sufficient, the FDA and Health Canada were not so sure. In June of that year, both countries made an about-face and moved to curb the possibility of mad cow disease making an appearance in North America by banning the practice of feeding rendered sheep and cattle back to ruminant animals. Although there had been no documented cases of mad cow disease or new variant CJD on this continent, the FDA announced: "The data and information raise concern that BSE could occur in cattle in the United States, and that if BSE does appear in this country, the causative agent could be transmitted and amplified through the feeding of processed ruminant protein to cattle, and could result in an epidemic." Because spongiform diseases take decades to incubate, consumers will have to wait to see if they have indeed been saved from that eventuality.

13

THE FOOD
ACTIVISTS

WAYNE GRETZKY AND THE NEW YORK RANGERS ARE AT THE
Calgary Saddledome. This is a big draw in a hockey town. But
an early burst of winter, with sub-zero temperatures and a blast
of blustery snow, has kept many potential fans huddled at
home on this November 1997 night in Calgary.

Nevertheless, about 150 people have overlooked the
inclement weather and the competing attractions to gather at
a University of Calgary theater normally reserved for dramatic
productions. They have come to hear American molecular biologist John Fagan speak about the perils of genetic engineering in food. He is an articulate and engaging speaker, his talk
peppered with metaphors. Genetic engineering is so impre-
cise, he says, it is like throwing a statue through the window
of an art gallery and hoping it will land right side up on the
appropriate pedestal.

But Fagan also takes pains to stress that his criticism of
genetic engineering is based on logic and science rather than
emotion and fear. Youthful-looking, almost boyish, he is dressed
in a trim business suit that seems designed to proclaim his

credibility as an academic scientist. "I do not come to you as a Luddite. I come to you as a scientist," he says, a shock of bangs falling over his eyes. "Science is not the problem. Let's go forward on the basis of science, not economics and politics."

His conventional appearance belies John Fagan's controversial background. Fagan astounded the international scientific community in 1994 when he returned $613,882 in grants to the U.S. National Institutes of Health on the grounds that his biotech cancer research might lead to dangerous applications in genetic engineering. Fagan, a graduate of Cornell, had been working with genetic engineering in medical research for more than twenty years. For much of that time, he led a research group at the NIH. But he became convinced that accidents could happen with genetic engineering and might be passed from one generation to the next. "I wanted to make a public statement," he says in explanation. "I don't say we should stop genetic research, but we are putting too much money into it."

From gene splicing, Fagan turned to what he called a more fruitful activity: research into traditional medicine, specifically Indian Ayurvedic healing. In his book *Genetic Engineering: The Hazards; Vedic Engineering: The Solutions*, he wrote, "There's been a great overpromotion of gene therapy techniques and these techniques are going to put us in the same place that nuclear power did—we got burned not realising the potential for side-effects." He called on fellow researchers to endorse a fifty-year moratorium on the most dangerous applications of genetic engineering and to demand full, comprehensive testing of all genetically engineered foods.

Fagan, like many scientists who have dared to speak out against biotechnology, has found himself ridiculed by his peers and the biotechnology establishment. On this evening, Maurice Moloney is here to challenge the speaker. Moloney is a former

Calgene scientist and now the University of Calgary professor who has discovered a way to insert valuable pharmaceutical protein genes into canola. He set up a company called SemBioSys to commercialize the technology; in a short time from this date, the company will receive the ultimate accolade, a significant financial investment from Dow Elanco. Moloney listens to Fagan's speech with barely contained irritation. When Fagan opens the floor to questions, Moloney leaps to his feet, brandishes a microphone in his fist, and begins to pace the edge of the stage, his long hair flying, finger pointing accusingly, sputtering with indignation.

Moloney attacks Fagan on the scientific front: a simple manipulation of genes in a canola plant is not transferred to oil drawn from the seeds. Fagan, in reply, assumes the calm, reasoned demeanor normally adopted by those who argue against him. He concedes that not every engineered food may be harmful, but asserts that more comprehensive testing is required. The showdown between academics dissolves into scientific jargon that few in the audience can follow, failing to deliver the theater for which Moloney's students in the audience had obviously hoped. Fagan moves on and Moloney and his entourage of supporters slip out.

The challenge is something Fagan has come to expect. He knows his credibility will be questioned. He has invited skepticism by teaming up with the Natural Law Party, a minor political movement that supports scientific endeavor as well as less conventional pursuits such as transcendental meditation and yogic flying. Fagan needs the financial and political support of an organization if he hopes to champion the cause against biotechnology, he says. "One scientist with a telephone in his office can't do anything." As an individual, he says he could never afford a speaking tour like the one that brought him to Calgary. "It is a very useful vehicle," he says about the party. However, Fagan does share the unconventional views of the Natural Law Party. He left the NIH twelve years ago to take on a professorship at the private Maharishi University of Management in Fairfield, Iowa. Days at Maharishi open and close with periods of transcendental meditation. Yet Fagan insists: "I am a mainstream scientist."

During the Industrial Revolution in the early 1800s, machinists, blacksmiths, and millers rose up to oppose the new technology that displaced people from family farms into factory towns. They were called Luddites. Today, the term has resurfaced: corporate biotechnology uses the word liberally to disparage its critics. In this age of kaleidoscopic innovation, a "Luddite" is someone who dares to question the march of progress.

In North America today, the academics who speak out against biotechnology are few and far between, largely because their credibility is constantly challenged. If they were talking in Europe they would be regarded as heroes; here they are routinely dismissed as flakes, lefties, or imbeciles. The biotechnology establishment argues that individuals and organizations who criticize biotechnology are obstructionist Luddites—scientifically ill-informed and emotionally overwrought. Fact, not emotion, say the genetic proponents, is the only way to assess the value of the new scientific technology.

Some researchers have told Fagan they admire what he is doing, but they fear exposing themselves to criticism from corporate biotechnology or from their departments. They say censure may take subtle forms—a missed appointment or loss of research opportunities—or perhaps be more direct—dismissal from university or public institutions. According to Fagan: "They say to me, I respect you, but I've got a mortgage and kids who have to go to college."

Jane Rissler of the Union for Concerned Scientists, a U.S.-based action group that is "sceptical of the promoted benefits of biotechnology," agrees a "biotech chill" has descended on many researchers in North America where the science has won such a firm foothold. She, however, has become so used to being called a Luddite, she is matter-of-fact about the criticisms directed her way. "It is part of what one has to tolerate. It comes with the territory." She says scientists who venture to speak out have always been criticized for using emotion rather than science to justify their positions. For example, Rachel Carson, the author of *Silent Spring*, the book that is credited with launching the ecological movement, refused to admit publicly she had breast cancer for fear that her findings would be dismissed as the rantings of an ill person.

Corporate biotechnology implies that people are not equipped to talk about biotechnology unless they have a Ph.D in science. Ann Clark has one, but when she told an audience she, as a mother, was concerned about the repercussions of genetic engineering, she says she could see the eyes roll.

The scarcity of scientists willing to question the current ethic means environmental groups, students, and food activists are left to do the job. These groups tend to use passion and rhetoric to make their points, and the biotech establishment has been quick to dismiss them as uninformed fear-mongers. Opposition to the well-oiled biotechnology machine is thus largely made up of a ragtag collection of individuals and often disorganized and underfunded groups. Fagan's Natural Law Party has put energy and money from its members into its "Campaign to Ban Genetically Engineered Foods," but its broader political objectives unfortunately undermine its credibility.

In the United States, the most visible opponent to biotechnology is Jeremy Rifkin, who *Time* magazine dubbed "The Most Hated Man in Science." Rifkin has spent twenty years as America's most vocal critic on a variety of economic questions ranging from the dangers of the space shuttle and beef consumption to the role of work in the fading years of this millennium. He has authored thirteen books, but he particularly likes to use a 1960s hectoring, take-no-prisoners, activist style that confounds many business operators and scientists. The Rifkin strategy includes lawsuits, boycotts, and guerrilla-like demonstrations. Henry I. Miller, former head of the FDA's Office of Biotechnology and now at the conservative Hoover Institution at Stanford University, told Gary Stix for *Scientific American* magazine, "One can't say enough negative things about a guy like that." Rifkin's Pure Food Campaign, renamed in 1998 the Campaign for Food Safety, is the most emphatic opposition lobby in the U.S. Its legal actions and boycotts have not managed to stop the release of any test-tube foods. However, it has prompted the federal government to increase its scrutiny of environmental risks.

Various other organizations voice their criticism of biotechnology when the new science intersects with their interests. For example, the Family Farm Defenders in the U.S. speak out against genetic engineering in crops and animals from the perspective that biotechnology undermines the family farm. The Environmental Defense Fund is concerned about the impact on the environment. The American Humane Societies address biotechnology from the perspective of what it means to animals.

Opposition forces do get together occasionally in their own "biotechnology working groups," but this cannot compare with the financial and organizational might of the Biotechnology

Industry Organization (BIO), which acts as an umbrella association for corporate biotechnology in the U.S.

The many advocacy groups might represent a more formidable assault if they did not allow petty grievances and competitions to sidetrack their interests. One environmentalist was just as dismissive of John Fagan as corporate biotechnology might be: "As soon as he starts talking about transcendental meditation, his credibility goes down the toilet." The Pure Food Campaign's so-called "Global Days of Action" in spring of 1997 did not earn the support of the international environmental lobby group Greenpeace until the campaign was virtually over. And when the Pure Food Campaign attempted to set up a satellite office in Canada, Canadian activists refused to work with the Americans, complaining they did not like their showy style.

Commitment to the campaign is often erratic and piecemeal, largely dependent on individual action. The environmental lobby group Pollution Probe hired a researcher in Canada to investigate where and what field trials of experimental crops were taking place. But funding dried up after a year, the researcher moved on, and the work was abandoned. The lobby against the introduction of bovine growth hormone in Canada fell largely on the shoulders of one individual at the Council of Canadians, an organization set up essentially to fight free trade with the U.S. After devoting nearly two years of his life to the cause, he was naturally exhausted and moved on to less demanding challenges. The campaign essentially disintegrated.

A further setback is that Greenpeace, the primary voice of opposition to genetic engineering in Europe, is suffering its biggest retrenchment ever in the U.S. In late 1997, the international lobby announced it was disassembling all ten of its branch offices in the U.S. and laying off 335 of its 400 staff.

To blame was a plummeting membership roll and a deficit of $2.6 million halfway through the year.

As for the Pure Food Campaign, it was at its apex in 1994, when bovine growth hormone and the Flavr Savr tomato were looming on the horizon. Thanks to generous contributions from the Foundation on Economic Trends, the lobby effort had a staff of fourteen people in its Washington office. It spent about $1 million on its campaign against BGH that year. It renovated Co-op Hall in the tiny community of Finland, in northern Minnesota, with plans to turn the building into a retreat for weekend food activist training conferences. However, by summer of 1997, the campaign was collapsing. Funding was down almost seventy-five percent, as charitable foundations moved on to different causes. Staff in Washington was reduced to five. The campaign could no longer afford to send mailings to its fifty thousand members.

The problem for food activists on this side of the pond, of course, is that however sincere and dedicated, they are a small group that is too easily written off as a lunatic fringe. Their protests and arguments have not won over the people they need to mount an effective barrier to the biotech juggernaut: the army of ordinary consumers with dollars to spend.

The contrast in consumer response to activism in North America and in Europe is truly remarkable. Corporate biotechnology likes to say that activists scare consumers with their uninformed and self-serving talk of Frankenfood. In Europe, consumers have decided the activists are right. A poll of respondents in the European Union rated independent consumer organizations, followed by environmental protection groups, as by far the most trusted source of advice on genetic engineering.

In Europe, Greenpeace, with its zealous, in-your-face brand

of activism, has led the charge against genetically engineered soybeans and other test-tube foods. Greenpeace organizers tried to stop the freighter *Ideal Progress* from loading soybeans in New Orleans by chaining themselves onboard the vessel. In Barcelona, they buzzed about the harbor in rubber dinghies in an attempt to stop another "soyship." Protesters from Germany arrived in Iowa to pose in front of a field of genetically engineered soybeans and decry in heavily accented English how biotechnology would "ruin the family farm." In London, dressed in white, hooded coveralls, with an "X" painted across their white-painted faces, Greenpeace activists stood in an eerie and solemn vigil in front of Unilever headquarters as the theme from *The X Files* played in the background. Demonstrators have paraded through European streets with inflatable Frankensteins. They have shivered naked on British rooftops. And at the World Food Summit in Rome in 1996, protesters pelted U.S. Agriculture Secretary Dan Glickman with genetically engineered soybeans and then peeled off their clothes to reveal bodies festooned with slogans like "no gene bean" or "the naked truth."

The destruction of field trials of genetically engineered crops has become routine right across Europe. For example, when Monsanto planted a one-acre experimental crop of Roundup Ready sugar beets near Carlow, Ireland, in 1997, the Gaelic Earth Liberation Front appeared in the early hours one morning to destroy the crop. Similar acts of "liberation" occurred just about whenever consumers heard about researchers trying out genetically engineered plants. As evidence of how rooted in the community these protests are, in 1998, a community-based initiative called Genetix Snowball rolled through the English countryside. The campaign took its inspiration from the "snowballs" peace movement of the 1980s in which two thousand people were arrested. Snowball participants each invite two others to join the next round of action, increasing participation exponentially. Participants inform police and farmers of what they are about to do and then leave a personal statement at each test site explaining the reasons for their actions. In an open display of civil disobedience, participants are willing to risk arrest and justify their actions in a court of law.

Gary Watson, who runs the largest farming operation in England, may seem an unlikely warrior, but his peaceful farm at bucolic Buckfastleigh in southwestern England has been on the front lines of an increasingly bitter struggle. He went to court in an attempt to stop the National Institute of Agricultural Botany from growing a trial of genetically engineered corn on neighboring land. Watson lost his court case but found himself and his farm the focus of intensive media attention.

Genetic engineering has also attracted the scorn of European celebrities—notably the Prince of Wales. Prince Charles, an organic farming enthusiast, launched his protest against biotechnology in September 1996 at the Eve Balfour Memorial Lecture when he urged that the introduction of genetically engineered organisms should proceed cautiously to ensure that any benefits would not be made at the expense of the safety and well-being of future generations. The prince noted that other new technologies, such as CFCs, asbestos, pesticides, and thalidomide, had led to unanticipated consequences. He concluded by saying, "I think we have reached a moral and ethical watershed beyond which we venture into realms that belong to God, and God alone." Prince Charles continued his campaign, launching a Web site in late 1998. The site received six million hits in its first week.

In North America, where money and individual achievement are often valued above community welfare, food activists are essentially forced to prove why they would dare to halt the pace of technological progress; the onus is not on companies to prove why genetic engineering should proceed. That has left the opposition trying to match the serious, scientific tones of corporate biotechnology. Caught in the industry's home court, it avoids moral debates as if "morals" or "ethics" were bad words. In Europe, Greenpeace activists climb to the top of a building to unfurl a banner. Nowadays, in buttoned-down, business-minded North America, the Campaign for Food Safety (formerly the Pure Food Campaign) calls a press conference.

For a while, the American lobby borrowed from Greenpeace's strategy book. There were tomato smashings to protest the Flavr Savr tomato and milk dumpings to oppose BST. These colorful demonstrations earned the activists the condemnation of the biotechnology establishment and some media attention, but not much else.

However, there are some recent glimmers of hope on the activist horizon. Ronnie Cummins, Pure Food Campaign's ever-optimistic director, says that the campaign's grim financial situation is perhaps "a blessing in disguise." The group is rethinking its strategy, trying to tailor it to the North American reality. It has come to realize it needs political support, he says, but that members of Congress will not take a stand against biotechnology until they believe it reflects the will of their voters. That means that at least five thousand people in each congressional district have to write a letter of protest or make a phone call before political leaders can be expected to speak out. And that demands grassroots organization.

In its new lean-and-mean incarnation, the Pure Food Campaign, now the Campaign for Food Safety, is taking its example from corporate America. For example, Cummins says the American Medical Association is able to launch a political response from 100,000 physicians across the country on just twenty-four hours notice. The association does this with just three staff members—and a sophisticated electronic mail system.

Cummins predicts the Internet will become the new equalizer in the battle over biotechnology. About twenty percent of American households already have e-mail addresses. By 1999, just about every company and every biotechnology association had a site on the World Wide Web. The voices of the opposition were just beginning to appear. A call for action from the new electronically minded Campaign for Food Safety can now be issued at little expense. Relevant news is posted each day on the campaign's Web site, eliminating the need for costly production and distribution of newsletters and press releases. And the campaign intends to study the success of direct marketers who have found a way to advertise products by tapping into mailing lists. And, in an effort at more coordinated action, the campaign held another set of Global Days of Action in the fall of 1997—this time with Greenpeace's support.

The experience in Europe shows that consumers do have the power to slow the pace of what might seem to be the inevitable march of corporate biotechnology. And it shows that scientific logic is not necessarily what is most persuasive. If North American consumers hope to make an informed decision on whether to buy test-tube technology, they must be open to the sound of different voices—even to those of Luddites.

14

THE NEW FRONTIER

THE AIR SURROUNDING TONY MCQUAIL'S FARM IS FILLED with the sound of thousands of insects rubbing their legs together. They have been given sanctuary here on this organic farmstead northwest of Toronto. From McQuail's perspective, the cicadas, crickets, ladybugs, and beetles are all beneficial bugs that have a role to play in the ecosystem. There is a jug of Dipel—the trade name for the organic pesticide *Bacillus thuringiensis* (Bt)—in the barn, but even that is pulled out only when there truly is no other way to deal with the cabbage loopers. When the rapacious striped larvae of the Colorado beetle appear on the leaves of the potato plants, they are picked off by hand and squashed between determined thumb and forefinger. Monsanto's New Leaf potatoes with the built-in pesticide will never bloom here.

The landscape of the neighboring farms around the haven of McQuail's "Meeting Place" holding is planted in seemingly endless, neat, ordered rows of corn and soybeans—the poster image of modern, industrialized agriculture. As Rachel Carson predicted nearly three decades ago in *Silent Spring*, there is an eerie silence here. In the world she imagined, DDT and other farm chemicals would strip the rural landscape of its bird and insect life. Although the pesticides used today are more benign than those of Carson's time, the fields of today's progressive farming are strangely silent.

By modern perspectives, McQuail's one hundred-acre operation is a throwback to times gone past. In defiance of the teachings of modern agriculture, he grows a little of everything. There is the community-share vegetable garden and the fruit tree orchard. A handful of cattle and sheep munch on grass in the pasture—no feed lot pellet for them. Geese strut about the farmyard, fluttering away in consternation at every approaching human. And a team of blond-headed Belgian horses takes the place of a mechanical John Deere in front of the plow. According to the teachings of our childhood picture books, this is what most of us would recognize as a farm.

"This farm sustains a lot of happiness," says McQuail. He, his wife Fran, and their two children seem content to live in tune with nature, just as their forefathers did, far from the lure of the local fast-food franchises. The members of the community-share garden arrive to pick up their produce each week in jaunty good spirits rarely seen in the urban supermarket. They collect lettuce in mid-summer, potatoes from the cold storage in the dead of winter. There is a strawberry celebration each spring and a corn roast each fall to honor the bounty of the land. Two apprentices have come here from as far away as Germany to learn how this contrary brand of farming manages to operate in industrialized North America in the waning years of the twentieth century.

Over a lunch of huge, glossy tomatoes and the snap of garden-fresh kohlrabi, Tony and Fran tell the story of how they were once tempted by the world of agribusiness. Each year, they take bushels of apples from their orchard to be stewed and pressed in nearby Goderich. The mash, spiced with a bit of cinnamon and a dollop of baking soda, becomes a creamy apple butter, the consistency of peanut butter with the full flavor of a freshly made jam. It is sealed in jars and sold under the label "Meeting Place Organic Farm Apple Butter." One enthusiastic customer raved about the creamy spread and told the McQuails he could place it in Japan. The prospect of a devoted though distant market was momentarily tempting. But then the McQuails remembered that the demands of mass production would strip away the very things that made the apple butter attractive in the first place. It would be impossible for the McQuails to grow and produce their organic fruit and at the same time become the McDonald's of a global apple butter industry.

For many urban dwellers whose impressions of farming have been shaped by nostalgia for times gone past, this is what they imagine agriculture is all about—not the modern hog farm with its massive internment barns, or a cash-crop operation where the endless miles of a single crop are doused with a synthetic rain of pesticides. City folk have an increased appetite for products, like the McQuail apple butter, that can be certified as being free of chemicals and biotechnology. The U.S. Organic Trade Association says the organic industry has experienced steady growth of more than twenty percent a year in the 1990s, even though organic products are more expensive. In 1996, Americans spent $3.5 billion on organic food and beverage products. More than forty percent of conventional supermarkets now stock organic goods. Even the *New York Times* jumped on the bandwagon, declaring on October 8, 1997, "Organic Food Industry Comes of Age." The U.S. government followed suit by approving new guidelines that would define "organic" produce. The guidelines were applauded by the industry—until it discovered the administration had failed to specify that organic foods would not be genetically engineered. (After the largest letter-writing campaign in the department's history, the USDA agreed to redraft its guidelines.)

But according to typical modern assessments of farming, the McQuail operation is a "subsistence farm"—a not very productive use of land. According to today's agricultural gospel, the McQuails represent a step backward into an unproductive past. They are Luddites in their century's revolution, opponents to progress.

Since the end of the Industrial Revolution, the grooves of change, the range forward, have become the fundamental essence of our time. Scientific progress is the altar at which our society worships. In our lifetime, the church of progress has regularly delivered miracles: everything from computers of increasing power and decreasing size, to the microwave, to instant banking, to a five hundred-channel television universe, to digital sound, to the Jacuzzi hot tub. Biotechnology tells us it can do the same with food by applying similar principles of scientific progress. It promises to produce better food, more efficiently and more productively, than the old-fashioned approaches practiced by the McQuails.

There is, however, a dark side to progress: the greenhouse effect, global warming, widespread chemical pollution, and nuclear accidents are some of its more ominous side effects.

The trappings of efficiency and productivity—automobiles, aerosol cans, air conditioners, and agricultural chemicals—all bring with them unexpected and unwelcome results.

We can no longer count on industrialized agriculture, that paragon of efficiency that defined farming since World War

Two, to produce the food we need. The old formula, based on chemicals, mechanization, and new varietal breeding, which was so spectacularly successful in expanding food production for nearly half a century, is no longer working particularly well. Grain production rose forty percent per person from 1950 to 1984. But from then until 1995, it has fallen about fifteen percent. In the last two decades, neither the output nor the number of people supported by an acre of land have risen as quickly as they did before. The biggest factor in the slowed gains is the soil's diminished response to chemical fertilizers; additional fertilizer use is having little impact on yields in many countries. The Green Revolution is coming to a close.

At the pinnacle of the Green Revolution, we produced enough food to feed the world. And yet, the television news was rife with reports of famine in faraway African countries. The difficulty has not been the amount of food we produce, but its distribution.

When many of us were growing up, our mothers used to urge us to eat up by reminding us of the starving children in Africa. But today in North America, families routinely throw away enough leftovers to feed a family in Ethiopia. Because most of us have never known hunger, we place little value on these scraps. According to the U.S. Department of Agriculture, Americans routinely toss away uneaten fruit, day-old bread and other pantry items, wasting one-quarter of the nation's total food supply—a total of ninety-six billion pounds of food. In the mid-1970s, the U.S. produced so much grain, the surplus was poured down the gullets of meat animals to fatten them for slaughter. In the late 1980s, so much surplus milk was produced, the U.S. Congress funded a dairy herd buyout and killed off or exported 1.6 million dairy cattle.

At issue is not just the distribution of food to developing

countries, but feeding the hungry right here at home. If just five percent of the wasted food that is nutritious and safe was recovered from restaurants, grocery stores, and residential kitchens, it could feed an estimated four million poor and homeless U.S. citizens. At the same time as this careless waste, the USDA spent almost $38 billion in 1996 to provide food aid to forty-five million hungry Americans.

On the affluent side of town, food is cheap, plentiful, and always available. We may complain about our weekly supermarket bills, but North Americans pay less of their monthly household budgets on food than any other culture in the world. It is no wonder we place so little value on something that costs so little.

However, the proponents of biotechnology insist the new science is the only way to refuel the Green Revolution. Dennis Avery, the latest in a string of proponents for industrialized agriculture, argues in his book *Saving the Planet with Pesticides and Plastic* that pesticides, the backbone of high-yield, industrialized agriculture, are already saving ten million square miles of wildlands from being plowed for food production. By 2050, he predicts pesticides and fertilizers could be helping to save as much as thirty million square miles of forests, prairie, and other prime wildlife habitat.

Avery, and the other disciples of industrialized agriculture, claim that biotechnology is the way to increase world food production. It is tempting to believe that biotechnology may somehow come to the rescue of starving millions and to an environment under siege. But when the rescuer is a corporate behemoth with a focus on profits and a portfolio of luxury products for high-paying customers, how likely is that? There is little profit in feeding a starving Ethiopia or North Korea.

Lester Brown of the Worldwatch Institute, who has written

extensively on the question of population growth and food production, says in his book *Tough Choices: Facing the Challenge of Food Scarcity*, that biotechnology "is not a magic wand that can be waved at food scarcity to make it go away." He says the optimism for the future comes from work like that being conducted by rice breeders at the International Rice Institute in the Philippines, who are relying on traditional breeding techniques to redesign the rice plant to boost its productivity. This work, although low-tech, promises to raise yields by twenty percent—enough to cover world population growth for thirty months. So there may be hope, albeit not from the engine of biotechnological progress.

Tony McQuail's indictment is still more emphatic: "Biotechnology is the next really big mistake," he says. The irony is that it is industrial agriculture itself that has created many of the problems biotechnology is trying to fix. For example, if a farmer chooses to violate the rules of common sense and plant the same crop in the same field, year after year, the soil will become depleted and weeds will invade. Genetic engineering's herbicide-resistant crops offer a chemical solution to a problem that could be resolved with basic crop rotation. Similarly, when you crowd thousands of chickens into a battery cage barn, they become bored and sickly, requiring their beaks to be cut off and necessitating numerous doses of hormones and antibiotics. Instead of improving these intolerable conditions, biotechnology proposes to make the birds less aware of them. In essence, biotechnology is being called on to patch up the problems caused by earlier technologies.

Nature has built-in checks and balances by which it holds species in bounds. Under so-called primitive agricultural conditions, the farmer usually had few insect or weed problems. Even these days, McQuail rarely has to deal with unmanageable pests or weeds. On the other hand, his neighbors, who have dedicated immense acreages to a single crop, often pull out the chemical sprayer. Monocultures, encouraged by the industrialization of agriculture, look beautiful, but they do not take advantage of the basic principles by which nature works. When industrialized agriculture plants huge fields of wheat, it provides a huge opportunity to insects that live on wheat. As Rachel Carson wrote, industrialized farming "is agriculture as an engineer might conceive it to be."

There was a time when cultivation by plowing, hoeing, or disking was the dominant strategy for coping with weeds in crop fields. This was quite simply achieved by hooking various implements to the back of a tractor and dragging them through the soil. This worked particularly well on perennial weeds, where cultivation disturbs the weeds above ground and eventually starves them to death. Annual weeds were cut apart before they could form seeds.

Today, a chemical mist clouds the farming sky. In the American Midwest, ninety-nine percent of corn and bean acreages are sprayed with herbicides. Although cultivation worked effectively for centuries, virtually no agricultural research has been done since the 1970s on mechanical strategies to control weeds. Instead, research has been aimed at the more glamorous options—chemical herbicides and, more recently, genetically engineered herbicide-resistant crops.

The sustainable agriculture practiced by people like McQuail may offer an option for the future. Rather than trying to dominate nature, sustainable agriculture mimics it. McQuail's farm is proof that farmers can produce a crop without the quick fix of chemicals or genetic engineering. He relies on wise management of crop rotation, replenishment of the soil with natural fertilizers, an understanding that some insects can be useful, and an appreciation for diversity, not monoculture. This kind of farming, in rhythm with the ecosystem, builds on the past—it does not relive it. It is an opportunity to develop an agricultural system that includes high yields, safe foods, and healthy environments—a future that coaxes, rather than assaults, nature. Tony McQuail makes us wonder exactly what problems biotechnology is intended to solve.

Can sustainable agriculture feed the world? Because most farmers in developing countries cannot afford chemical inputs, they follow the same rhythms Tony McQuail does. Developing countries must find ways to encourage higher-yielding, sustainable systems that can produce the food they need. The industrialized world has a role to play in offering research support to those countries. Biotechnology, with its profit-oriented conditions, is not the answer. Perhaps sustainable agriculture is the road to the future.

Every revolution brings negatives. No matter what your perspective, it would be naive to think this latest one will not. However, in this case it will be impossible to put the genie back in the bottle once the dubious realities become evident, because biotechnology proposes to unleash living things that can duplicate themselves. Critics use the phrase "genetic pollution" to describe a world in which artificial life overwhelms the natural world.

Ann Clark asks some fundamental questions: Who will be responsible for cleaning up any biotechnological mess in the future? Will the proponents of genetically engineered crops be held accountable? "Will society once again be obliged to assume responsibility for the ecological and health repercussions, if any, from genetically engineered organisms, leaving the proprietors to capitalise on the benefits without absorbing the risks?" she asked at a National Farmers Union conference in Saskatoon in 1997.

Corporations operate on the basis of short-term gain, Arthur Schafer notes. By the time long-term repercussions appear, companies, their principals, and their shareholders are often long gone. "The crucial decisions about our health and well-being and the health and well-being of future generations are being made primarily by multinational corporations solely on short term profit considerations."

Although decisions may be made by the corporate sector, with the acquiescence of government, consumers have more control over the course of biotechnology than they may imagine. Europeans have proven that. As Shafer says, "We vote with our dollars." Of course, it is difficult for consumers to vote with their dollars if they do not know what they are buying. In North America, labeling of genetically engineered food is required only if the nutritional value or toxic level is significantly altered or if the food contains genetic material from a known allergen.

The simple "no labels" stance has been the foundation for the success of the biotechnology industry. Corporations know if foods are labeled "genetically engineered," shoppers will likely reach for the other package on the supermarket shelves. In 1994, Norman Bradsick, then president of the Asgrow Seed company, told the *Kansas City Star*, "If you put a label on a genetically engineered food, you might as we put a skull and crossbones on it." Corporations may know that, but they do not often explain it that way. At a farm conference in Oxford, England, in early 1998, U.S. Agriculture Secretary Dan Glickman told Europeans to stop "defaming" American-produced food. "Mandatory labelling implies a potential health or environmental risk. In the absence of scientifically proven risk, labels only serve to mislead consumers." In other words, the fight to keep labels off is a service to consumers!

Consumers feel very differently. In poll after poll, even those conducted for the industry, consumers say they want labels. In Canada, the Natural Law Party collected ten thousand names on a petition requesting labeling. In 1997, a group of prominent Americans formed a group called Consumer Right to Know; Gillian Anderson, who stars in the television series *The X-Files*, lent her high-profile name to the effort.

In 1998, corporate biotechnology watched with helpless loathing as the European Union moved to require labeling on all GMOs. Somehow, Europe had managed to resist the vigorous industrial lobby. All that business could do was to hope the labeling bug would not spread to its most important market in North America. There, test-tube foods were supposed to arrive in the supermarket stealthily and unannounced.

In an effort to stop the spread of the appetite for labeling, corporate biotechnology has begun to focus on the global political arena at the Codex Alimentarius Commission. This United Nations group, charged with the task of coming up with international laws on labeling, meets every spring in Canada. It struggled throughout the 1990s to find a solution to the labeling question that would satisfy all 147 member countries, with the primary line of conflict set between the U.S. and Europe. In classic diplomatic style, it gave no quick answers, even after seven years of discussion. Whether or not to label genetically engineered foods would become an issue for the future.

Meanwhile, North American consumers continue to sleepwalk toward the biotechnological revolution. Thomas Hoban, associate professor and extension sociology specialist at North Carolina State University, has done much work in the area of consumer acceptance of biotechnology. In a review of five national polls from 1992 to 1995, Hoban found that public awareness of biotechnology remained low despite extensive media coverage. This is dangerous, since corporations have established the principle that biotechnology is safe until proven harmful. Therefore, the burden of proof lies with the public. And "proof" is elusive.

There is no way of predicting what may happen in the future. We were told there was no proof that industrial pollution, nuclear energy, chemical use, food additives, and a host of other modern essentials were harmful to us. Sandra Steingraber writes powerfully in her book *Living Downstream* that there is no proof that the degradation of the environment is to blame for incidences of human cancer. She says the true courage of our time is to make decisions on impartial evidence. Many scientists say this "precautionary principle" (basically, better safe than sorry) should guide us in making difficult decisions about biotechnology.

Bioethicist Arthur Schafer acknowledges it is difficult for society to make a decision on test-tube foods—particularly if scientific information is incomplete. "The potential consequences are not only horrendous, but we have to make decisions behind a veil of ignorance," he says. The proponents of genetic engineering say biotechnology is all about scientific findings, not ethics or emotions or fears for the future. In the face of an ethical discussion, they retreat quickly to more comfortable ground—what they call the facts.

But surely the power to manipulate life poses many ethical questions beyond the basic facts of did it do this, and did it do that. These are questions that everyone is entitled to ask: Is biotechnology a violation of the old taboos about meddling with nature? Is it cannibalism to eat food with a human gene in it? Can a vegetarian eat a tomato with a flounder gene in it? Isn't the labeling of bioengineered food just a question of our right to choice? How do we weigh animal versus human welfare? What are the consequences of future generations growing up in a world of engineered nutrition?

Shafer says every new test-tube food has to be assessed according to a risks/benefit analysis. "We have to ask: Is it necessary? Will it work? What are the risks and benefits? What does it harm? Who benefits? Who suffers?" he suggests. For instance, many people would feel that a gene-spliced drug that cured cancer was worth the potential risks. But they might feel very differently about milk produced by cows boosted with a growth hormone that had no apparent benefits, except for the pharmaceutical companies that produced it.

In some views, biotechnology is a high-speed train running on a track of purported progress. A derailment seems inevitable. Michele Brill-Edwards says that kind of train wreck has already happened, with an even less intrusive technology. She is referring to mad cow disease and its jump to the human population. "Britain used to say it had one of the safest food systems in the world. This is the kind of glib reassurance that is offered by ministers, and it generally works."

In the world of science fiction, Dr. Frankenstein learns his lesson about the short-sighted hubris that led him to think he could control nature and create life. And the bleak existence Aldous Huxley described in *Brave New World* suggests that unbridled scientific progress will lead to a grim future.

In real life, science has succeeded in creating a universe more fantastic than the writers could imagine. We are standing on the brink of a new millennium and a new revolution. Biotechnology beckons, offering us the world of our dreams— or a nightmare of horrors. Food, that essential of life and the heart of every culture, promises to be for ever changed. Will we rush in, or hold back?

Epilogue

For those with apocalyptic inclinations, 1999 was a year of pre-millennial foreboding. Nature served up a bitter menu of disasters. Its rumbling forces crumbled buildings and lives in Turkey; swelling waters swept over the banks of the Yangtze River; hurricane-force winds and rain pelted the American seaboard with disturbing frequency and severity.

Seemingly not to be outdone, human beings devised their own potential cataclysm: the threat of the Y2K bug loomed over almost every aspect of computerized modern life. And when it came to food, human error matched nature's disastrous offerings. Hundreds of Europeans fell ill after drinking contaminated soda pop. Belgian chocolate, along with Belgian beef, pork, chicken and all other dairy products, was banned throughout the world when it was revealed that dioxin-tainted oil had ended up in animal feed.

In the climate of anxiety that characterized the last year of the millennium, it was perhaps no surprise that consumers, even in North America, finally awoke to the revolution in biotechnology that had been quietly transforming their food. In 1999, genetic engineering was the subject of articles and news reports in a wide range of publications — everything from *The Economist, The New York Times,* and *The Globe and Mail* to *Adbusters* magazine. The headline references to *Frankenstein* and *frankenfoods* became ubiquitous. The stories of the impact of science on our daily bread led to the wide-spread acceptance of a new vernacular. The acronyms GM for genetic modification and GMO for genetically modified organisms became part of everyday language.

In Europe, particularly in Great Britain, anxiety reached a frenzied pitch. Travelers returned from England with stories of how the menu at the Piccadilly McDonald's proclaimed its food was GM-free or how otherwise mild-mannered individuals were transformed into "eco-warriors" in the battle to tear up trial plots of engineered crops. Charles, the Prince of Wales, upped the stakes in his war of philosophies with Prime Minister Tony Blair by submitting an article to the *Daily Telegraph* that denounced the technology that tampered with the natural order of food. In May 1999, the 115,000-member British Medical Association issued a report that called for a moratorium on genetically engineered food and declared that more independent research was needed to study its safety. Even the government's own chief medical officer and science advisor called on ministers to set up a panel to see if GMOs could cause birth defects and create new cancers.

European governments and retailers responded decisively to the new consumer apprehension. European Union environmental ministers moved to implement the legal equivalent of a three-year moratorium on any new approvals of engineered crops or foods. Acknowledging the old adage that "the consumer is always right," seven of the U.K.'s largest grocery chains pulled genetically modified products from their in-house brands. Zeneca's altered tomato puree, which had once sold briskly, disappeared from store shelves. Unilever, the largest processor in Britain, Nestle and Cadbury Schwepps, all declared themselves GMO-free.

In North America, 1999 began with the same optimism and

enthusiasm that had characterized the first years of commercial biotechnology. Sixty percent of Canada's canola crop was genetically engineered; one in three acres of corn, twenty-five percent of the soybeans, and twenty percent of the potatoes were modified. Canada continued to authorize crops born in a lab — by fall of 1999, the number of approvals had climbed to forty-five. And North American governments continued to press for international rules under the World Trade Organization and the biosafety protocol that would force countries to accept genetically modified foods, even if their consumers did not want them.

But by mid-year, as crops ripened in the fields, the European controversy reverberated across the Atlantic and there were reports of "guerrilla gardeners" here at home, wading into field trials of genetically engineered plants, scythes in hand. The Mothers for Natural Law presented Washington with half a million names on a petition demanding labeling for GM foods. Groups like the Council of Canadians and Greenpeace warned that shoppers would have to become accustomed to seeing protesters dressed up as vegetables or farm animals outside their grocery stores handing out leaflets decrying genetic engineering. And the magazine *Consumer Reports*, with a readership of 4.7 million readers, took the spirit of labeling and consumer's right-to-know to a new level when it listed in its September issue which brands of tortilla chips, muffin mixes, and baby foods contained genetically modified ingredients.

Consumer anxiety was fueled by growing indications of genetic engineering's impact on human health, the environment and animal life. The most disturbing information came when an expert on plant toxins declared on British television that he would not eat modified foods and that "it was very,

very unfair to use our fellow citizens as guinea pigs." Arpad Pusztai, a researcher at the Rowett Research Institute in Aberdeen, was referring to the damaging effects genetically modified potatoes had on the immune systems and the internal organs of his lab rats. Pusztai had fed the rats a diet of potatoes engineered with a gene from the snowdrop plant and a commonly used viral promoter — the cauliflower mosaic virus.

As there had been virtually no tests on the effects of genetically modified foods on mammals and humans done anywhere, Pusztai's television appearance sent shock waves around the world. Although he had spent thirty-five years at the Rowett Research Institute and had 270 published scientific papers to his name, there was a concerted effort to discredit him. Pusztai was dismissed from the institute on the basis that he had been "muddled" on his findings.

Throughout 1999, biotechnology proponents and critics debated whether Pusztai's research proved genetic modification could have an unforeseen impact on health. A specially convened group of the Royal Society condemned his work, saying it was flawed and unjustifiable. On the other side, twenty scientists from around the world signed a letter demanding Pusztai be reinstated. In October, he published his findings in *The Lancet*, provoking another round of debate. By the end of 1999, Pusztai was left defending his case on the Internet and there was still no definitive word on whether engineered potatoes, or any other GMO, were safe to eat.

However, evidence mounted that biotechnology was indeed polluting the environment. The most alarming indication came with the release of a scientific study in *Nature*'s May issue that showed genetically engineered corn could ravage the Monarch butterfly. Researchers at Cornell University reported that the pollen from corn with a built-in resistance to pests, spliced with a gene from *Bacillus thuringiensis*, and then sprinkled on milkweed killed nearly one-half of young Monarch larvae before they were transformed into butterflies. Milkweed, a common weed that often surrounds corn fields, is the exclusive source of food for the extravagantly colored butterflies. Corporate scientists found themselves arguing that the research was not conclusive as it was based in a laboratory and might not translate into the field. But their protestations seemed hollow — many people interpreted the research as proof of an unnecessary assault on the "Bambi" of the insect world.

In the U.K., scientists reported that bees could spread GM-tainted pollen much further than early proponents had predicted — up to four kilometers. In Canada, farmers had practical experience that backed up those findings. For example, organic farmers were told not to bother planting organic canola as it would be sullied by the engineered versions that were grown throughout Western Canada.

On the animal front, the news was rife with pre-millennial portent. "Dolly," the sheep that made headlines three years earlier as the first mammal to be cloned from an adult, was aging unnaturally. Her cells were actually nine years old. Somehow Dolly had absorbed the age of her "mother" as well as her own.

In 1999, the BBC and *The Globe and Mail* reported that about twenty transgenic pigs had been exported from Britain to Canada, after the U.K. outlawed experiments in xenotransplantation. The Canadian government did not have a policy on animal-to-human organ transplants, nor did Health Canada inspect the transgenic pigs when they arrived. Yet Canada quietly began the experimental work that was banned in the U.K.

Consumers responded to these reports of biotechnology's progress with concern. And that in turn, spurred a very pragmatic fallout. After inquiries from Greenpeace, the Gerber baby food company, a subsidiary of the European biotech firm Novartis, declared it would eliminate all genetically engineered sources from its products. H. J. Heinz quickly followed suit. "I want our mothers to be comfortable," Al Piergallini, president of Novartis's U.S. consumer health operation told the press. Appealing to the "mothers" of four-legged offspring, Iams, the pet food company, said it would not use varieties of altered corn that hadn't been approved by European regulators to produce its animal foods.

Those who had been staunch supporters of biotechnology began to soften their line. In July 1999, U.S. Secretary of Agriculture Dan Glickman tempered his position when he told a Washington audience that the biotech giants should listen to consumer concerns and consider voluntary labeling. Gordon Conway, the president of the Rockefeller Foundation, which had helped to bankroll the development of biotechnology, warned Monsanto's board of directors that it could not "force-feed" consumers genetically engineered foods. And the United States and Canada found themselves outnumbered at the 1999 G-8 meetings, when the world's most powerful leaders agreed to an inquiry into genetically modified food.

Also increasingly in 1999, international export markets were closing the door to genetically engineered crops. Japan, South Korea, Australia, and New Zealand all announced they would join Europe in its policy requiring the labeling of modified food. The segregation of altered crops from conventional varieties became a reality of doing business. Agri-business giant Archer Daniels Midland told suppliers in the fall of 1999 that they would have to separate harvests, no matter how cumbersome and expensive it might be. The Consolidated Grain and Barge Company followed the example, telling its producers that consignments containing GMO contamination "no matter how trivial" would not be eligible for premium prices.

Japan's labeling laws would not come into effect until April 2001, but Japanese companies were already avoiding genetic modification. Japan's largest maker of soybean protein food products, Fuji Oil, said it would stop using modified soybeans. Japan's largest and third-largest beer makers declared they would no longer buy manipulated corn. The Honda Trading Corporation, a wholly owned subsidiary of the Japanese carmaker, took matters into its own hands and began to build a plant in Ohio to sort and bag non-modified soybeans.

For several years, many North American farmers had been enthusiastic champions for biotechnology. But by late 1999, key export markets were suddenly off-limits and domestic consumers were becoming increasingly hostile to genetic modification. The American Corn Growers Association acknowledged the new reality and advised farmers to consider conventional varieties. "GMOs have become an albatross around the neck of farmers on the issue of trade, labeling, testing, certification, market availability and agribusiness concentration," the association wrote in its newsletter.

To add to the irritation, producers began to find themselves without the consolation of the bumper crops that had been promised by corporate science. In 1998, Charles Benbrook, an environmental consultant and former director of the Board of Agriculture at the National Academy of Science, reviewed the yields of 8,200 U.S. university-based soybeans varietal trials and found that conventional varieties produced on average ten percent more than that from Roundup Ready varieties. Benbrook also found that up to five times the chemicals had been used on the herbicide-resistant crops compared to natural varieties. The reports of limited returns from biotechnology were bitter news for farmers who were already struggling with the impact of dismally low commodity prices.

In 1999, corporate science began to flounder in the shifting sands of public opinion. The critics it had dismissed as scaremongering Luddites seemed to be winning the public relations war for the hearts of consumers. Biotech giants AstraZeneca and Novartis spoke openly about shedding their agricultural biotech divisions. Monsanto found itself in the glare of an increasingly harsh public spotlight. In October, the company gave in to pressure and announced that it would not commercialize its sterile seed technology the critics had dubbed the "Terminator." Despite blockbuster sales of a new arthritis drug, the company's stock was falling. In September 1999, Monsanto shares were selling for $37 compared to $62 the year before. Germany's influential Deutsche Bank even went so far as to produce a report for investors advising them to steer clear of companies associated with engineered crops. Tim Ramey, the U.S.-based author of the report, wrote "GM organisms are dead. We predict that GM, once perceived as the driver of the bull case for this sector, will now be perceived as a pariah."

Despite years of support for the biotechnology industry, the Canadian government began to backtrack. In September 1999, Ottawa helped bankroll a project by the Canadian Council of Grocery Distributors and the Canadian General Standards Board to develop standards for the voluntary labeling of GM foods. Agriculture Minister Lyle Vanclief broke with his administration's past when he said "the Government of Canada believes in the right of consumers to have access to information as it relates to biotechnology and food." Of course, the government was talking about voluntary, not mandatory, labeling.

In the early 1990s, corporate science proponents had proclaimed biotechnology would rule the next century. Although the biotech industry was still defiantly stiff-necked, by late 1999, it seemed as if genetic engineering was unraveling. The opposing forces promised no rest for the industry. In Great Britain, for example, activists were not satisfied with turning off the supply to consumers; their next focus would be stopping the use of GMOs in animal feed.

The activists had struck a chord with consumers. Even in the supportive North American cradle of biotechnology, people were finally asking questions they had never asked before. The anxiety that shadowed the last year of the century seemed to rouse many citizens from their slumber. It seemed that the future might be defined by consumer efforts to reclaim control over their most important daily sustenance — their food. But they could not afford to doze again if they did not want corporate science's version of biotechnological progress — for the sake of profit, not the betterment of society — to characterize the new millennium.

Reading List

This is not intended to be a comprehensive bibliography, but rather a list of interesting reading.

Avery, Dennis. *Saving the Planet with Pesticides and Plastic: The Environmental Triumph of High-Yield Farming.* Indianapolis: Hudson Institute, 1995.

Busch, Lawrence, William Lacy, Jeffrey Burkhardt, and Laura Lacy. *Plants, Power and Profit: Social, Economic and Ethical Consequences of the New Biotechnologies.* Cambridge: Basil Blackwell, 1991.

Carson, Rachel. *Silent Spring.* Boston: Houghton Mifflin Co., 1962.

Gussow, Joan Dye. *Chicken Little, Tomato Sauce and Agriculture: Who Will Produce Tomorrow's Food?* New York: TOES Books, The Bootstrap Press, 1991.

Fagan, John. *Genetic Engineering: The Hazards; Vedic Engineering: The Solutions.* Fairfield, Iowa: Maharishi University Press, 1995.

Grace, Eric. *Biotechnology Unzipped: Promises and Realities.* Toronto: Trifolium Books, 1997.

Hardy, W.F. and Jane Baker Segelken, eds. *Agricultural Biotechnology: Novel Products and New Partnerships.* Report 8 for the National Agricultural Biotechnology Council. Ithaca, New York: 1996.

Ho, Mae-Wan. *Genetic Engineering—Dream or Nightmare?* London: Gateway Books, 1998.

Kimbrell, Andrew. *The Human Body Shop: The Engineering and Marketing of Life.* San Francisco: Harper Collins Publishers, 1993.

Kneen, Brewster. *The Rape of Canola*. Toronto: NC Press, 1992.

Mather, Robin. *A Garden of Unearthly Delights: Bioengineering and the Future of Food*. New York: Penguin Books, 1995.

Miller, Henry I. *Policy Controversy in Biotechnology: An Insider's View*. Austin, Texas: Academic Press, R.G. Landes Co., 1997.

Mooney, Pat and Cary Fowler. *Shattering: Food, Politics and the Loss of Genetic Diversity*. Tucson: University of Arizona Press, 1990.

Mullen, Michelle. *Biotechnology: Social and Ethical Issues, Industry's Commitment and Public Policy*. Report for the Biotechnology Council of Ontario, Toronto: 1994.

Office of Technology Assessment, Congress of the United States, Washington, D.C. *Commercial Biotechnology: An International Perspective*. New York: Pergamon Press, 1984.

Powell, Douglas and William Leiss. *Mad Cows and Mother's Milk: The Perils of Poor Risk Communication*. Montreal: McGill-Queen's University Press, 1997.

Raeburn, Paul. *The Last Harvest: The Genetic Gamble that Threatens to Destroy American Agriculture*. New York: Simon & Schuster, 1995.

Rampton, Sheldon and John Stauber. *Mad Cow U.S.A.: Could the Nightmare Happen Here?* Monroe, Maine: Common Courage Press, 1997.

Rifkin, Jeremy. *The Biotech Century: Harnessing the Gene and Remaking the World*. New York: Jeremy P. Tarcher/Putnam, 1998.

Robbins, John. *Diet for a New America*. Walpole, New Hampshire: Stillpoint Publishing, 1987.

Steingraber, Sandra. *Living Downstream: An Ecologist Looks at Cancer and the Environment*. Reading, Massachusetts: Addison-Wesley Publishing Co., 1997.

INDEX

108613